Steel, Skill ar
Rugby in Ebbw Vale
and the Valleys
Vol. 1 1870-1952

Steel, Skill and Survival

RUGBY IN EBBW VALE AND THE VALLEYS

Volume 1

1870-1952

David Boucher

With a Foreword by Cliff Morgan

Ebbw Vale Rugby Football Club Ltd.

Published by Ebbw Vale Rugby Football Club Ltd.,
Eugene Cross Park,
Ebbw Vale, Gwent, NP3 5AZ
Telephone: 01495 302995

ISBN
Hardback 0-9539293-0-2
Paperback 0-9539293-1-0

British Library Cataloguing in Publication Data.
A catalogue record of this book is available from the British Library

Printed in Wales, UK, by Dinefwr Press, Llandybie

Contents

List of Illustrations

Foreword

by

CLIFF MORGAN

The warmth and the welcome at the Former Player's reunion of the Ebbw Vale Rugby Club; the joy of being with Clyde Best with whom I played for the Welsh Secondary Schools Team in 1949; the faces of Ebbw Vale players of the past who had played for fun and friendship made me feel good. It was living proof that the adventure of rugby played with toughness and style and with the laws has been a privilege that we all share.

Today the game is so much more different for the players who are expected to be super fit and dedicate so much time to the game. The game is a better spectacle. What Ebbw Vale and every other rugby club must never forget is that there are so many young people – gifted young people – who should be cared for so that in the years to come we can be certain that they have the opportunities and wisdom to plough a precise furrow that spells out the history and traditions of this great club.

We should never forget Eric Finney who gave his all for the game – a number eight who was always at the heart of the Vale pack. His inspiration and masterful knowledge of rugby made him so highly respected by all opposition. Not only a terrific scrummager and lineout man, he was so good around the field. I played with Eric at a Welsh Trial at Abertillery and it astounded us that the Welsh Selectors overlooked one of the finest forwards ever to play in our game. Not only did he know the ins and outs of forward play but he was proud of Ebbw Vale and was such a good guy to be with . . . the selectors must have been mad. But in the words of Mark Twain: "A difference of opinion is what makes horse races".

Capped by Wales 36 times, leader of the Welsh pack in 1971, Denzil Williams flew the flag of Ebbw Vale so proudly in the front-row. His rock-like presence made him a key member of the Triple Crown squad of 1966. He was like an ancient rock on which a team could build. And there was Arthur Lewis – a formidable centre, who played the game for fun. Yet he was very much admired as a class player by all the British Lions who toured with him. He had a theory. Use an excess of embrocation. If you're not fit, you should smell fit. My first cap for Wales was against Ireland in 1951 as it was for big Ben Edwards – playing at the time for Newport – who kicked the goals to enable us to draw the match. I recall standing behind him that night in a line to claim our expenses. Ben claimed two third class returns on the train – for Friday's training and the match and then Eric Evans asked me what mine was. "Five shillings sir," I said. He looked up at me and said, "you liar and cheat. It's two shillings and four pence return from Trebanog and that's four shillings and eight pence." He gave me a half-a-crown, a two shilling piece and two pennies!

Documented in these pages are the names and deeds of fine rugby men of Ebbw Vale. Take down and read and the memories of the Steelmen will be as sweet as the Wild Honey of the *Mabinogion.*

25 September, 2000

Preface

Obtaining the material to write this book has involved a great deal of assistance from others who have been generous in giving their time. Much of the material I have been given relates to the period after 1950 which is covered in volume two, and due acknowledgement of its sources will be given there. In relation to this volume I would like to thank Kim Stinton for tracking down the document of incorporation of the Northern Union Ebbw Vale Rugby Club at the Public Records Office. The Welsh Rugby Union granted me permission to consult its minute books and I am grateful to Angela for her help. I am deeply indebted to Nina Whitcombe of the inter-library loans section at University of Wales, Swansea for obtaining invaluable books and articles for this project. Irene Heakin kindly offered her research skills in searching the newspaper archives at Newport Public Library. I am very grateful for her many hours of painstaking searching trying to find the elusive match reports in the *South Wales Argus* and other newspapers, including the *Star of Gwent.* She managed to uncover much interesting and important information on the early history of the club. Duncan Thompson gave me considerable assistance in searching through the *Western Mail, South Wales Echo* and the *Football Echo* for reports on games after the First World War. He was able to compile a fairly comprehensive list of fixtures and results and discover reports on the condition of the rugby ground during its re-surfacing period. I am indebted both for the many hours spent at the microfilm reader at Cardiff Public Library, and for the valuable information he uncovered. The staff at Newport and Cardiff public libraries also deserve a vote of thanks for their assistance. I spent many hours going through the *Merthyr Express* at Merthyr Public Library and would like to thank the staff there for their generous help and unfailing assistance. I would also like to thank the staff at Collingdale Newspaper Library in London for helping in my search of other newspapers. David Williams very kindly read and commented upon chapter two and gave me the benefit of his keen interest in the subject. It goes without saying that I take full responsibility for all the imperfections that remain.

I am extremely grateful to Marcus Russell for inviting me to write this history, and giving me the opportunity to give something back, in the form of applying my skills as an historian, such as they are, to the Club that has given me so much pleasure (and pain!) over the last thirty five years. I am also grateful to Alun Evans for overseeing the final stages of production. Finally, it would be remiss of me not to thank all of the volunteers, committee members and staff who have given their services to Ebbw Vale Rugby Club in times of adversity and success.

David Boucher
School of European Studies,
Cardiff University

Introduction

On Monday 11 April, 1960, at the Welfare Ground, Past and Present Ebbw Vale teams played each other for the first time in the history of the club. Ebbw Vale had won the Unofficial Championship three times and looked on course to win it for a fourth time in a decade. Players from the past included Ebbw Vale's first Welsh international Graham Powell, and the Welsh Trialist and substitute Eric Finney. In the Present team were such memorable players as the twenty year old David Nash, and the Scottish international and British Lion, Arthur Smith. Eighty years after its inception Ebbw Vale Rugby Football Club was quite rightly celebrating its outstanding achievement of surviving one of the most turbulent histories of any club in the Union. The historical notes to the programme, written by the eighty-three year old Percy Miles (Glynfab), conclude with the refrain, 'I think the time is overdue when a full and complete history of the Club is attempted.'

This book traces the first seventy years or so of that history against the background of changing economic and social conditions, and in the context of the development of the game of rugby union and rugby league in the South Wales valleys. Rarely has a team had such a turbulent history, marked by a constant struggle for recognition of its worth and claim to play a higher standard of rugby. The aloofness of the southern clubs and their disinclination to play against valley teams was detrimental to the game in Wales. The Welsh Football Union, later to become the Welsh Rugby Union, steadfastly refused to intervene to require the top clubs to play less fashionable teams. The lack of top quality competition gradually had devastating consequences for attendances at the games, and at the turn of the century, despite being a highly successful team, Ebbw Vale was forced to play junior rugby.

On its return to second class rugby the situation did not improve, and the patience of Ebbw Vale was tried by being required to play a season before its application for re-admittance into the Union would be entertained. Like its English counterpart the Welsh Football Union was not prepared to acknowledge the difficulties faced by working class men in taking time off work to play rugby. Clubs were forced to make payments under the table in order to compensate men for loss of wages. With allegations against Merthyr and Aberdare instigating a full scale enquiry, and a call from the WFU to see the Ebbw Vale books, both Merthyr and Ebbw Vale took the hugely courageous step of turning professional. The Merthyr club broke away from the Union club, but in the case of Ebbw Vale the Union Club converted itself into a Northern Union Club (rugby league) and became a limited liability company. Ebbw Vale was certainly the most successful of the Welsh Northern Union teams. It won the Welsh League twice, and outlasted all the other Welsh teams in the Northern Union. Although it was initially successful as a spectator sport the odds were stacked against its success. First, the Welsh Football Union conducted a campaign of vilification and belatedly promoted Rugby Union in the valleys by persuading teams such as Cardiff, Newport and Swansea to play the likes of Merthyr Rugby Union. Second, the rise of Association Football in the area began to capture the imagination of the youth and press to a greater degree than either Northern Union or Rugby Union. Third, and perhaps the most important factor, was the costs and distances involved in participating in the Northern Union League. When the Welsh League was established this alleviated the problem only to create a new one, less attractive fixtures and falling attendances. Ebbw Vale ceased to play Northern Union in 1912, but the ghost of professionalism re-emerged from time to time to haunt the club, as, for example, in 1926 and 1927 when league games were proposed by the Welfare Association. The second of the proposed games was played on the Welfare Ground despite objections and legal action taken by the Rugby Club. Ebbw Vale was once again expelled from the Union and reinstated when the weight of the press was put behind its case.

It was the establishment of the Ebbw Vale Steel, Iron and Coal

Company Welfare Association in 1918 that enabled Ebbw Vale to apply successfully to the WRU to allow rugby union to be played again at Ebbw Vale after the Northern Union interlude. Although the Works Welfare Association only lasted for three years it gave impetus to the new Ebbw Vale Welfare Association. The transfer of the Welfare playing fields and grounds at a nominal rent to the new Association, despite problems in recruitment and difficult times during the Depression, enabled an extensive programme of development to be carried out on the provision of leisure facilities in the area. The Welfare Ground was continuously improved, the most significant investment being the relaying of the pitch at the end of the 1940s, and the relaying once again two years later when the initial work was deemed to be a failure.

This period coincided with Ebbw Vale's determined bid to become a first class team, and despite having seasons disrupted and having to play home games on neighbouring grounds, the club succeeded, and even won, the unofficial championship in the 1951-2 season. The Welfare Association became the central focus of sporting activities in Ebbw Vale and provided facilities for such diverse activities as pigeon racing, baseball, cricket, hockey, bowls, tennis, shooting, and swimming. It was responsible for constructing, among others, a cinder race track, the Bowls Pavilion, an ornamental fish pond, and the Lido during the Depression by using voluntary labour, and also playgrounds at various community locations. As more and more people became unemployed pressure on the facilities increased, as the revenue from weekly subscriptions decreased. It was able to survive as a result of grants from the Miner's Welfare Federation, the good will of local businessmen in providing some materials and transport free, and through the enormous good will of the inhabitants who readily lent their skills and muscle to the variety of schemes for a few Woodbines and a meal a day.

After the re-establishment of the Rugby Union Club in 1919 Ebbw Vale once again became a formidable force, and the traditional rivalries between such teams as Abertillery and Tredegar were resumed. In the early 1920s Ebbw Vale regained its reputation as the champions of the hills, but played inconsistently thereafter. It was generally acknowledged that Ebbw Vale was a class above other teams in the area and that it was unjustly treated in having such a struggle to get decent teams from South Wales to visit the area. Ebbw Vale compensated by building-up an attractive list of encounters with English clubs such as Nuneaton, Bristol and Wolverhampton, and gradually came to establish connections with Neath, Aberavon, and Cardiff, as well as Pontypridd, Mountain Ash, Newbridge, Pontypool and Maesteg.

For the twenty years between the two world wars the town's economic fortunes fluctuated considerably, and from 1923 to 1937 there was almost continuous depression. Miners throughout the country were targeted by the Press for allegedly holding the country to ransom in resisting the continuous erosion of their working conditions until the Marine Colliery Disaster in 1927 when fifty miners died. From then on there was a greater social recognition of the dangers of working in the deplorable mining conditions. All clubs struggled for funds during the Depression years and sought to diversify sources of income, including introducing 'electric hare' racing at some stadiums. Association Football and Rugby Union in Ebbw Vale was badly hit by the economic depression for a number of reasons. Numerous young men left the area to seek work elsewhere, and those that remained could ill afford even the reduced entrance prices and were forced to watch games from vantage points around the ground.

It was not until the late 1930s that Ebbw Vale could lay unequivocal claim to be recognised as a first class club when it consistently beat teams in the higher bracket. In fact, because of the Steel and Coal production in Ebbw Vale rugby was strengthened in the area because of the Second World War. There was a pool of young men to be drawn upon working in the vital industries which were not required for active military service. Even though the activities of the Welsh Rugby Union were officially suspended teams were allowed to make their own arrangements. It was during this period that Ebbw Vale played all of those clubs that tended to be aloof before the War, and consistently beat them. Teams such as Cardiff and Newport were able to put out strong teams because of the greater catchment areas they covered, and many Welsh international players visited Ebbw Vale while representing these teams. The fixtures were not recorded in the official records of the clubs. Ebbw Vale achieved its only invincible season in 1940-41, winning all of its thirty games. The post-war period saw Ebbw Vale capitalise on the momentum of the War years and the new prosperity that the Steel Works had brought to the area. The aloofness of the South was still a considerable problem, and it was only by consistently beating English teams and the less fashionable strong teams in Wales that the Valians, as they were called, managed to force the more famous teams to take notice. In 1949-50, against all the odds, Ebbw Vale succeeded in its seventy year struggle for first class recognition and finished fourth in the championship table, and went one better in the following season in coming third to Cardiff and Newport. The ultimate accolade came in 1951-52, after numerous problems with the ground, in taking the title of the premier club in Wales for the first time.

Chapter One

Establishing the Game

It is not entirely established that William Webb Ellis fortuitously invented the game of rugby football when he picked-up the ball at Rugby school in 1823 and ran, but the modern game certainly began to develop shortly after this. It was initially an ill-disciplined, and violent, contest among an unlimited number of men intent on causing damage to the opponent in the process of chasing the ball. The rules were not uniform throughout the areas that played the game, and even the scoring was not fully agreed until the late 1880s. Historically it is now accepted that the Romans, as well as leaving us the legacy of straight roads, concrete, under floor central heating, heated baths with attendant food vendors, and sporting amphitheatres, also introduced the game that predates rugby football, Harpestrum.

An early form of rugby at an army barracks, published in 1827.
(Source, J. B. G. Thomas, *The Illustrated History of Welsh Rugby*, 1980).

Ellis's departure from traditional football was not as radical as all that. In football players were allowed to catch the ball and pick it up for the purpose of punting it towards the goal. The person holding the ball could be charged to prevent clearance. The player holding the ball could not pass it, nor run with it towards goal. What Ellis is reputed to have done is to have breached the rule preventing him running towards goal. It was perfectly legitimate for him to have handled the ball. There was a game closer to rugby, called 'Hurling', already being played in Cornwall. There are reports in 1602 that the game was played between 15-20 players, and that the goals were two bushes 8 to 12 feet apart. The ball was thrown in the air and caught by a player who could then be challenged by one player at a time, and could defend himself by striking the chest of his opponent with double fists. This was called butting. If he broke free of the first tackle, he was tackled by another, the object being to force him to spill the ball, called 'hurling'. The aim was to place the ball through the opponents goal. One observer commented that: 'The ball in this kind of exercise is endowed with a kind of magical property; for each who catches it becomes immediately like a madman; fighting and struggling with those who go about to hold him; and no sooner has the ball left him, but his fury goes with it to another, and he becomes immediately peaceable and calm himself.'[1]

Initially the game of Rugby football was very unlike that which we have come to know today. The Laws of Rugby School, for example, state that the game is won if either side scores two goals. The game was declared a draw if no goal was scored after three days play, or if either side failed to reach the two goals after five days. In response to the more inventive players' attempts to deflect the ball from goal it was declared that 'no player may stand on the goal bar to intercept it going over'.

In 1874 the Rugby Union rule book gives specifications of the field of play. The only dimensions mentioned are the goal posts which should not exceed eleven feet in height and should be placed

1. Cited in Admiral Sir Percy Royds, *The History of the Laws of Rugby Football* (Twickenham, Walter and Co.,1949), 63.

18ft 6" apart, with a cross bar at ten foot from the ground. The posts were to be equidistant from the sides of the field. The field of play was enclosed by a touch line on both sides and goal lines at each end, cut out of the turf. There were no other lines on the field. The dimensions of the pitch do not become specified until 1879 and were not to exceed 110yds in length and 75yds in breadth, and should be as near as possible to these measurements. At the same time the dead ball line is introduced, and in 1905 the Rugby Union adds the 25yd and 10yd lines to the plan of the field. In 1926 a broken 5yd line is added on each side of the length of the field of play.

Although Ebbw Vale Rugby Football Club was not officially established until 1880 there are signs of rugby in the area before then. According to J. B. G. Thomas there was a Blaenau Gwent side in 1869. Certainly by the mid 1870s matches were being played against teams in the Tredegar Valley, with rival supporters clashing on the mountain tops. Rugby was a very different game in those days. The period 1871 to 1895, the year in which Ebbw Vale became recognised by the Welsh Football Union, saw the standardisation of rules, the value of scores, size and weight of the ball, and the size of the pitch.

Challenge Cups

In 1871 the English RFU was established at a time when few working men were able to participate in the sport because of the long working day. By the 1880s, however, a whole spate of northern teams had been instituted by businessmen, and working men were having a significant impact on the playing field. Working class participation in the North injected a greater degree of competitiveness than in the South where the idea of challenge cups was wholly rejected. The Yorkshire Challenge Cup was established in 1877, closely followed by Northumberland, Durham and Cumberland. Local leagues also developed in the North, but were rejected in the South. In Wales rugby clubs sprang up throughout the 1870s, and the WFU was formed in 1881 and presided over the mushrooming of the number of clubs playing Rugby Football Union.

Rugby football was a predominantly middle class game almost unknown in Wales before 1870. In fact association football looked the more likely candidate to take deep root. Indeed, Cardiff, Newport and Swansea were established with the intention of playing association football, but converted to rugby union rules in order to take advantage of English competition. Those clubs within travelling distance of the Severn were dominated by rugby. When rugby did become established, like in the North of England, competition was an essential part of the game. In October of 1877 the South Wales Challenge Cup was instituted by the South Wales Football Club, holding out the prospect of a 50 guinea prize for a 2 guinea entrance fee. On their way to the final Newport beat Pontypool, Llanelli and Carmarthen, and defeated Swansea in the final at Bridgend by one goal to nil on 2 March, 1878. It was a ferociously contested competition, which in 1880 created the East West division which has been a permanent characteristic of the game in Wales. Indeed Welsh trials themselves were based on this regional principle. In 1893, for instance, the East trial was held in Penarth and the West in Aberavon, with the final held in Neath. In that year the competition was divided into two districts, ensuring that the final would always be a battle between East and West. Interest in the cup waned in favour of more local competitions, and the last final was staged in 1887. In the meantime from 1885 challenge cups had been established in Monmouthshire, worth thirty guineas, in Cardiff, Swansea and Llanelli. There was no question, however, of the WFU forming a league.

There is one report of Ebbw Vale competing in the inaugural Monmouthshire Challenge Cup against Monmouthshire Rangers at Abergavenny on 12th February, 1885. Ebbw Vale achieved a decisive victory against a team that played less cohesively than their opponents. The game was vigorously contested by both sides, but Ebbw Vale's superior qualities won through. The report credits Ebbw Vale with 17 points and Monmouthshire Rangers with 10. However, the reporter's description of the scores, one goal, one try, and three touches down, to one goal, nowhere near accounts for the points tally. The *Merthyr Express* reported that Ebbw Vale would go on to meet Maindy at Pontypool in the next round, but there are no further accounts of Ebbw Vale games until April 7th when Merthyr played host. Almost a decade later Ebbw Vale played Abergavenny Steam Press in the Monmouthshire Challenge Cup at Baily Park. Abergavenny won decisively by 2 tries and 3 minors to 3 minors. Abergavenny Steam Press progressed to the final against Newport 2nds. The game was postponed three times, and eventually was scheduled for 22 April 1893, at Newport. On that occasion Newport refused to play because the ground was too hard and the game was awarded to Abergavenny by default. Abergavenny once again progressed to the final in the following year, but this time succumbed to the superior power of Pontnewydd.

Ebbw Vale also participated in the Union Challenge Cup in 1895. Eight teams entered, Penarth, Risca, Neath A, Llanelly A, Blaenau Gwent, Crumlin, Pontymister and Ebbw Vale. Ebbw Vale met Pontymister on 23rd March in the first round. In driving rain Pontymister kicked off down the field, with Ebbw Vale immediately returning the 'leather' to the half way line. The first few scrums demonstrated that Ebbw Vale had the dominant pack, and throughout the forwards played 'a hard dashing game'. Tom Jones and Kerton (called Curtin in the first few reports), kept the pressure on Pontymister from the backs, and looked dangerous all afternoon. The pair were responsible for the move that resulted in the first try touched down by Jones after a short kick over the line by Kerton. The conversion only just missed. After the interval Pontymister re-group and mounted a concerted campaign to cross the Ebbw Vale line, but the counter-attack was short lived thanks to Kerton who, seeing his chance, ran strongly and scooped up the ball carrying it over the visitor's line. Ebbw Vale won by 2 tries and 4 minors to 2 minors. In the second round Ebbw Vale met Neath A at Neath, the eventual winners of the competition. In a hard fought contest Ebbw Vale went down narrowly by 1 try and 1 minor to nil. Neath A went on to beat Crumlin in the final by 1 goal to nil.

In the early years of rugby in the hills Merthyr tended to be the focus of the occasional match report. It was after all the largest town in Wales, whose population exceeded that of both Newport and

Cardiff. In the absence of an official capital city, Merthyr laid claim to the unofficial title with its population of over sixty thousand people.

Rationalisation of the Game

In 1871 a limit was placed of 20 players in each team, thirteen of them forwards, three half backs, one player at three quarter, and three defending at full-back. Passing the ball was largely confined to the forwards, who were also expected to be skilful at dribbling the ball. Usually the ball was kicked from a maul to the half backs who were small and agile, either running for the line, or much more preferable, dropping a goal if they came in range. The bigger heavier ball, like a lead weight when wet, made goal scoring quite an achievement. The three quarter would be a specialist drop goal kicker, and also expected to tackle the opposition halfbacks. In 1876 there was a major revolution in the game, the number of players was reduced to fifteen and the object of the game gradually changed. There were now usually ten forwards, without a standard formation, and five backs. It was not uncommon, however, to have a combination of nine forwards and six backs. By the 1890s it was standard practice to have eight forwards and seven backs.

It was not until 1875 that it was agreed a try should have a value in the game, but goal scoring was still the most important aspect of the contest. At this stage in the development of the game no points were awarded, and no number of tries could match a drop goal. Tries, especially those underneath the posts, which were listed separately in the result, were essential because they were the prerequisite for a kick at goal. Minors, dribbling the ball over the line but failing to touch it down, were also listed in the score, but seem to have carried no weight.

It was at Oxford that the role of the backs came to be a more prominent feature of the game after 1881-2. Generally speaking, up until this time the scoring of tries relied upon the pure strength of the forwards who ran with the ball until they were brought down. The Oxford captain Vassel effected the most inventive transformation when he devised the plan of breaking up the pack and moving the ball rapidly from hand to hand among the backs. Such open play required more agile forwards who were there to clean up the ball at tackles, and hence developed the need for a 'wing' off the scrum, whose role was to dribble, pass and follow-up. The success of Newport and Cardiff in the early 1890s was put down to the fact that they had developed these skills into a fine art.[2] This reassertion of the dominance of the forwards was counteracted in Wales by moving from three to four three quarters players, which was reputed to be the reason why the Welsh national team won all its matches in the 1892-3 season.

The points scoring system of Cheltenham School was adopted in 1886 and a numerical value was given to each score, three for a drop goal and one for a try, with three tries equalling one goal. In 1888 penalty goals were introduced, and could be taken from free kicks or off-side infringements. It wasn't until November 1888 that the WFU decided that a game should be won by a majority of points, and that a try be valued at two points. The International Board followed suit in 1889, but because of the settlement terms of a dispute over recognition between the RFU and the IB, a try was reduced to one point for the 1890-1 season. It was then restored to two points and upgraded to three in 1894. The drop goal continued to be more valuable than a try until 1947-8. In the following season it became worth three points, and it was not until the 1970-71 season that a try became worth four points. A penalty goal has remained constant at three points since 1891-2. Up until 1879 it was legitimate to obstruct a player who didn't have the ball, and it wasn't until 1893 that the size and weight of the ball became standard, and that the referee's word became final. Touch judges had been introduced in 1889 to reduce the conflict generated by partisan umpires.

Living in Ebbw Vale

What was Ebbw Vale like around this period? Because of the abundance of iron ore, coal, and limestone, the three essential components

2. Creston, 'Football', *The Fortnightly Review*, vol. 55 (1894), 27.

for making iron, Ebbw Vale, Cwm and Beaufort were at the forefront of the industrial revolution in Wales. The new Steel Works was opened in Ebbw Vale in 1870 which rolled the first steel in December. Fluctuations in employment were unpredictable, and sometimes there were even shortages of labour in the area. In the late Spring of 1871 the various works around Ebbw Vale were finding it difficult to recruit labour and resorted to the novel idea of importing about twenty black men from Liverpool Docks, principally to work at the steelworks. They aroused a great deal of curiosity in the town, and appear to have been treated with courtesy, mainly because people were surprised by their manners and command of the language. The *Merthyr Express* of 3 June, 1871 commented that: 'The men are treated very kindly on all hands and they appear to be an intelligent and well conducted class. They speak English with considerable fluency, and the girls at the works are highly amused with the many peculiar antics of the "Darkey" company'.

This, of course, was before governments attempted to regulate the economy through Keynesian economics. There were regular cycles of boom and depression in the iron and steel industry, with considerable uncertainty of tenure. Wages were reduced in times of depression, and would rise again in times of labour shortage. In 1878-9 the iron and steel industry went into depression and Ebbw Vale experienced a severe downturn in fortunes. The management at the steel works attempted to reduce wages by 10%. The semi-skilled and skilled men went on strike bringing the operation to a complete standstill, over Christmas and well into the new year. Relief funds were established in order to alleviate the 'great amount of distress and privation'. Many of the fitters and boilermakers were members of societies and received 15s per week from the strike fund, those who were not members got 10s, but ordinary labourers had nothing and relied upon charity. In early March at Beaufort the Distress Committee distributed 1,500 rations of bread, but was unable to give soup because its funds were nearly exhausted. It was in this month that news of emigrations to Australia began to appear. After April the industry began to pick up again and by September there were once again reports of labour shortages at the steel works.

Life was precarious, and danger lurked at every opportunity; the danger of disease, the loss of one's life in work, and what was statistically as likely, the death of young women in childbirth, and not least among the worries was the loss of one's company owned home. Owners of the various industries were ill disposed to invest in expensive safety measures, and the workers themselves had ill-adjusted to the savageness of the new technology. Men, women and children daily risked their lives, almost oblivious to danger. Serious accidents at work were frequent, and fatalities not uncommon. The new mode of transportation, the steam train, was treated by many with little respect. People would board and jump off trains in between stations, or at stations before the train had fully come to a halt, resulting in the most horrific injuries, including loss of limbs and life. The nature of the iron and steel industry inevitably resulted in some of the most gruesome and shocking deaths imaginable. On 24th April, 1870 a man was roasted alive at the furnaces in Ebbw Vale after the surface material on which he stood in a kiln gave way. His body sank up to his chest into the white hot materials, while his colleagues used planks and ropes in an unsuccessful rescue attempt. They managed to secure hooks below the neck, but succeeded only in wrenching the head from his body.

The coalmines in Ebbw Vale had a reputation for being reasonably safe. The most serious accident occurred in Number One, Victoria Colliery, 2nd March 1871 (note that the illustration overleaf wrongly gives the date as 3rd March), an explosion that killed 19 men. In Beaufort, under Crawshay Baily's auspices, conditions were deplorable. Despite frequent attempts to prosecute the Beaufort owners and managers for neglect of safety standards it was almost impossible to secure a conviction because it was managers of iron works and other industries who comprised the board of magistrates.

The headstones in the graveyard of St. John's, New Church Road, testified to the impersonal brutality of burgeoning, barely regulated industry, poor sanitation, and poor diet. Headstone after headstone stated the name, age – many sixteen or seventeen – and the name of the ironworks to which the departed belonged. The average ages of those buried in the graveyard in 1844, 1855, and 1865 were

COPY OF VERSES ON THE EXPLOSIONS AT PENTRE YSTRAD AND EBBE VALE COLLIERIES,

February 24th & March 3rd, 1871.

The following is a list of the names of the persons who lost their lives at Ebbe Vale

John Price, aged 18. single
James George, 24, married
Thomas James, 21, single
George Gallop, 25, married
David Philips, 21, single
Samuel Cook, 18, single
William Plumber 24, widower
Joseph Harries, 12, boy
Francis Adams, 21, single
James Turner, 50, married
G. Turk, aged 18, single
J. Chapman, 23, married
John Gallop, 30, married
Charles Ford, 20, single
Thomas Mitchell, 39, married
John Evans, 31, married
Philip Philips, 59, married
George Williams, 23, single
Jonathan Price, 50, married

Fathers, mothers, sisters, brothers,
Listen to this mournful tale,
Of the fate of those poor Colliers,
At Pentre Ystrad and Ebbe Vale;
More than 60 fellow-creatures,
Men who felt no care or woe,
In the evening left tgeir dwelling,
And in death were soon laid low.
Farewell friends and dear relations,
These poor Colliers may have cried,
Where at Ebbe Vale and Pentre Ystrad
Scarcely a week has gone aside.

More than 70 hardy Colliers,
On them fatal afternoons,
Went below the earth's bright surface,
To labour in the pit's deep gloom;
The fiery damp soon came, upon them,
And carried death both far and wide,
Till scorched or stifled by the vapour,
Sixty of their number died.

The frightful sound of the explosions,
Cast a gloom on all around,
And many a prayer went up to Heaven
For those poor Colliers underground.

The fatal pits were soon surrounded,
Hundreds stood in blank despair,
With trembling hearts and anxious faces,
Watching for the dear ones there.

The fiery damp had come upon them.
In manly strength and youthful pride,
And some poor fathers and their children,
In death's embrace lay side by side,
Some were stifled at their labour,
Others as they turned to fly,
Some so burnt that no one knew them,
What a fearful death to die.

The air was rent with cries of sorrow,
As the bodies did appear,
Wives lamenting for their husbands,
Children for their fathers dear.
Aged mothers for tocir offspring,
Perhaps their best support and stay,
Many more with grief were trembling,
For some dear one passed away.

H. Disley, Printer, No. 57. High Street,
St. Giles, London.

A Broadsheet Ballad commemorating the deaths of miners at Pentre Ystrad and 'Ebbe' Vale Collieries.

St. John's Church (New Church) about 1917 with Morgan James' Field in the background.

twelve-and-a-half, eighteen, and seventeen years and five months respectively. The low average is accounted for by the high rate of infant mortality.

St. John's Church is also the site of one of the most deeply moving folk tales of spirits in Monmouthshire. According to legend an Ebbw Vale woman in Victorian times fell in love with a wealthy farmer's son way above her station. His parents wanted him to marry the daughter of a sea captain, but in the meantime he courted the woman of lower status. She refused to submit to his sexual desires unless they were married. Not to be outdone, he arranged a fake ceremony, had his way with her and left her abandoned and pregnant.

He refused to do the right thing by her even though his father demanded it. Instead, under threat of his father's curse, the son persisted with the plan to marry the sea captain's daughter. In a last desperate attempt to get him to change his mind the rejected young girl, with his baby daughter, made a heartfelt plea, which fell on deaf ears. The mother and daughter were later found dead in the mill stream, suspected murdered. The son died in a storm at sea shortly afterwards, leaving a widow and baby. On cold misty nights the ghost of the jilted lover with the baby in her arms can still be seen walking down the mill stream towards the site of St. John's Church.

Benefit Matches

While accidents were commonplace, people were never desensitised to tragedy. The sense of community spirit and feeling of social cohesiveness that arose in adversity engendered a strong belief in social responsibility. Ebbw Vale became notorious for its benefit concerts which raised funds for afflicted workers, or for the widows and orphans of the deceased, and if this proved insufficient, there was always the Workhouse at Tredegar! Ebbw Vale Football Club was undoubtedly supportive of the community, just as the community supported it. In order to raise money for worthy causes the rugby club played invitation teams designed to draw big crowds. They played many benefit matches which generated big gate receipts. Among the teams they played were a 'Select Team' comprising the cream of players from neighbouring clubs; 'A. M. Rickett's Cardiff Team', and most impressive of all, such was Ebbw Vale's undoubted reputation, that they succeeded in attracting the famous Newport team to the valleys for the first time. Ebbw Vale had a particularly good season during 1893-94, immediately predating its affiliation with the WFU. With the exception of Newport and Nuneaton, Ebbw Vale played none of the prestigious clubs. Its opponents included four teams from Cardiff, Cardiff Northern, Maindee, Canton, and Hibernians, all of which failed to defeat the Valians. Of the thirty-two games reported Ebbw Vale was defeated only six times, all by narrow margins. Their victors were Pontymoile, Pontnewydd (twice), Risca, Penygraig, and Newport.

It was on 3 January 1894 that the club played a 'Select Team', the best players from Tredegar, Brynmawr, Nantyglo, Blaina and Abertillery. The match was played in aid of the relief fund for the tin workers of Brynmawr and Nantyglo. Ebbw Vale was the most formidable team in the area, only losing three of its fourteen previous matches. Five of the team failed to turn-up and they had to be replaced by players from the seconds. One of the backs was obviously the worst for wear, having been 'Christmassing' in the morning. He put in a distinctly seedy performance. As a result Ebbw Vale didn't play impressively. It was a disappointment to the spectators because Ebbw Vale had such an impressive record to defend. Although there were obvious highlights, such as a brilliant performance from D. J. Richards, the captain, the game was marred by 'too much of a rough forward game'. The game ended in a draw with Ebbw Vale one minor, and the select team nil. The gate receipts amounted to £24.

By far the most impressive of the benefit matches was the clash between Ebbw Vale and Newport. It is testimony to Ebbw Vale's record and reputation in the 1893-4 season that they were able to attract such a famous club, which fielded an extremely strong team, including Arthur J. Gould as captain and his brother Gus. Arthur Gould was already a seasoned Welsh international and continued to represent his country as player and captain until January 1897, collecting 27 caps. He captained the Welsh team 17 times. Gould was the Welsh equivalent of W. G. Grace in cricket. His was a household name, with his face appearing on match boxes, and his exploits being celebrated in music hall songs. When Newport came to the hills for the very first time it had had a very strong season, playing 31 games, winning 26, drawing 2, and losing 3, twice to Cardiff and once to Blackheath. At this time Newport played Cardiff at least four times a season, and was not to play Ebbw Vale as a first class club until the 1953-4 season, and then only once at home each season until 1964-5, when an additional Floodlight Alliance fixture was scheduled, the exception being 1956-7. Ebbw Vale played home and away fixtures to Newport in two seasons prior to their elevation, 1923-24 and 1939-40.

The 1894 clash was one of the most eagerly anticipated games in the history of Ebbw Vale. The benefit was arranged for the widow of the late Sergt. Instr. Keefe. One of the Dauncey brothers of Newport acted as referee and organised the Uskside contingent, which was described as 'a very warm side indeed'. D. J. Richards captained the 'Valians', as they had come to be known. The large crowd gave a standing ovation as Newport ran on to the field, renewing their enthusiasm as the home team followed. It was an uncharacteristic lapse of concentration on the part of Ebbw early in the opening minutes of the game that resulted in a soft Newport try, which made the difference to a game of which the home side were commonly conceded to have had the better in the closing stages. The Gould brothers, having a natural instinct for each other's play, put on a scintillating show of passing, capitalising on the skills of all the Newport backs to play fast open and attractive rugby in their onslaught on the Ebbw line. Heroic tackling and counter attacks by the Valians put Newport under pressure. Ebbw Vale frequently looked dangerous, as for example when Bainton found touch close to the Newport line from a free kick way up the field. Pressure was relieved when Bowley, Packer, Day and Groves, effected a marvellous move which pushed Ebbw right back and forced them to touch

J. Arthur Gould, captain of Newport and famous Welsh International.

down. From the drop-out Arthur Gould gathered up and cut right through the three quarter defence, but the opportunity was lost when his pass failed to connect with his brother. Newport won by one goal to two minors. The *Merthyr Express* of 21 April, 1894 contends that: 'The game was admitted by all to be one of the finest displays of football ever witnessed on the Bridge End Field. From the moment the ball was put in motion until the expiration of the game, there was not a dull minute'.

On Saturday 2nd March 1895, after a lay-off of five weeks because of severe frost Ebbw Vale played an unusually strong Newport 2nd team, which included Bert Gould, defeating it with a fast open display of rugby by one try and three minors to nil. Two days later they were on the field again for a benefit match in aid of the widow of John Morgan, a locomotive driver from Beaufort. Before a large crowd the A. M. Ricketts' Cardiff Team ran onto the Bridge End Field and immediately asserted its authority, threatening the line on a number of occasions in the first few minutes, but with some fine dribbling and skilful play from the half-backs, Williams and Simmonds, the game was turned around. The final score was Ebbw Vale 2 tries and five minors to the visitors' four minors.

Social Conditions in Ebbw Vale

The state of the roads and pavements in Ebbw Vale in the last quarter of the 19th century was typical of an industrial town. Open drains and communal water pumps helped to foster disease. Housing was meagre, unsanitary and overcrowded. The overcrowding was usually because of having to take in lodgers, whose amorous escapades were often reported in the *Merthyr Express.* Instigated by an enraged husband, a wife and her lodger would appear in court for crimes associated with 'elopement', such as theft, which really amounted to the taking of some of the woman's possessions from the family home. Company houses were built without indoor or outdoor privies, and either a hole in the back garden, a dry ash closet, or open cesspits served to dispose of the human waste. Where there were outlets for sewerage it was discharged directly into the rivers and streams. Pig sties and cow sheds were reported to be filthy and a hazard to both animals and humans. Local Government Board reports throughout the 1880s lamented the lack of progress in improving sanitation and in making the large number of houses declared uninhabitable fit to live in.

It is not surprising that in these conditions infectious diseases were rampant. There were five hundred cases of measles during the latter part of December 1870, and during the last week one doctor alone issued five death certificates, warning that it was injudicious exposure of the children to cold air rather than the measles itself which proved fatal. The last of the Cholera epidemics occurred in 1866, but there was a severe scarlet fever epidemic in 1882, with a 132 deaths out of a population of 14,700, a mortality rate nearly twice that of the surrounding areas. There were milder recurrences in 1887, 1891, and 1898.

Drink was part of everyday life, and a legitimate expense for quenching the thirst of men at the furnaces. The beer allowance was the normal expectation of a worker, with double rations for forge and furnace men. The miners were given the allowance in cash in 1890, but it was not until the 1914-18 war that it was abolished in the local iron and steel industry and instead factored into the wage structure. Pubs were a focal point of the community even for those attending evening meetings at chapel. Each had a local pub where the congregation would retire afterwards to discuss religion and politics, or to watch a game of skittles or coits out the back. Pubs were not only places to drink, but were also meeting places and venues for entertainment. On 9th July, 1870 an advertisement for the newly opened Belle View at Briery Hill appeared in the *Merthyr Express*, boasting the finest Pontycapel ales and porter. It also announced the imminent opening of an assembly room claiming to be the largest in Wales. The long rooms in pubs served as meeting places, and venues for travelling balladeers who sold their sheet music for a penny on the streets. The pub was also where employers distributed wages. It is not surprising, then, that drunkenness in the streets, and bare knuckle fighting was a severe problem.

The Temperance movement flourished in the town. It was still the case, however, that visitors to the town in the early 1870s commented that they had not seen the likes of such public drunkenness anywhere outside London. Temperance did not mean total abstinence. In 1838 the 'Two Pints a Day Temperance Society' was formed, allowing members to drink everyday except Sundays. By the time rugby was being played in Ebbw Vale total abstinence had gained considerable headway. In 1870 'The Independent Order of Good Templars' established a local lodge, and by 1880 the Band of Hope was formed in most non-conformist chapels. Liberal reformers throughout the country, as well as advocating better education and conditions of work, also linked much of the social degradation to the evils of drink. T. H. Green, the famous Oxford Philosopher and Social reformer, was instrumental in setting-up coffee houses as alternatives to the pubs, and Ebbw Vale was not slow in following the fashion. In 1881 Mr Samuel Davies, a leading figure in the temperance movement in Ebbw Vale, opened 'The Ebbw Vale Coffee Tavern', which was run by his wife and daughters. In the latter part of the 1880s the Emlyn Palace coffee shop was opened next to the Institute, but only lasted until about 1908, when Italian cafes began to serve the same purpose. The Emlyn Palace was the venue where the Ebbw Vale Wednesday Football team was established 8 September, 1887. It was a team made up of shop assistants who were unable to play on Saturday afternoons because of work commitments. Mr E. Prosser was the chairman and J. Edwards the president. The team began training on Wednesday 14th September. It played some of the same teams as Ebbw Vale, and its matches were more frequently reported in the *Merthyr Express* during the 1887-88 season.

The incidence of arrests and convictions for drunkenness decreased in the latter part of the century, despite the increase in the number of public houses. In Bewellty, which included Ebbw Vale, Rhymney and Tredegar, during the last two decades of the century the number of public houses increased from 84, one per every 418 persons, to 146, one per every 398 persons. The records of the Bedwellty Sessions Division show that in 1883-4 out of a population of 34,625 one in every 74 persons were convicted, totalling 469. In 1900-1 out of a population of 53,777 there were 596 convictions, that is one in every 398 persons. Notorious habitual offenders were placed on a Black List, and if caught in a public house subsequently both the offender and the landlord would be fined. At the time of Aneurin Bevan's birth in 1897, Michael Foot maintains that '"Drink" was the enemy which appeared to exploit and to ravage more mercilessly than any coal-owners'.[3]

The life of the mind did not go unattended. The Literary and Scientific Institute, built by the Ebbw Vale Company in 1853, was the first public building. It developed a museum and library, and hosted numerous lectures on subjects, ranging from the ancient Egyptians to the fall of Louis Napoleon. One of its purposes was to teach technical subjects to people in the locality, but because of the high rate of illiteracy, it found that most of its evening classes were devoted to teaching the three Rs. The chapels and philanthropic iron works provided rudimentary education, and held regular lectures and discussions on biblical, and sometimes controversial themes. The *Merthyr Express*, at this time a four page broadsheet, carried national and international news, and the reader could keep himself or herself well-informed on such subjects as the Franco Prussian War, the benefits of temperance, Socialism versus Individualism, as well as reports on local events by local intelligence gatherers.

Such time as there was for recreation revolved around competitions. Just as the life of a citizen in an Ancient Greek polis revolved around religion and organised contests, most of the Greek plays, for example, with which we are familiar were written to be performed in competitions, the lives of Ebbw Vale men and women centred on the chapel and competitions, many of them organised by the different religious denominations. It is no co-incidence that there should be such a resemblance. Education that aspired beyond the three Rs was dominated by the Classics. Henry Jones, an eminent Welshman, who rose from being a shoemaker to the occupant of the chair of moral philosophy at Glasgow University, the chair that Adam Smith had distinguished, once commented that the Eisteddfod was the Welsh equivalent of the Olympic Games. In 1868 an annual

3. Michael Foot, *Aneurin Bevan 1897-1945*, vol I (London, MacGibbon and Kee, 1963), p. 15.

'Ebbw Competition Meeting' was instituted offering prizes for a wide range of literary and craftsmanship skills. At the third meeting, for example, prizes were offered in literary composition, singing, reciting, drawing, reading, writing, geography, sewing, knitting and parsing. Parsing is the activity of resolving sentences into their constituent parts of speech, and describing them grammatically. The principal prize on offer was £5-00 for the best history of Ebbw Vale.

A local proprietor of a public house, Jack Sykes, capitalised on the popularity of competitions in August 1870 by staging a 'grand music' contest outside his establishment for the prize of a silver cup. There were eleven competitors, but none who sang with such clearness of expression as William Thomas, 'an old gentleman of eighty summers'. He won the cup for his rendition of 'Ellen the Fair', and Jack Sykes achieved his design in attracting large audiences to his pub. Between Christmas and the New Year there were annual geese shooting contests, and the competition was described as 'spirited'. About sixty geese were purchased to be used as game for the competitive riflemen of Ebbw Vale.

Recreational competitive sports also began to develop at the town level, with the satellite villages of Cwm and Beaufort preserving their own autonomy and identity. Beaufort and Ebbw Vale formed cricket clubs in 1860. By 1871 local cricket had become popular enough to merit reporting in the newspapers. The Ebbw Vale Cricket Club played its matches at Duffryn Fields and provided a 'sumptuous supper' for its opponents after the game. In the 1871 season Ebbw Vale beat Beaufort both at home in July and away in August: home by over a hundred runs, and away by 3 runs and seven wickets. This was a season in which the Ebbw Vale cricketers 'exhibited undoubted signs' of 'earnestness and energy'. Friendly competitions also flourished among Cricket teams of different sections of the community, including the Steel Smelters. Most sociologists of sport maintain that clubs at the town level do not spring out of thin air. Instead, they have their origins in smaller community teams, often associated with the chapel, or place of work.

In 1870 the Bridge End Inn was leased to Mr Dobbs. It served as the centre of the community in being used for all sorts of purposes

Ebbw Vale Steel Smelters Cricket Club Season 1903.

from social gatherings to public business. It was the regular venue for inquests, and meeting place of the Philanthropic Lodge, which also held its annual feast and procession there. The Bridge End Inn was intermittently to become the club house of Ebbw Vale Rugby, under Union and Professional rules, and served the purpose until a new facility was erected in the early 1950s. Mr Golightly succeeded Mr Dobbs as landlord of the Bridge End. He captained a team called Hills United which played other local teams such as The Crusaders, The Lilly Whites, The Bake House Rovers, and Briery Hill Rovers. He also played for Ebbw Vale in the 1882-3 season.

The Formation of Ebbw Vale RFC

It is not unreasonable to assume that these local teams formed the foundation on which the town side was built. In the mid 1870s there are reports of games between teams from rival collieries in different valleys. Horse breaks would collect the unwashed miners from the pithead and transport them to the games. The games and their sequels were bitter and bloody, with the competition on the field spilling over into raging battles between supporters on the hillside. It was not an uncommon sight to see a procession of players and supporters winding their way up Tredegar Road to the Hill Top carrying the goal posts with them. When Ebbw Vale Rugby Club became established in 1880 it played its early games on Dobb's Field at Pontygof, south of the Bridge End Field, and was captained by L. Williams. Soon afterwards Ebbw Vale moved to the Bridge End Field.

Reports on the first decade of Ebbw Vales' existence are rather sketchy and infrequent. The announcement of the formation of Ebbw Vale football club appears in one sentence on 30th October, 1880 in the *Merthyr Express.* The newspaper had weekly reports on local and district intelligence. The correspondent for Ebbw Vale was Mr Jacob Wall, who worked for the paper from its inception until his death in 1883. He wrote: 'The lovers of outdoor recreations will be pleased to learn that a football team has been established in the town, their ground of practice being Dobbs's field, adjacent to the Bridge End, Pontygof'.

Ebbw Vale Rugby Football Club 1883. Ebbw Vale's first captain, L. Williams.

The reporting of football matches was infrequent, despite their evident popularity. Cricket, the gentleman's game, was much more favoured in the columns of the press. It was not until 1883 that a small intermittent section appeared in the *Merthyr Express* devoted to football, Nevertheless, Ebbw Vale's first game against Tredegar Working Men's Football Club merited one column inch. The game was played on 2nd December, 1880 and reported on 4th. The full report reads:

> 'FOOTBALL MATCH – Ebbw Vale is not without its football club. Mr. Thomas Wood, engineer is president. On Thursday afternoon the first match of the season was played between the Ebbw Vale and Tredegar clubs. The heavy rains that fell for several days previous to the play, contributed to make the play ground wholly unfit for a pleasant contest. The skill of the contending parties could not be developed to any high degree. The victory, if it may be so termed, inclined to the Ebbw Vale club, and was by a draw decided accordingly, the Tredegar team making five touch-downs in self defence'.

It is evident that the writer did not have a firm grasp of the principles governing the game.

After its first season Ebbw Vale began to use the Bridge End Field as its home ground. The playing field at this time had no fence around it, there were no terraces on the bank, and no stand, and was susceptible to severe flooding. During periods of heavy rain the water flowed right down the bank and directly onto the pitch, the surface of which was one and half feet lower than it is today. Time and time again reports talk of games being marred by heavy rain which resulted in atrocious conditions under feet, dangerous for both the players and spectators. The ground also had a pronounced slope, sufficient enough to give a side an advantage. Winning the toss was important in order to get the advantage of the slope in the first half.

Ebbw Vale's initial affiliation was to the County Hotel, reflecting the fact that the game was not wholly working class, and still deferred to its public school origins. For the last game of the season on

5th April 1885, for example, Merthyr was treated to 'an excellent tea' provided by Mrs Lewis of the County Hotel. After the cloth was removed from the table, formal toasts were proposed, including a raising of glasses to Queen Victoria. The formalities were followed by solo renditions of 'capital songs' concluding 'one of the most enjoyable outings the Merthyr [team] has had' (*Merthyr Express*, April 7th, 1885).

Without adequate fencing around the Bridge End Field it was difficult to prevent those disinclined to pay from viewing the game from the tram road across the river. At times attempts were made to screen-off the tram road, especially when the gates were expected to be high. In February 1894, for example, the president of the club, Mr. J. W. Holmes, who ran the County Hotel, arranged a benefit match against Bert Taylor's Team in order to raise finances for the club and to enhance the prospects of a better fixture list for the following season. In anticipation of a large crowd the enterprising Ebbw Vale committee took the precaution of fencing the tram road with canvas sheets in order to obstruct the view of those too mean to hand over a few coppers for the game they professed to love. Those whose view was obstructed missed, in the words of the correspondent, 'the best contested event that I have had the good fortune to witness for some time, and the result reflects the greatest credit upon the victors', namely Ebbw Vale winning by a margin of one goal and three minors, to one minor.

Ebbw Vale was not a WFU recognised club in its early days. Its play was more noted for its ferocity than its skill, but it did exhibit more open and more attractive rugby than any other team in the district. The rugby club immediately became a force to be reckoned with in the valleys. Early in its second Season, which didn't begin until October in those days, Ebbw Vale was said to have a strong team destined to become 'very efficient, judging by past successes'. The season was short and the number of games few. In a match report of a game between Ebbw Vale and Merthyr which took place on 5th April, 1885, an indication is given of a typical season's play in the valleys. The match, which ended in a draw, concluded Merthyr's finest season so far. Its record was 12 matches played, 6 won and 5 drawn. The one defeat was at the hands of Ebbw Vale at Merthyr, going down 2 goals and 1 touch down to 2 tries. Three of these 12 games were against Ebbw Vale. The Merthyr 2nd team played only 7 games, winning 4 and drawing 1. Given that Merthyr and Ebbw Vale were comparable teams, there is no reason to believe that the Valians would have had a significantly heavier fixture list.

The season that gave Ebbw Vale the fullest coverage in the *Merthyr Express* was in fact that of 1884-5. Other newspapers do not carry any accounts of Ebbw Vale rugby before the 1890s. From the reports we can piece together that Ebbw Vale played Rhymney and Merthyr before Christmas, beating Merthyr by two goals and two touch downs to nil at Ebbw Vale. The result of the Rhymney game is unknown. On January 24th, 1885 the return game was played at Rhymney. The early reports refer to the ball as the 'leather', which in this game found itself for the most part in the Rhymney 25. Rhymney had a stronger pack, but was constantly put on the defensive by Ebbw Vale's kick and chase tactics in the first half. The Ebbw Vale forwards were able to capitalise on Richards' huge punts by following-up with a combined attack. In the second half Rhymney was wholly on the defensive, hardly entering Ebbw Vale territory. Ebbw Vale won decisively by 20 points to nil.

The return match with Merthyr took place on Wednesday 11th February on the Merthyr ground which was in such a deplorable condition that both sides agreed to limit the game to thirty minutes each way. This probably suited Ebbw Vale, which was able only to muster 14 men, who were: E. Whislade, back, three quarter backs, D. J. Richards (captain), H. Jones, and D. W. Morgan; half backs C. Williams, J. Morgan and Sandbrooke; forwards L. Clarke, Golightly, L. Coombes, D. Roberts, Parry, T. Morris, Morgan and E. Davies. For most of the game Merthyr dominated, penning Ebbw Vale in its own half, with only the occasional opportunity being created by D. W. Morgan and D. J. Richards. Ebbw Vale went down 2 goals, 4 tries, and 3 touch downs to nil. On February 12th Ebbw Vale played Monmouthshire Rangers in the Monmouthshire Cup at Abergavenny, winning by 17 points to 10, and went on the meet Maindy at Pontypool in the next round. This match was not reported. Ebbw Vale met Merthyr for the third time on 5th April. Rain fell throughout the game as Merthyr played with the wind in the first half and secured an early try, converted by J. Williams. Ebbw Vale hit back strongly after being forced to touch the ball down. Richards attempted a drop goal which the full-back failed to gather-up, providing the opportunity for Sandbrook to fall on it and score a try. Richards converted. The final score was a draw with both sides scoring one goal and one touch down each.

It is the Tredegar game for the first three seasons that attracts press coverage. On 10th December 1881 Ebbw Vale easily beat Tredegar at home. The kick-off was at 3-30pm and by the time it finished the ball must have been barely visible. The score was one goal, eight tries, 7 touches down and one touch down in goal to nil. In their next two meetings, away on 21 October, 1882 and home on 20th January, 1883, Ebbw Vale was an irresistible force, but it did not so easily defeat Rhymney on 13 January, 1883. The away game against Tredegar went all Ebbw Vale's way in the first half, and although the home team exhibited some resistance in the second half, it couldn't prevent Ebbw Vale putting a greater distance between them. Ebbw Vale's passing and running was far superior, and L. Williams, the captain was said to have had a 'very fine' game. The result was 2 goals, 3 tries, 2 touches in goal, and 5 touches down to nil. The return on home ground was almost embarrassing, and the correspondent says with a hint of exasperation: 'To give full details of the game would be mere repetition of the facts as Ebbw Vale carried all before them try after try, being secured in rapid succession.' Even the advantage of the down hill slope did not arrest the onslaught for more than a few minutes. All of the team played so well that none were singled out for special praise. Ebbw Vale won by two goals, nine tries, and seven touches down to nil. The Rhymney game, however, was not so easy. Rhymney, playing away from home, vigorously contested the game, holding Ebbw Vale to a much narrower margin, one disputed try, one touch in goal, and three touches down to nil.

The interesting thing about the two Tredegar match reports for the 1882-3 season is that the Ebbw Vale teams are named. In the

Ebbw Vale Rugby Football Team 1892/3. T. Jones, captain.

first of the games the players fielded were: J. Parry, back; T. Richards, A. D. Henry, three-quarter backs; L. Williams (captain) and L. Nicholas, half backs; R. J. Jones and C. E. Jones, quarter backs; H. Skinner, E. Needham, D, Morgan, J. Marchant, D. Richards, W. Golightly, D. Bevan, and L. Evans, forwards. For the second game, T. Richards moved to half back, replacing C. E. Jones, to make way for Dr Mason, who was joined at three quarter back by the captain L. Williams, moving from half back. While in the forwards H. C. Williams, T. Morris, D. W. Morgan, and T. Jeffries replaced D. Bevan, L. Evans, and W. Golightly. In the first game there were eight forwards and in the second nine.

The fixture still remained eagerly anticipated in 1887 when large numbers of spectators turned up on a cold February afternoon to see Ebbw Vale win 2 goals, three tries, and five minors, and one dropped goal to nil. W. J. Owens, the full back, W. Hughes at three quarter, and W. McCarthy, at forward, were praised for having 'splendid' games. By the early 1890s the Tredegar fixture ceased to be a feature of the Ebbw Vale calendar, and when the Monmouthshire League was instituted in 1896-7 Tredegar played no part. The fixture resumed in 1899-1900 season when Ebbw Vale beat its rivals away by 2 goals (a penalty, and a drop goal from a mark) to 1 try, and at home by 3 tries to nil. During the 1900-1901 season the match was being billed as the 'International of the Hills', and Tredegar was widely thought to be a distinct threat to Ebbw Vale's undisputed claim to be champions of the valleys.

In the following season Ebbw Vale rejoined the Monmouthshire League, having defected at the end of the first season. Both Ebbw Vale and Tredegar were now in the Monmouthshire League together, battling for supremacy. They both enjoyed exceptionally good seasons, with Tredegar taking first blood in the first skirmish between them. In a close game Tredegar won by 1 goal to nil. Pill Harriers topped the League, but second place was not decided until the last game of the season. The 'International of the Hills' was to decide second and third positions. Tredegar won comfortably by 1 goal and 2 tries to nil.

Throughout the 1890s Ebbw Vale was the most formidable team in the valleys. The 1893-4 season, for example, was described as a 'remarkable success'. Applications to join the WFU came from all sorts of rugby clubs of dubious status, necessitating the establishment of a vetting procedure in 1892. Ferndale and Merthyr were recommended to the AGM in 1893, and Ebbw Vale, Pontnewydd and Glamorgan County Football Club were found to have satisfactory credentials in 1894 and went through the AGM at the Angel Hotel, August 30, 1895. There were twenty-three club 'belonging' to the WFU in 1895 which rose to 47 by the end of the 1896-7 season.

Given the social composition of the Ebbw Vale team, and the necessity to take time off work in order to play, it seems that the club found itself in a number of disputes over paying broken time money to players between 1895 and 1907. It was investigated by the WFU in 1894-5 to ensure that it adhered to the rules of amateurism before being admitted to the WFU, and was again threatened with having its books inspected in 1907 as part of a general attempt to eradicate professionalism from the game. The issue of professionalism versus amateurism was in the news quite frequently, both in Wales and nationally, because in 1895 about half of the clubs broke away from the RFU and formed the Northern Union. The issue of

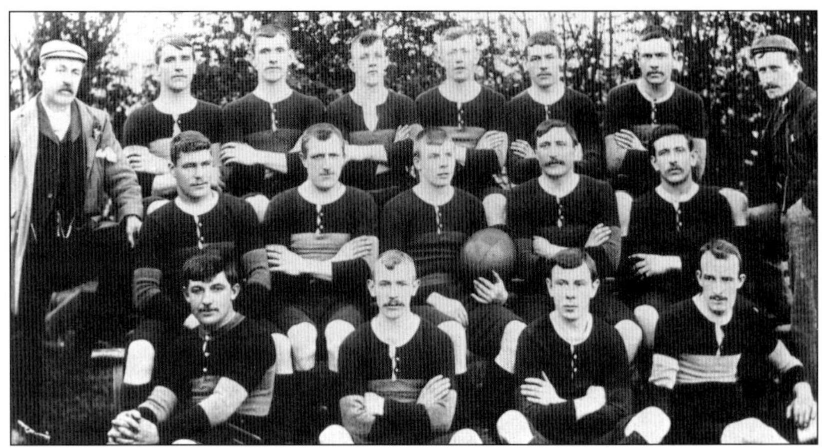

Ebbw Vale Rugby Football Club, 1895-6. E. J. Giles, Captain.

the distinction between amateurism and professionalism was particularly sensitive because of the testimonial match of Arthur Gould, just two years after he played at Ebbw Vale. The English Union made it clear that it could not support the testimonial if the gift to Gould was to be monetary. The WFU therefore suggested that the proceeds of the game be used to buy the deeds of his house, which were presented to him on Easter Monday, 1897. The WFU had pledged money but was forced to withdraw the offer under pressure from the International Board, but eventually decided that Gould would not be in breach of its rules and reinstated the 1000 shillings, and allowed others to subscribe. The RFU declared that Gould would technically be in breach of the rules and would become a professional player. In consequence the WFU withdrew from the RFU and IB and international matches with Wales were suspended. One of the conditions of re-admittance was that Gould could no longer represent his country. He did, however, serve as a loyal member of the WFU for many years after.

During the 1890s Ebbw Vale became one of the most formidable 2nd Class teams playing in Wales. They are variously described as 'the Champions of the Hills', the 'premier team of the Hills', 'local champions', and 'invincible'. This success was built on a solid foundation in the 2nd team, which had an equally impressive record. In the 1894-5 season the reserve team was praised for having an even better record than the Firsts. The team lost only one of its first thirteen, scoring 128 points and conceding 13. On 15 December, 1894 'Leatherum', the *Merthyr Express* football correspondent, remarked that: 'The Ebbw Vale 2nds are the possessors of a remarkable record, in fact, I question whether there is a 2nd team in the district that can boast of such wonderful doings'.

The Monmouthshire District of the Rugby Football Union was formed in 1896-7. Ebbw Vale was playing its games on the Bridge End Field at a rent of £2.00 per game and finding it difficult to balance gate receipts against expenditure, despite the fact that Ebbw Vale was undoubtedly the biggest draw in the area, attracting large crowds for both 1st and 2nd team appearances. This season was badly hit by atrocious weather, especially during important games. Besides those teams in the Monmouthshire League Ebbw Vale played such opposition as Roath, Abertillery, Abergavenny, Newport Seconds, and Cardiff District, defeating them all. Ebbw Vale's overall record was 33 matches played, 20 won, 5 drawn, and 8 lost. Marchant topped the list of try scorers obtaining 13, with Kerton a close second on 11, plus a dropped goal and penalty.

The final positions in the first season of the Monmouthshire League were:

	Played	*Won*	*Lost*	*Drawn*	*For*	*Against*	*Points*
Pontymister	16	14	1	1	160	12	29
Crumlin	16	10	3	3	104	97	23
Ebbw Vale	**16**	**8**	**3**	**5**	**121**	**68**	**21**
Abercarn	16	7	3	6	59	34	20
Cwmbran	16	8	7	1	105	64	17
Blaina	16	4	9	3	39	135	11
Abertillery	16	4	9	3	43	91	11
Pontnewydd	16	4	11	1	42	106	9
Cwmcarn	16	1	14	1	42	166	3

Source: *South Wales Weekly Argus,* May 8, 1897.

Despite achieving an enviable position in the League during the first season the range and reputation of teams were not high profile enough to increase receipts sufficiently to match expenditure. Despite its creditable performance Ebbw Vale decided to withdraw from the League in order to seek more attractive opposition. The *Weekly Argus* lamented the departure of the Valians describing it as a 'great loss' which would be 'severely felt'. In particular the committed play of Kerton, Marchant, Waterfield and Simmons of the backs, and Parfitt, Keates and Walters of the forwards would be sadly missed. Brynmawr replaced Ebbw Vale in the competition.

Regardless of being termed the 'recognised champions of Monmouthshire', and 'the finest team in Monmouthshire outside Newport' good quality opposition was still proving difficult to attract even after leaving the Monmouthshire League. Teams such as Brecon, St. Peters, Chepstow, and Cinderford, all of which were beaten by Ebbw Vale in the 1898-1899 season, didn't have the drawing power of the likes of the fashionable teams in South East and South West Wales. The latter part of the nineteenth and the early years of the twentieth centuries were turbulent times for Ebbw Vale. Against Crumlin and Blaina in 1899 Ebbw Vale was cited by the WFU for fielding second XVs instead of their first team. In addition, Barry complained to the WFU that Ebbw Vale had failed to honour its debt of £5-00 in lieu of a fixture at Barry, and the Valians lost one of their best players, Jack Foley, to Brynmawr. In the same year two of Ebbw Vale's captains were suspended by the WFU, the first in January, Kerton, for two weeks following an incident at Barry, and the second, in December, J. H. Pugh, following a match at Mountain Ash. He was suspended until the end of the season for 'using disgusting language' to the referee H. J. Taylor. Pugh's team-mate, D. J. Thomas was suspended for two weeks for the same offence.

The 1898-99 season saw Ebbw Vale vacate the Bridge End Field for the cheaper option of playing on the Beaufort Fields. Towards the end of the season reports of Ebbw Vale's financial difficulties began to circulate. Debts were accruing largely because of the failure of opponents to fulfil home commitments. Brecon, Treherbert, Machen, Treorchy, and Pontypridd failed to honour their commitments because they couldn't raise teams. The rescheduled game with Treorchy resulted in Ebbw Vale having to pay Chepstow compensation for cancelling its fixture. The *South Wales Daily News* reported on 27 March, 1899 that the 'Monmouthshire champions have been exceptional sufferers in this respect . . . Not only pecuniary loss, but also the moral effect on spectators and players is likely to be of a permanent character.' And on the 17th April the newspaper suggested that: 'The non-appearance of Pontypridd plunged Ebbw Vale into financial difficulty and they were in a way depending upon this match to clear their debts'. In 1900 the Club defaulted on the payment of its dues to the WFU. It was 'struck off the Union list', but readmitted in the same year, just before the start of the new season. At the end of the 1900-1901 season Ebbw Vale complained to the WFU that Pontymister, Treorky (Treorchy), and Blaina had failed to fulfil their fixtures with it.

In spite of its financial difficulties Ebbw Vale enjoyed a very good 1901-2 season on being readmitted to the Monmouthshire League, finishing third in the table. This, however, was an Indian summer, because the 1902-3 campaign turned out to be a disaster. Out of the 18 League games played the Valians managed to win only three, drew 3 and lost 12. The team conceded 147 points while scoring only 26. Ebbw Vale was placed last in the table, with Pill Harriers and Tredegar retaining their previous season's placings at first and second. *The South Wales Daily News* reported on Monday 3rd August that there was 'talk that Ebbw Vale will not be as strong as usual next season'. It looks as though the team completely folded at the end of 1902-3. The explanation, according to the *Merthyr Express*, was that 'Ebbw Vale fell upon evil days, owing to a ground difficulty' (Nov. 3rd, 1906). However, junior rugby was still played in the town and the Ebbw Vale Crusaders, capitalising on the senior club's demise, went on to win the Monmouthshire Junior League in 1904-5 and 1905-6.

In 1905 Ebbw Vale made an application to the WFU for formal recognition once again. The application was rejected and Ebbw Vale told that it must field a team for a season before re-consideration. Ebbw Vale regrouped, and although failing to be re-admitted to the

Monmouthshire League, played most of the teams in it. Ebbw Vale now returned to the Bridge End Field for the first time in over five years, sharing the ground with Ebbw Vale Crusaders, who played on alternate Saturdays. Entering the new season Tredegar was no longer the force it once was, and Abertillery was the most formidable of the valley teams, whose prospects, according to the *Merthyr Express* (1 Sept., 1906), were 'exceptionally rosy'. Abertillery had won the Monmouthshire league the previous season.

Ebbw Vale was not daunted by the task of having to re-establish itself, indeed, because of its former glory, expectations were high 'that the once famous club will again be seen high on the ladder of sport' (1 Sept., 1906) Supporters were not disappointed. During its first season back in senior rugby Ebbw Vale remained unbeaten at home, and overcame some of the most powerful sides in the Monmouthshire League. Ebbw Vale had a disappointing start to the season losing its away games to its old rivals Abertillery and Merthyr. Relying on some of its old veterans, including J. Kerton, Danny Beynon and Alf Rodway, and new inexperienced, but talented recruits, such as Jack Puts on the wing, play was not always consistent, but when the whole team fired on all cylinders some outstanding victories were achieved. Against the Pill Harriers on 6 October, 1906, Ebbw Vale continued a winning streak by scoring six tries, two of then converted. Only Danny Beynon among the veterans showed his age in his painfully slow delivery to the backs. Two weeks later Ebbw Vale achieved 'a ridiculously easy victory' over Cardiff Albions in very wet conditions, by an even more impressive score, running in 10 tries, and converting 1.

It was on the back of this run of success that the local rivalry between Tredegar and Ebbw Vale was resumed on Monday evening, 29th October. Tredegar, on the other hand had succumbed to the superior forward strengths of Brynmawr and Abertillery. It was a nostalgic occasion, evoking memories of former struggles before mass crowds. In front of a good, but much smaller crowd, Ebbw Vale had a heavier, more experienced pack which played with determination. Its opponents' forwards, on the other hand, lacked vigour and keenness. It was in the front five that the game was won, starving the much sleeker Tredegar backs of possession, and forcing them on the defensive. The score of 1 goal to nil did not reflect the superiority of the Valians. The superiority of the Valians was confirmed at the return match on February 24th, 1907. This return 'international of the hills' was eagerly anticipated, but the enthusiasm and passion for rugby in the area had not yet returned to its former levels. The crowd was the largest of the season, but still far below those attendances when the rivalry was at its most intense.

The game was described as 'fast and furious' between extremely fit and well drilled players, with both sides 'exerting every nerve and resorting to every legitimate tactic to secure the lead' (*Merthyr Express*, 3rd March, 1907). A mistake by the Tredegar defence mid way through the first half gave Ebbw Vale a scrappy try which won the home side the game. The forwards were again formidable, and the commentator doubted whether any pack in Monmouthshire could match them. Hudson, Monks and Saunders were the outstanding forwards, with Saunders resorting to a bit more force than was necessary on occasions. The Tredegar pack nevertheless gave a good account of itself, and was once again beaten by its lack of weight.

After the first Tredegar game Ebbw Vale continued its winning run by beating Llwynypia by 1 goal and 3 tries (13pts) to nil, but then succumbed to a combined Rest of the League side, going down by 11pts to nil. By mid November the boys from the Bridge End Field had re-established their traditional reputation, and perhaps had become a little too over confident. In facing Aberdare, Ebbw Vale predicted that it would comfortably win the game by 16 points. The 'Darians' picked up the gauntlet and mounted a strong offensive, led by the talented half-backs Rhys Rees and Gibbon who outclassed their counterparts. Ebbw Vale countered the half-back pairing by reverting to 'smart tactics', and some tactics that were considered 'rather dirty', to out manoeuvre them, The Valians saved face by managing to achieve a no score draw. Aberdare was delighted to have fought such an even battle 'against such a powerful new Monmouthshire organisation as Ebbw Vale' (*Merthyr Express*, Nov. 17th, 1906).

Draws were obtained in the following two matches against Blaenavon and Bristol, but Mountain Ash away proved too strong for the Valians who went down 11 points to nil, in a game that was a model of fluent and exciting rugby. Ebbw Vale was outclassed in the back division by players with superior speed and tactical thinking. While the Vale forwards gave good account of themselves, and gave exhibition demonstrations of how to wheel the scrum, they could not contain P.C. Dick Thomas, a Welsh international, who scored the try of the season when he gathered-up the ball from a poor field by Young, the visiting centre. He shot for the line, side-stepped the Vale skipper, W. J. Thomas on the wing, and cut back inside Giles, the full back. The cheering was deafening as Thomas crossed the line.

For the rest of the season Ebbw Vale maintained its unbeaten home record, and put on some very strong performances against some tough opposition. Against Abertillery, for example, the leaders of the League, Ebbw Vale secured a draw, despite having to play with fourteen men for most of the first half because of an injury to Irwin. The veteran Kerton had an outstanding game scoring both of the Ebbw Vale tries. The final score was 6 points each. There were, of course, disappointments, one of which ended in ugly scenes at the end of the game after the referee disallowed a drop goal which would have secured the match for Ebbw Vale. The visiting crowd 'groaned and hooted vigorously' at the decision, and made for the referee 'in a threatening manner' at full-time. After some delay the police managed to escort the referee away unharmed. Brynmawr emerged the winners with 1 try and 1 drop goal, 7 points, to one try, 3 points. Ebbw Vale beat Blaina and lost to Abertillery in the last two games of the season.

Ebbw Vale's return to senior rugby was a resounding success both on and off the field. Financially the club made a profit and was comfortably able to pay a heavy £10 fine for failing to field a team against Blaenavon. It was suggested that most teams would have been bankrupted by such a heavy penalty. The accounts at the annual general meeting showed a healthy balance, but there were still difficulties to be overcome in meeting the criteria of the WFU for re-admittance into the League. In addition, Ebbw Vale remained concerned about its inability to attract first class opposition, which it felt that its record over the years richly deserved. It is in this context that we turn to the most notorious period in the history of the club.

BIBLIOGRAPHY

Primary sources

The Minute Books of the Welsh Rugby Union.

Newspapers

The Merthyr Express, The South Wales Gazette, Western Mail, The South Wales Weekly Argus Supplement, The South Wales Argus, The Times, The South Wales Daily News, Monmouthshire Merlin, Star of Gwent.

Books and Articles

Arthur Gray-Jones, *A History of Ebbw Vale* (Risca, The Starling Press, 1970).

Anonymous, 'The Ups and Downs at Ebbw Vale over the Years' in *Welsh Rugby*, January, 1966.

Jack Davies, *One Hundred Years of Newport Rugby 1875-1975* (Risca, Starling Press, 1974).

Michael Foot, *Aneurin Bevan 1897-1945*, vol. I (London, MacGibbon and Kee, 1963).

Roy Palmer, *The Folklore of (old) Monmouthshire* (Herefordshire, Logaston Press, 1998).

J. B. G. Thomas, *The Illustrated History of Welsh Rugby* (London, Pelham Books, 1980).

J. B. G. Thomas, ed., *Rugby in Wales* (Llandybie, Christopher Davies, 1970).

David Smith and Gareth Williams, *Fields of Praise* (Cardiff, Wales University Press, 1980).

Roy Lewis, *Rugby Vale: A Brief Account of Ebbw Vale Rugby Football Club* (Ebbw Vale, EVRFC, 1979).

Steve Lewis, *Newport Rugby Football Club* (Stroud, Tempus Publishing, 1999).

Wray Vamplew, *Pay Up and Play the Game* (Cambridge, Cambridge University Press, 1988).

Gareth Williams, *1905 and All That* (Llandysul, Dyfed, Gomer Press, 1991).

Admiral Sir Percy Royds, *The History of the Laws of Rugby Football* (Twickenham, Walter and Co.,1949).

Chapter Two

Amateurism and Professionalism

The single most important issue in sport for the Victorians and Edwardians was the question of playing a game for its own sake, or playing for money. It is a very little noticed fact how closely the Victorians associated sport with morality and character building. The idea of a healthy body leading to a healthy mind was for them an indisputable fact, and therefore central to the curriculum of the public school. This means end relation between exercise and mental health was thought to be considerably tainted by the merest hint of professionalism, except in relation to cricket in which the professional could be gainfully employed. While not playing the game the professional could be involved in coaching, tending to the wicket and doing odd jobs around the club house. The relationship was very much felt to be one of master and servant, and the professional was expected to know his place. N. L. Jackson maintained that 'generally the professional cricketer is a good fellow, not spoilt by praise and rarely failing to show due respect to his employers'.[1] Cricket professionals did not enjoy the same privileges as the amateurs, and in some clubs entered the field by a different gate.

Rugby and Character Building

Rugby Union was thought to be the pre-eminent game because it displayed all the qualities of a contest and developed the strength of character necessary for military service. Rugby was the backbone

1. N. L. Jackson, 'Professionalism and Sport', *Fortnightly Review*, vol. 67, 1900, p. 156.

Ebbw Vale Cricket Club Season 1909.

of imperialism and inextricably associated with patriotism. Cecil Rhodes himself financed the first English Rugby Union tour to South Africa in 1891, and touring teams came from both Australia and New Zealand. Professionalism in rugby union football was viewed not only as a contagious moral disease, introduced into the game by the lower classes, but also tantamount to treason. In selecting men from working class backgrounds for the national team Wales was deemed to be lowering the whole tone of the game. In 1903 the Scottish referee Crawford Finlay was disturbed that Wales selected miners, steelworkers and policemen for the national side. He contemptuously suggested that they should clear off and join the Northern Union.[2]

It was argued that in the English Union the reason why rugby had remained amateur for so much longer than association football was that it was dominated by the public schools and universities of the south. The game simply attracted a better class of people.[3] Indeed,

2. David Smith and Gareth Williams, *Fields of Praise* (Cardiff, 1980), 124.
3. Ernest Ensor, 'The Football Madness', *The Contemporary Review*, vol. 74, July-December 1898, p. 757.

the better classes were dissociating themselves from association football and taking up rugby and hockey,[4] except in the North where unfortunately the 'labourer diverted his attention from quoits and rabbit coursing and pigeon flying, and turned it to football'.[5] Indeed, one commentator went as far as to blame the growing interest of the working man in football as the cause of the decline of the Liberal vote. As long as men were thinking of nothing else but football, they couldn't at the same time be thinking of politics: 'not properly understanding their interests, and , moreover, being indifferent towards them they passively vote Tory.'[6]

There was a fear that with the increased flow of migrants from the countryside into the towns and cities that the working classes would be subject to less exercise, and as a consequence their strength of character would be diminished. Working men and boys were to be encouraged to play football in order to develop their sense of chivalry and honour, which could be severely undermined by the introduction of monetary rewards. While it was difficult to deny the success of professionalism in association football, it nevertheless had its vociferous critics, and rugby enthusiasts argued that the objections against professional association football had even greater force in relation to rugby. Because of the nature of the game the career of the full-time professional rugby player would be shorter, and hence ruinous to his long-term job prospects. Whereas in association football the referee was in a position to detect and punish unfair play, it was much less easy to spot in rugby. Professionalism, some argued, would lead to an increased incidence of unfair play in the rucks and mauls because of the overbearing desire to win submerging the more gentlemanly attitude of fair play. The more extreme critics advocated banning the award of first and second team jerseys, blazers, ties, and scarves. Competitions for challenge cups were viewed as particularly pernicious because they 'introduce

4. N. L. Jackson, 'Professionalism and Sport', *Fortnightly Review*, vol. 67, 1900, p. 157.
5. Creston, 'Football', *The Fortnightly Review*, vol. 55, 1894, p. 30.
6. Robert J. Sterdy, 'The Ethics of Football', *The Westminster Review*, 165, January to June, 1903, p. 184.

a fictitious sort of keenness, which is only too apt to lead to tricks of all descriptions. The cup ties in Yorkshire and other counties have done this.'[7] Competition was thought by some to be thoroughly evil.[8]

It is no coincidence that during the early years of Northern Union players were also required to work in respectable jobs, and strict limits were put on remuneration in order to prevent allegations of indolence being levelled at professional rugby players. The aim was to demonstrate that the moral fibre of the professional was just as strong as that of the amateur. The trait of under the table payments had become endemic before the formal change of code, and the rules were systematically violated despite the imposition of heavy penalties upon those who were caught.

The Northern Union and Migration of Players

The sheer dishonesty of having to deny what was a thinly veiled practice of paying broken time money to working class players in the North of England led to 22 clubs breaking away from the Rugby Football Union in September 1895. It was not meant to be a professional game, and allowed for only six shillings broken time to be claimed for one day per week. It was in fact an attempt to curtail professionalism more effectively than Rugby Union had done. Even though three years after the split, and nine before Ebbw Vale became professional, in 1907 the Northern Union had bowed to pressure for a fully professional game, it still retained the work clause which required team members to be in recognised employment. This clause was aimed at the large number of Welshmen in the Union, many of whom had drawn wages for their services since before the split. The *Athletic News* smugly exclaimed in 1898 that 'It will be a treat to see some of those Taffies work'.[9] The Northern Union employed private detectives to ensure that the rules were not

7. Hely Hutchinson Almond, 'Football as Moral Agent', *The Nineteenth Century*, vol. 34, July–December, 1893, p. 909.
8. Ensor, 'The Football Madness', 758.
9. Old Ebor, *Athletic News*, 8 August, 1898.

broken, and one of the most severe penalties was imposed on Dai Fitzgerald, who played for Batley and Wales. He was banned for eighteen months in 1898 because his coal agent's job didn't entail any work.[10] Even though the regulations were abolished in 1905, the poor financial position of most of the clubs meant that wages were low and that it was almost impossible to make a living out of Northern Union rugby. Ebbw Vale players throughout the five years of professionalism still held down regular jobs in the collieries and steel works.

The WFU took a firm line on Professionalism before the formation of the Northern Union in 1895. The link between the North of England and South Wales was forged in the early 1880s when teams from Wakefield Trinity, Batley, Hull and Dewsbury visited Cardiff, Newport, Neath, Llanelli and Swansea. Very soon these prosperous Northern clubs were recruiting the best Welsh players. The first recruit seems to have been D. H. Bowen an international full-back from Llanelli who went to play for Dewsbury in 1884, followed closely by the Wales and Newport back James Bridie who went to Manningham. In 1886 the Wales and Cardiff half-back William 'Buller' Stanton shocked the WFU by joining Dewsbury. The migration of players to the North of England was perceived as a serious problem in early 1892. When David and Evan James left Swansea to play for Manchester's Broughton Rangers it was amid rumours that they had been recruited and enticed with monetary inducements of £250. The WFU asked the Rugby Football Union not to grant the transfer. They were declared professional by the RFU, much to the delight of *The Cambrian*, Swansea's local newspaper, which gloated that 'to talk about these players being non-professionals is absurd' (6 January, 1893). The writer mocked the opposition to the decision by Yorkshire and Lancashire, maintaining that they will never get the decision overturned. Ironically, it was the WFU which pressed to have the decision reversed in 1896 when the James's had returned to Wales only to leave for good in 1899 for a fee of £200 and £2-00 a week, with employment as warehousemen. The brothers James were

10. Tony Collins, *Rugby's Great Split* (London, Frank Cass), 179.

so legendary that when professionalism came to Wales their names, despite their ages, were linked with the Ebbw Vale club. The *Merthyr Express* suggested on 27 September, 1907 that: 'The latest is that the brothers James are in negotiation for places in the Valians ranks. The rumour came from the right source, and it may be taken for granted there is something in it'. Nothing, however, came of it.

Numerous clubs were experiencing difficulties in keeping their best players in the face of lucrative offers from the North of England. In 1892 Ebbw Vale lost one of its most gifted players, W. Gameson, to Wakefield Trinity, and Pontypridd complained to the WFU about one of its players going to Yorkshire without permission. At a Committee Meeting at the Angel Hotel, February 25, 1893 the WFU adopted a resolution to deal with all similar cases equitably. Any player who moved from a Welsh club to a club in another Union without the permission of the WFU would be deemed professional.

South Wales was an obvious recruiting ground for the newly professionalised game, and a general paranoia was generated by the operations of scouts in the area. Northern Union clubs made it worthwhile for members of established rugby clubs to encourage players to turn professional. The WFU attempted to eradicate this practice by banning from Welsh grounds anyone deemed to be acting as an agent for the Northern Union. This was the penalty imposed upon a Newport official, Mr. Twist, who was caught recruiting players for the professional game. In January 1898 Ebbw Vale complained to the WFU about someone attempting to recruit their full back Waterfield for Huddersfield and asked that the person be dealt with in the same manner as Twist who had been banned from Newport's ground.

The WFU found it necessary to be more precise in its rules relating to professionalism as individual cases arose which needed a response. In September 1897, for example, Mountain Ash asked for clarification on the issue of a player who had signed to join a professional club and had received payment, but did not actually play. The WFU decided that in such circumstances a player would still be eligible to play in Wales. This ruling was overturned in 1900, and the mere signing of an agreement constituted professionalism. Furthermore, it had in October 1898 declared that any player playing in the same team as a professional would himself be deemed professional.

The professional game obviously gave rise to players who wished to seek reinstatement as amateur players. The WFU drew up its own blacklist in 1896 by requiring all clubs to supply the names of players who had gone North. It declared all players on this list professional. One such player was W. Gameson, formerly of Ebbw Vale. Gameson's case was unusual in that he went to Wakefield Trinity before the establishment of the Northern Union. Ebbw Vale wrote a lengthy letter to the WFU to persuade the Committee to reinstate him, but on October, 15, 1896 it resolved 'that Gameson having played for a club in the Northern Union he is thereby constituted a Professional and his reinstatement was accordingly refused'. Almost two years later Barry made representations on Gameson's behalf, and he was called to appear before the General Committee on October 4, 1898. He satisfied its members that he had played as an amateur and received no payment while playing for Wakefield Trinity. He was accordingly reinstated. In November of the same year Gameson applied for a transfer back to Ebbw Vale.

By 1905 the Northern Union was feeling the effects of competition from Association Football which was becoming extremely popular in the heartlands of the North. It was felt that in comparison with soccer Northern Union football might be suffering because it was not a national game. The *Leeds Mercury*, on 22 October, 1905 argued that the Northern Union operated in too limited an area to constitute a real force, and in its defection had weakened the Rugby Union. Only Association Football, it suggested, was national in scope and had the propensity to attract mass appeal.

It is in this context that the establishment of Northern Union in Wales has to be understood. It could be no easy task because of the unprecedented success of the Welsh national rugby union team, and the strength of the leading clubs which were based on the south coast. Teams in the valleys, however, found it difficult to establish attractive fixture lists because of the reluctance of the likes of Cardiff, Newport and Swansea to play in the industry scarred valley towns. To a large extent it is the neglect of the WFU to appreciate the problems of developing the game in the valleys without regular fixtures with the popular coastal clubs, and the refusal to acknowledge the necessity of having to compensate workers for time lost in playing the game that made Ebbw Vale, Merthyr, Mid Rhondda, Treherbert and Aberdare susceptible to the overtures of the Northern Union. It was only when the Northern Union was established in Wales that the WFU made a conscious effort to annihilate it by staging games designed to win back support in the industrial heartlands of Wales.

Professionalism in the Valleys

Ironically it was the unprecedented success of Welsh rugby union between 1900 and 1905 that precipitated the move to professionalism in the valleys. The three quarter line of 1905, comprising Morgan, Gabe, Nicholls and Llewellyn, were awesome in attack and spearheaded the 3-0 defeat of the touring highly successful New Zealand team. Wales was the only country of the four home nations to defeat New Zealand. The tour was such a huge financial success that it led to a movement in Australia and New Zealand to explore the possibility of staging a tour from which the players would benefit financially. One of the principal inducements for Welsh clubs to join the Northern Union was the prospect of a fixture with Albert Henry Baskerville's touring professional All Blacks team of 1907-8. It should not be underestimated, however, the extent to which the Welsh success of 1905 reinforced a sense of national identity and patriotic pride, and therefore to turn away from the amateur code was tantamount to treason, and those who turned professional were vilified by the public school educated leaders of the WFU and the patriotic Welsh press.

Initially it looked as if Aberdare would be the first to field a professional team, but complications over the use of a ground delayed its entry into the Northern Union. It was a former secretary of the club, E. H. Rees, who made allegations in the *South Wales Daily News* which panicked many clubs to contemplate a future outside of the WFU. He claimed that professionalism was rife in South Wales. In a printed statement he furnished the WFU with an extensive list of instances where players had been paid for their services, and clubs had engaged in false accounting to disguise it. Such was the extent of the publicity surrounding the allegations that the WFU was forced to make a through investigation. These enquiries were viewed with some trepidation in the valleys where it had long been the practice to pay more than reasonable expenses, and to disguise the payments by submitting a false set of accounts to the WFU.

In July 1907 there were allegations that Merthyr was paying some of its players and the WFU set up an enquiry to investigate. This prompted officials from both Merthyr and Ebbw Vale to make approaches to the Northern Union. Aberdare players were already under investigation, along with players from Morriston and Usk. Aberdare, like Merthyr and Ebbw Vale was actively pursuing the possibility of joining the Northern Union. In the case of Merthyr it was claimed that 'the success of the club over the last two years was gained by poaching the best players from other towns; by liberal payments under the table; by paying more than other clubs could afford.' The sudden explosion of enthusiasm for Northern Union in the valleys invited the wrath of the WFU which disparaged the coalmining areas and the men who converted to professionalism. These areas, it was contended, were less than patriotic, and the men were hardly of the calibre which constituted the national team. Such views were disingenuous because the WFU planned a campaign to win back the valleys by staging matches between the top southern clubs, and by strengthening the fixture list of those clubs that remained loyal. The irony is that the very attitude that the WFU expressed towards the valleys and their inhabitants, and the difficulty of getting competitive fixtures with the likes of Swansea, Cardiff, Newport and Llanelli, was what drove clubs like Ebbw Vale to turn professional in 1907.

Only in the previous season had the NU reduced the number of players in a team to 13, taking two from the forwards, and the year before had dropped the work clause which required players to prove that they had worked in respectable jobs during the week prior to the game on Saturday. The rule led to the ironic situation that some players who hadn't worked for years because they were able to live on the money they received from their Rugby Union club, when they went North actually had to get a job. The game did not adopt the name of Rugby League until 1922.

Both Ebbw Vale and Merthyr Alexandra enjoyed successful seasons in 1906-7, although Merthyr thought Ebbw Vale second rate. They both showed healthy surpluses on their balance sheets. Merthyr was already playing in the Monmouthshire League, but Ebbw Vale was in the process of having an application considered by WFU for re-admission. The fortunes of Ebbw Vale Rugby Club and Merthyr Rugby Club are closely parallel in that they both became established around the same time, but did not gain WFU recognition until 1894-5. They were both heavily industrialised areas and relied upon the ordinary working man for fielding their teams. It was well known that it was beyond the means of most men with responsibilities to take time off work to play rugby. Rumours circulated throughout the early 1900s that both clubs practised a veiled professionalism in paying broken-time money to their players. Before the annual general meetings of the clubs the WFU had already made its intentions known to investigate the books of both of them, and Ebbw Vale had in fact discussed the issue at a meeting of about forty people on 15 July, 1907. In this context the annual general meetings, at the Assembly Hall, Angel Buildings, Merthyr, and the Bridge End Inn, Ebbw Vale, generated eager anticipation because it was rumoured that proposals to turn professional would be tabled.

The arguments in favour were presented on grounds of principle. It was distasteful and dishonest, it was argued, to feign amateurism while payments were being made to players and officials under the table. Merthyr Alexandra rejected professionalism, while Ebbw Vale adopted it with enthusiasm. A breakaway group of Merthyr supporters and officials did, however, create a new professional team immediately following the defeat.

The Assembly Hall at Merthyr was packed with townspeople and players on Tuesday, 9th July, 1907, and the retiring president, W. W. Green, anticipating a hostile reception, wisely decided to stay away. A. J. Howfield was elected to the chair. After the usual pleasantries from the chair the secretary W. T. Jones read out the accounts which showed a surplus of £206.2s.3d. from income receipts of £826. The accounts were eventually passed after detailed and heated questioning about some of the categories of payment, such as the sum of £31.18s.3d for clerical services. Jones was accused by E. H. Rees of demanding £7.5s from Aberdare Rugby Club to take a team there from Merthyr. He further alleged that two players had been paid 24 shillings and 18 shillings per match, a matter that was under investigation by the WFU. He also intimated that there were plans at Aberdare to institute the professional game. Then came the proposal from Mr. Leonard openly to adopt professionalism. Amid objections to the constitutional status of the question at issue, the proposer argued that everyone knew men were not travelling long distances for the love of the game, and that he wanted to see a line drawn between bogus amateurism and open professionalism. If money was to be paid it should be done honestly, over the table rather than under it. The motion was seconded by a school teacher, W. Harris, who had resigned from the committee because of the veiled payments made to players. He argued that every club in South Wales were up to it, but it would be Merthyr who would be sacrificed in the WFU enquiry, a view which proved to be rather naïve. On the same evening the WFU met in Cardiff to investigate a number of players, including three from Aberdare, and found that 'the answers of the several men called before the committee were more or less satisfactory'. In an attempt to arrest the drift towards professionalism the WFU later found that in the case of Merthyr Alexandra although they were not entirely convinced that the rules had always been upheld, there was no evidence that they had been breached. The committee of the WFU met in Merthyr on 9th August and suspended one committee member of the Merthyr club, he was Mr Leonard who had made the proposal at the AGM to pay the players.

Against attempts to silence him, Harris shouted that Merthyr should take the lead and be the first in Wales to adopt professionalism openly. Those who opposed it pointed to the difficulty of finding a new ground at such short notice, and maintained that Merthyr would be out on a limb with there being no evidence of any other team imminently about to adopt the Northern Union code, except for Ebbw Vale, a second rate team that could not be compared with Merthyr. An amendment moved by Percy C. Williams that the club continue with its amateur status was overwhelmingly adopted. It is clear, however, that during the following week defectors from the club, including two officials elected at the AGM, managed to persuade a large number of the best players to join the new Merthyr Northern Union team, and had also found a ground to stage the games. They were entered both for the league and challenge cup. At the annual meeting of the Seconds team of Merthyr Alexandra at the Tiger Inn in Merthyr on 16 July, the defectors were denounced as traitors.

A week later on 15 July a meeting was held at the Bridge End Inn to consider the question of professionalism. Before about forty people William Morgan Evans, the club joint secretary, who had resigned his position, announced that he had made enquiries about joining the NU and had been to Manchester to meet with officials. The chairman of the club, Mr Joseph Davies, made it clear that Evans had acted in a private capacity. The Northern Union had indicated to Evans that they were already in negotiations with Aberdare and prepared to offer the same terms, with the exception that Ebbw Vale would be offered £10 subsidy per away match in the first season. It was also communicated that Merthyr had been given an undertaking to enter the league with the inducement of a game against the touring New Zealanders, at a rate of £50 and 50% of the gate. Evans argued that 'the so-called amateurism in South Wales to-day was a farce, and professionalism was admitted to be rampant in the Monmouthshire League teams.' In view of the fact that Ebbw Vale had decided to submit a 'straight' account sheet turning professional was the honest thing to do 'in the face of bogus amateurism in the Monmouthshire League'. Before voting on a motion to submit Ebbw Vale into the Northern Union fixture list for the following season, objections were raised and the meeting became rowdy. Assurances were given by Mr Jones, the landlord of the Bridge End Inn, that he had no objections to professional rugby being played on the field. A resolution was passed to make application to the Northern Union, and that no action be taken on the questions of the Bridge End Field until after the annual general meeting. Mr Jones, however, had no authority to give assurances about the use of the field. The Bridge End Inn and the Bridge End Field were leased by Phillips and Son, Brewers, from the Ebbw Vale Company. Arthur Phillips, a member of the firm and the mayor of Newport, was initially vehemently opposed to professional rugby being played on the field. After receiving a deputation he maintained his hostility to the Northern Union game, but was prepared to treat the matter as a business proposition, and would therefore consider the terms offered.

On 22 July the AGM adopted, by a vote of 63-20, the motion to turn professional. From the line of questioning and the fact that the WFU had deferred a decision on Ebbw Vale's application to join, pending receipt of the books of the club, one of the reasons for turning professional was the belief that the club's accounts would not bear scrutiny, and as a consequence that the application to join the Monmouthshire League and Welsh Union would be rejected. During the meeting players admitted that they had been paid, and officials admitted that there was a big discrepancy between the figures as they were publicly stated, and what they actually were. This was in order to disguise the fact that the players received £153 in wages clear of expenses. What differentiated Ebbw Vale from Merthyr was that a rugby union club decided to convert itself into Northern Union, whereas at Merthyr a new club was formed and the amateur club re-grouped and continued to play union, at first struggling, but soon to hold their own against distinguished opposition such as Llanelly, which was then always spelt with a 'y' at the end.

Ebbw Vale Northern Union

The Ebbw Vale Football Club Limited was formed on 16 August, 1907, and registered as a company on 11th October with capital of £250 divided into 500 ten shilling shares. The certificate of incorporation is dated 14 October. The players and officials were all suspended for life by the WFU. This caused a great deal of amusement at Ebbw Vale because the club was not affiliated to, nor connected in any way with, the Welsh governing body. It is difficult to

Name of Club or Member.	Punishment.	Offence.
FREDERICK GEORGE SCRINE, ... Swansea	Suspended to Dec. 31st, 1907	For receiving expenses in excess of amount actually disbursed on account of reasonable hotel or travelling expenses.
ALBERT JAMES THOMAS, Usk ...	Ditto	Ditto.
Police Constable ARCH, Penarth ...	Suspended for whole of Season 1907-8	Ditto.
GEORGE TAYLOR, Morriston ...	Suspended for One Month from Sept. 3rd, 1907	Ditto.
W. THOS. TAYLOR, Morriston ...	Ditto	Ditto.
H. J. WHITTLE, Hirwain	Suspended to Dec. 31st, 1907.	Ditto.
A. PICKERING, Aberdare	Ditto	Ditto.
DAVID JONES, Aberdare	Permanent Suspension.	(1) For receiving Money consideration for playing Football. (2) For refusing to give evidence and assist in carrying out the Professional Rules when requested by the Union to do so.
CHARLES LEONARD, Merthyr (on Merthyr Committee).	Ditto.	For moving a Resolution for payment of Players.
T. ARNOLD, Swansea	Ditto	(1) For playing under an assumed name whilst suspended. (2) For receiving a Money consideration for playing Football.
Merthyr Club	Although not satisfied that the laws against professionalism have been adhered to as closely as might be wished, no proof adduced of the actual breach of such rules. All officials of the Club who have recently joined the Northern Union of course are suspended permanently.	
Ebbw Vale Club, Officials and Players, who have recently joined Northern Union.	Permanent Suspension.	For joining Northern Union.

The Welsh Football Union's Official Findings and pronounced punishments.

DUPLICATE FOR THE FILE.

No. 95202

Certificate of Incorporation

I Hereby Certify, That the

Ebbw Vale Rugby Football Club Company Limited

is this day Incorporated under the Companies' Acts, 1862 to 1900, and that the Company is **Limited.**

Given under my hand at London this Eleventh day of October One Thousand Nine Hundred and Seven

Fees and Deed Stamps £ 4" 5" 0

Stamp Duty on Capital £ —" 15" 0

H. F. Bartlett

Registrar of Joint Stock Companies.

Certificate received by G. C. Hayward for Jordan & Sons, Ld. 120 Chancery Lane.

Date 14th Oct. 1907.

The certificate of incorporation.

identify what colours Ebbw Vale adopted for the professional game. Circumstantial evidence from a match report against Huddersfield suggests that in the 1908-9 season Ebbw Vale played in Yellow and Green hoops

The Northern Union fixtures of Merthyr and Ebbw Vale were arranged in such a way as to ensure that when the one played at home the other played away. Their first commitment was on 7th September, 1907. Merthyr was at home to Oldham, one of the leading Northern clubs, and Ebbw Vale away to Keighly. The highlights of the season were to be the games against New Zealand, at Merthyr on 2nd November, and at Ebbw Vale on 22nd January, 1908. There was also to be an international match between Wales and New Zealand at Merthyr on 1st January, comprising Welsh players from any of the NU teams.

After the initial uncertainty about playing at the Bridge End Field Ebbw Vale managed to secure its use on favourable terms through its negotiations with Messers. Philips and Sons, Newport. A wooden fence and turnstiles were erected in 1906, more or less on the line of the current Club House, and improvements were made to the changing rooms, which were in the Bridge End Inn itself. In turning professional Ebbw Vale was obliged to erect fencing around the ground, but not around the pitch, and build some wooden stands. 'The Rambler' covering the first home fixture against Salford in the *Merthyr Express*, congratulated the committee on having the enclosure 'well roped, the lines well defined, and the field in almost perfect order'. It was not until early November that the fencing around the ground was almost complete, but there was still no stand nor adequate press box. Because the ground was leased on an annual basis the incentive to invest large sums on improvements was largely absent. Despite this, it was estimated that the ground could easily hold 25,000 people.

The popularity of the game had economic consequences for the railway. The platform of the Bridge End railway station was extended and an extra entrance erected. It also had the only gas street light in the vicinity of the ground. The railway station was convenient for transporting miners, brickworkers and coke workers to the games straight from work. The men covered in coal dust from head to toe, and the women covered in brick dust, faces smeared with the brown clay, or smudged with the dust from the coke ovens, drank in the Bridge End before going over to the ground to be led in their chanting by Billie Shae, who throughout the afternoon shouted 'Are we downhearted?', to which the crowd would reply, 'No we are not downhearted'. The *Merthyr Express* reporter 'The Rambler' covered all the Ebbw Vale Northern Union games and the 'Linesman' covered the Merthyr games.

Playing in the Northern Union League

The difficulties of playing in the expanded Northern League cannot be exaggerated. Communications were far more primitive than today, and travel to the North of England by road was prohibitive. Away matches were a three day excursion, starting on Friday evening and arriving mid-Saturday morning, returning on Sunday. On their second visit to the North, and their first to Lancashire, fog lights were placed on the track as the train left the GWR station. On their arrival the Ebbw Vale men were described as 'fagged and seedy' after a tedious all night journey. The Northern teams found the travelling just as arduous. They did nevertheless receive excellent treatment at the County Hotel which all the teams made base camp.

Ebbw Vale played its first game on 7th September 1907, an away fixture against Keighly and lost 26-3. Ebbw Vale's momentous entry into the fray of Northern Union football was a great occasion for the town. On Friday night the GWR station was packed with cheering supporters and well wishers as speeches were delivered from the carriage hired for the team. The players travelled for twelve hours overnight, and were not really familiar with the new code. Ebbw Vale's very first Northern Union rules try, and the only one for the Valians in this game, was scored by Evans from a lovely passing movement started by Chappel. The first home game against Salford proved to be even more of an embarrassment with 'The Rambler'

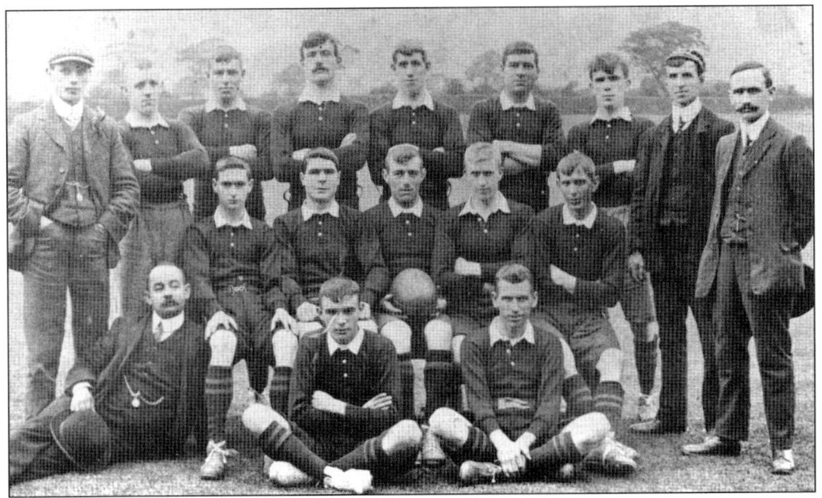

Ebbw Vale Northern Union Rugby Club 1907.

commenting that: 'It was a case of an untrained team, with crude knowledge of a strange system, having to go under to a well trained, nicely balanced lot, well versed and schooled in all the niceties and tricks of a system of which they are past masters'.

In both of the opening games of the season the backs were at fault. Against Keighly they were out of their depth, playing against the sun and the slope of the field in the first half, and consistently failing to capitalise on the spirited work of Rodway, Saunders and Hitchins among the forwards. Against Salford they were accused of being the main culprits in the 'worse exhibition of tackling [that] has ever been witnessed on the ground'. The half-backs Chappel and Lewis were singled out as not being up to the game. The three quarter line was also particularly weak because of the absence of Kerton and 'Chick' Jenkins, two of Vale's most gifted players. The forwards put in spirited performances in both games. Despite the heavy defeat Ebbw Vale fans turned out in droves to give a 'hearty send off' to the visitors at the L & N.W.R station.

The third game of the season, away to Oldham, one of the strongest teams in the League and second in the championship the previous

Ebbw Vale's first visit to Lancashire. From the Athletic News.

season, was viewed with trepidation. A sound defeat by 26 points to 5 was welcomed with relief because of the expectation of a complete humiliation. Ebbw Vale held its own for three quarters of the match, but was outclassed at the end. Dan Beynon, despite the fact that age was not on his side, and Kerton, the try scorer, proved a remarkable half-back pair. The forwards, while playing solidly, were exposed as much slower than the opposition. The following home game against Bramley saw a considerable improvement in Ebbw Vale's performance, and despite losing, reports generally agreed that it was in the kicking department rather than in the general level of skills that the home team was found to be wanting.

Out of 30 games in their first season Ebbw Vale won only 6 and drew 2. Ebbw Vale beat Merthyr, Swinton, Hull, Leeds, Dewsbury and Keighly, to finish one from the bottom of the League at 26th.

The game against Merthyr on October 12 was obviously eagerly awaited because it was the first clash against the professional clubs. Merthyr was the favourite and the disappointing weather drew less than the anticipated crowd. Nevertheless, nearly 4,000 paying spectators witnessed Ebbw Vale's very first win, and the first ever win by a Welsh side. The Valians won by a goal to nil which the spectators greeted with a display of 'wild excitement, seldom equalled even in Welsh football'. Kick-off was delayed by 19 minutes because the Merthyr train was delayed in Beaufort by a coal train blocking the line. When they arrived the players had to run straight on the field in 'a starved condition' to avoid incurring greater penalties for lateness.

Ebbw Vale maintained its form the following Saturday against the Swinton 'Lions'. In defeating them 10pts to 2pts Ebbw Vale became the first Welsh team to beat a Northern Union side from England. The Welsh fans were ecstatic and displayed their 'hysterical enthusiasm' when the whistle was blown for time. Hitchins kicked off against a strong wind, and the forwards charged after the ball immediately posing a danger. After strong scrimmaging near the Swinton line Dan Davies forced himself over the line. The Ebbw Vale forwards were superb and the game was won by all round superiority. Once again Kerton and Chick Jenkins gave heroic performances, but the real find of the match was Reuben Carpenter. Against Merthyr the goal kicking was distinctly suspect, but this weakness was rectified by drafting-in Carpenter whose speed and goal kicking gave Ebbw Vale an added dimension. He kicked a goal from a mark made by Dan Davies, and added the goal points to a try scored by Arundal. This winning run came to an abrupt halt the following week when the Valians faced Hull away, losing by 22pts to 2pts.

Ebbw Vale played Merthyr in the Northern Union Challenge Cup on 14th December. It was the first time that Welsh teams had taken part in the competition. Despite the inclement weather a crowd of 3000 turned out to see Merthyr gain its revenge and beat Ebbw Vale by 9pts to 6pts. The weather and condition of the ground were atrocious. A strong wind howled down the ground giving Merthyr complete territorial advantage in the first half and a lead of 6pts at the turn around. Rees, Page and Jenkins scoring tries for Merthyr, while Kerton and Tom Davies reciprocated for the Valians in the second half, while Merthyr added to its points tally with a try from Smith. Despite a spirited second half in which Ebbw Vale threatened to score throughout, it were unable to make up the deficit. Merthyr dealt a double blow by beating Ebbw Vale again on 26th December, and once more there were mitigating circumstances. Higgins, Burgham and Penny failed to turn up, and there were no travelling reserves. Two spectators, Dan Beynon and Jim Wilcox, who had not played for five years, were pressed into taking the field. Wilcox had walked from Ebbw Vale to Merthyr to see the game, and was therefore not at his best for the duration of the game.

Undoubtedly the highlight of the season was the visit to the Bridge End Field by the touring New Zealand team. It attracted a crowd of nearly 8,000 people and grossed £350. Of the Monmouthshire clubs only Newport had ever attracted a larger crowd. Frederick Mills, the steel works manager, was called upon to kick-off. With a mighty thump he sent the ball hurling down the field amid comments that Ebbw Vale might do well to sign him for the next season! Ironically, it was Mills who was so instrumental in persuading the WFU to re-admit Ebbw Vale to the Union fold after the First World War.

In a tense first half the Valians gave good account of themselves, looking more menacing than their opponents for most of the time. At the turn around New Zealand led by one try (3 points) to one goal (2 points). In the second half Ebbw Vale played like a team possessed and so vigorous was the forward play that despite the New Zealanders crossing the line twice the ball was held up off the ground. The New Zealanders responded with some pretty rough tactics provoking the referee from Swinton to caution them. At full time the score line remained the same and Ebbw Vale despite losing by one point, certainly attained the moral victory. New Zealand was severely criticised for a lack lustre performance that did no credit to the Northern Union game.

Ebbw Vale completed the season in style with the final official fixture against the team which it played in the opening match, Keighly. The game was originally scheduled for 4 January, but was rearranged for 18 April, 1908. Revenge was thought to be unlikely because both Kerton and Llewellyn had to pull-out, but the Valians rose to the challenge and won 13 points to 10. This high point was tempered by the news that Kerton was to retire because of the severe facial injury he sustained the previous week at Hull. The 'Rambler' exclaimed that: 'His retirement is the passing of a great player. He has been to the Ebbw Vale team what Gwyn Nicholls and Arthur Gould were to the Cardiff and Newport teams. For the last 15 years he has been the shining light of Ebbw Vale's back division' (*Merthyr Express*, 4 April, 1908). News of him hanging-up his boots was premature, and he continued to play a prominent role in the Ebbw Vale team. Two seasons later he was out again for a prolonged period, but returned for the final match against Broughton Rangers in which he played 'wonderfully well for an old un' (*Merthyr Express*, 23 April, 1910).

To finish off the season in style a hastily arranged evening match between Ebbw Vale and Merthyr was played at the Bridge End Field which attracted a 'splendid attendance'. The kick off was scheduled for six o'clock in order to allow time for the soccer match to be completed. The game was prolific in scoring and Ebbw Vale came out on top with 3 goals, 6 tries (24 points) to Merthyr 4 goals, 4 tries (20 points). The game was described as having 'a particularly brilliant character'

Despite a poor record, to survive the first season with healthy spectator support was an achievement. Financially, the club made a healthy profit, taking £1,600 in gate receipts of which 46% was written off as depreciation. After paying the legal costs of setting-up a limited liability company the club was able to pay a 10 per cent dividend and carry over a surplus.

The 1908-1909 season saw the introduction of four additional Welsh teams, sufficient to establish a Welsh League which would to some extent alleviate the pressure of having to travel long distances up North. The Northern Union guaranteed at least 4 home and away fixtures with the top Northern teams and underwrote travelling

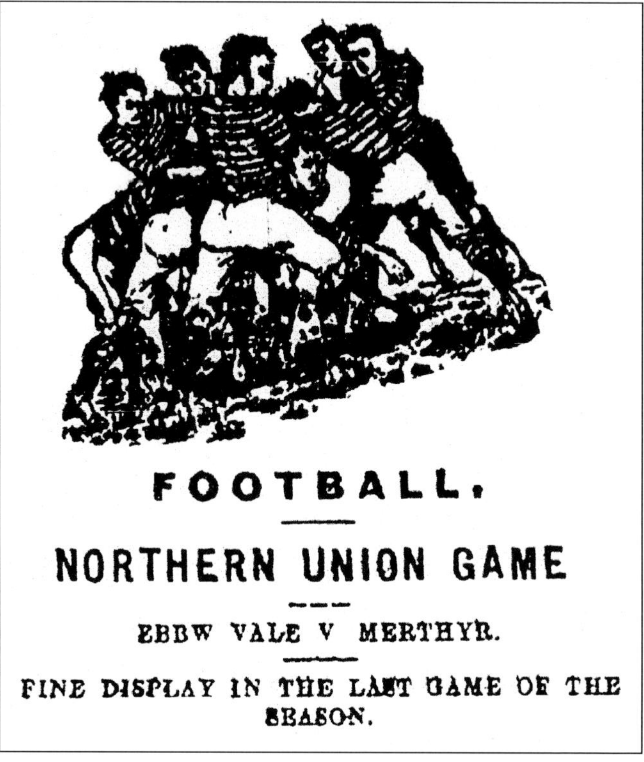

FOOTBALL.

NORTHERN UNION GAME

EBBW VALE V MERTHYR.

FINE DISPLAY IN THE LAST GAME OF THE SEASON.

The illustration heads the rugby reports in the Merthyr Express.

costs by £5-00 per match, a considerable reduction from the £10 of the previous season. Ebbw Vale's fixture list initially had only five Northern clubs, Hunslet, Bramley, Salford, Rochdale Hornets, and Hull Kingston Rovers. Each of the sides in the Welsh League were to play each other four times, but only two of those meetings were to count in the Northern Union League. W. M. Evans the secretary thought that such a small number of English clubs would reduce the attractiveness of the game for spectators and he travelled North to persuade the authorities to include more fixtures with the top English clubs. He succeeded in securing additional games including Wigan, Halifax, St. Helens and Warrington. Ebbw Vale's fortunes took a remarkable turn for the better, helped by their obvious superiority to almost all of the Welsh clubs. The Valians comfortably won the Welsh League, and finished a very respectable 14th out of 31 clubs in the Northern Union League. Its most embarrassing moment, described as a 'Welsh disaster', was defeat at the hands of Beverley, an amateur club, on 27 February, 1909 in the Challenge Cup. It was the 1990s before this achievement was equalled again in Rugby League.

In the opening four games of the season Ebbw Vale twice made credible shows against Hunslet, but went down on both occasions, and also lost badly to Wigan by 5pts to 36pts. Following this poor start a remarkable transformation took place. Out of the next eleven Northern League games Ebbw Vale remained unbeaten, winning ten and drawing against Warrington 10-10, but also beating Bramley and Rochdale Hornets who were trounced on their first visit to Ebbw Vale before a crowd of nearly 4000. The game was played with passion and little restraint: 'The Hornets were like demons let loose, but were met by sturdy and resolute tackling that did not savour of the drawing room.' (*Merthyr Express,* 7th Nov. 1908). The referee temporarily lost control of the game and players laid into each other to their heart's content, with occasional interventions from the spectators. At full-time the Hornets were booed off the field for their rough play.

After nine games Ebbw Vale stood eleventh of thirty one in the table with a 61.11 percentage, and after fourteen games they rose to eighth place, winning nine and drawing one with a percentage of 67.85. After this high point things began to unravel, and by mid January Ebbw Vale had slipped back to thirteenth place with a percentage of 55.26. The team nevertheless rallied for the game against Australia, losing by the narrowest of margins 9pts to 8pts. The Kangaroos were full of admiration for their opponents commenting that no side in Wales, and few in the North could match Ebbw Vale for their cultured and scientific approach to the game. At the close of the season Ebbw Vale was placed a creditable fourteenth, but easily won the Welsh League by failing to lose any of its games in this competition. The Welsh cup was three foot high and solid silver crowned with a dragon. Other Welsh emblems were engraved around the outside of the cup. It was presented on top of the press box by the President of the Welsh League, Mr Kent, after Ebbw Vale defeated the pick of Wales team at the end of the 1908-9 season. Players each received a gold medal. The jubilant crowd carried Higgins the captain shoulder high from the ground.

The 1909-10 season saw Ebbw Vale take the Welsh League title for the second year, but against a considerably reduced cohort of teams with Aberdare, Mid Rhondda and Barry all pulling out of the Northern Union after one season because of financial difficulties. In this season, however, Ebbw Vale produced the most successful cup run of any of the Welsh clubs. Ebbw Vale beat Merthyr in the challenge cup 12-7 and went on to produce the biggest cup upset of the competition in beating Huddersfield away. The loss devastated the Huddersfield players, supporters and press. It was described in the *Huddersfield Examiner*, 14th March, 1910, as the 'Fartown disaster'. The Fartown Lakers, as Huddersfield were known, and their supporters, approached the match rather complacently. Having beaten the formidable Oldham in the first round, Ebbw Vale did not appear so daunting an obstacle. Reports indicate that the score line of 8pts to 5pts flattered Huddersfield, and that it was a great relief to them when the whistle blew for full time. To rub salt in the wound, Dai Davies played a significant part in the defeat of his ex-club. Fans of Huddersfield had their laments printed in the paper, one of which included the lines: 'No more the famous claret and gold in the cup tie will be see. For they've fallen easy victims to the yellow and the green.' So shaken by the defeat were the Fartown Lakers that they changed their method of selecting the Football sub-committee, and reduced the number of members to five.

In retrospect Ebbw Vale made a foolish decision in giving up home advantage in the quarter final against Salford. In the previous round they had played before a crowd of 10,000 and made a comfortable profit. In trying to emulate their success Ebbw Vale found Salford too tough to beat on their own turf, losing by 2 pts to 8pts.

Ebbw Vale finished a respectable 17th out 28 clubs that season in the 1909-10 season.

The managers and players almost went into hibernation during the close season which was all too evident when play resumed. The start of the 1909-10 season saw Ebbw Vale in indifferent form, beating only Treherbert in the first six games. Ebbw Vale could not afford to alienate the support with such a poor performance, given the growing competition of Association football, with Ebbw Vale Town in the first division and Ebbw Vale United in the second division of the Monmouthshire League. Prospects of beating a Northern club looked remote, and Ebbw Vale was not financially secure enough to purchase players for positions in which it found itself weak. The selection committee was forced to experiment bringing Enoch Jones from Waunlwyd in at full-back and moving Harvey from centre to fly-half, replacing the injured Shiglo Thomas. Chistison was brought in at centre, and a new signing from Dewsbury, Bowen, was given a chance in the forwards. Before a crowd of 3,000 '13 dashing Welshmen' were able to register their first win of the season. Enoch Jones had a dream debut making a crunching tackle on Batley's Ward to stop what would have been a certain try. Ebbw Vale won 6pts to 2pts with the visitors displaying increasing bouts of ill-temper as the game appeared to be slipping away from them. On the next three occasions that Ebbw Vale met a Northern club, twice at home and once away at the end of November and beginning of December, the Valians came out on top beating Hunslet 8-3, Leigh 6-0 and Widnes 3-0. By the end of the season, largely due to the successful cup run, only just missing out on a place in the semi-final, Ebbw Vale had regained the admiration of its opponents and supporters. The final game against Broughton Rangers was a huge morale booster. The forwards dominated a tired and jaded Broughton team which went down 20pts to 8 pts. The end of season round-up praised Ebbw Vale for redeeming it reputation as a force to be reckoned with. The correspondent commented that 'towards the end of the season the Monmouthshire club gave such a striking object lesson to their most formidable rivals that they were no longer looked upon as "small fry", but was treated with the respect that was due to a club of the first rank' (*Merthyr Express*, 23 April, 1910). The completion of three seasons was a significant landmark

Ebbw Vale's defeat at Warrington from the Athletic News, *January 1910.*

for Northern Union rules in Wales because it constituted a moral victory over the Welsh Rugby Union which predicted the collapse of the professional game in that period. The game was nevertheless unable to sustain itself across a broad base. Treherbert became a further casualty because it was unable to fulfil its fixture list. Despite applying for re-election to the competition for 1910-11 the Northern Union turned the application down and admitted Coventry in its place.

The new season saw Ebbw Vale with its strongest fixture list yet. With the exception of Merthyr, the sole remaining opposition in Wales, all of the games were against the top English sides. Ebbw Vale had a disappointing start to the season losing its first three games, the second in the last minute against Dewsbury. The Dewsbury game saw Ebbw Vale play fast attractive rugby with strong defensive tackling. The loss was all the more bitter to swallow because what appeared to be a perfectly legitimate try was disallowed. The Valians were seriously weakened by the absence through injury of Chick Jenkins, Dai Davies and W. Harvey.

Out of the next seven games Ebbw Vale had four good wins against Rochdale, Runcorn, Swinton, and Hunslet, making them 20th in a league of 28. There were, however, rumblings of discontent in the North. An article in the *Yorkshire Evening Post*, Saturday, 5 November complained of the burden that the Welsh clubs put on the league. They were unable to draw big crowds playing away from home, and the cost of travel to Wales was hardly justifiable for the Northern clubs, who found the journey increasingly tedious. It argued that the Northern League had done all it could to promote the game in Wales, including providing a travel subsidy, and that if the Welsh clubs could not make a success of it, the English clubs should not be taxed to make up for Welsh deficiencies.

Out of the next seven games Ebbw Vale won an impressive four, giving reason to be optimistic about attaining a high place in the ratings. On December 10, for instance, the Valians achieved a comfortable win against Bramley. It was unfortunate that the weather deterred the crowd for a game that was doubtful to start because of the conditions. Against a full strength Bramley a depleted Ebbw Vale team, missing Chic Jenkins, Llewellyn and Foley, put up a courageous performance. The Valians dominated the first half coming out on top 13 points to nil. They had the opportunity to reduce the aggregate score against them by piling the points on, but the per-

Ebbw Vale Northern Union Club, circa 1908-9.

formance fell away in the second half with a notable indifference among the forwards who were not putting the effort into the scrummaging, leaving the backs few opportunities to shine. The new winger, Shepherd was starved of the ball, and had no opportunities to prove himself. Despite the less than enthusiastic performance Bramley were well beaten by 19 points to five.

Downturn in Fortunes

After fifteen games Ebbw Vale had crept up the table to sixteenth place. Their fortunes then collapsed. With the exception of beating Merthyr on 26 December by 25 points to 3, only to lose against them by 2pts to nil the following day, Ebbw Vale did not win another game until the final fixture of the season against York on 18 April. Llewellyn set an Ebbw Vale record in the first Merthyr game by scoring five out of the seven tries. He scored 24 tries in all that season and finished 12th in the rankings, a considerable achievement while playing for a struggling side. Just four days after playing Ebbw Vale for the second time Merthyr played its last game in the league against Coventry. In January 1911 it was forced to withdraw because of financial difficulties, leaving a number of clubs with unfulfilled return home fixtures after having travelled to Merthyr.

The demise of Merthyr must have been dispiriting for Ebbw Vale which was now the only Welsh side left in the Northern Union. It nevertheless put up a valiant effort in its next game against Hull, with Foley and Burgham playing the games of their lives. Some players, however, were less than impressive. Llewellyn and Shepherd were passengers who like Mr Micawber were always waiting for something to turn up. The penultimate game of the season showed distinct promise with Ebbw Vale holding Oldham to 5pts to nil, in what was described as sensational play. By now however, attendances were poor and the following falling away. The last game of the season was played against York at home on a Tuesday evening in weather which depleted the crowd. It was a meritorious win, but did little to abate the speculation that the Monmouthshire club might not be able to start a fifth season. Ebbw Vale finished 25th out of 28 in the League, their worst season to date. It was nevertheless the longest serving of all the Welsh clubs, and determined to carry on.

Ebbw Vale started the 1911-12 season positively, losing their first game to Huddersfield, but winning home ties against Wigan, Swinton and St. Helens. They could not, however, rescue their credibility by securing an away win. Ebbw Vale had a lamentable run towards the end of the season and was struggling to field a full team. The Valians were only able to field twelve men in each of the games against Halifax and Hull Kingston Rovers, and were reduced to the indignity of having to borrow a reserve player from the Rovers because Llew Llewellyn had been injured against Halifax. Their pride was partially restored by beating York in the final game of the season by 17 points to nil. Ebbw Vale once again finished a disappointing 25 out of 27, winning only four of its games over the season.

Speculation mounted during the close season about Ebbw Vale's ability to carry on in the League. Players became nervous and secured their futures elsewhere. Llew Llewellyn moved to Wigan and W. Higgins to Hull in August 1912. Two days before the opening fixture against Huddersfield on 7 September, 1912, Ebbw Vale withdrew from the league. When the Club folded in 1912 there was speculation about whether it would start the 1912-13 season. Ebbw Vale failed to meet its first match commitment and was officially dissolved as a company 26 March, 1915. Ebbw Vale was the longest serving of the Welsh Rugby League teams. The raw statistics, as always do not tell the complete story. Although Merthyr has the highest winning percentage of 63.9, the fixture list of Ebbw Vale was always tougher, comprising the top teams in the League.The first experiment in Northern Union football was over, with few tears shed up North at the prospect of no more arduous trips to Wales.

The Northern Union game did not flourish in isolation in Ebbw Vale. The professional team encouraged the development of Northern Union rules amateur rugby. The club established a medal competition for local works teams which attracted quite a lot of interest. In March, 1908 for example, a Northern Rules game between the Steelworks and Waunlwyd Colliery attracted a crowd of about 1,000 to see the miners win 27pts to nil. The final of the medal competition was held on Saturday, 16 May before a crowd which equalled that of the professional games. The Marine colliery was represented by 'The Record Team' and Waunlwyd colliery by the Crocks, the favourites to win. In a close and exciting game the Marine boys won 3pts to 2pts.

THE RECORD OF WELSH RUGBY LEAGUE TEAMS

Team	*Period*	*Mean Winning* %	*Highest Winning* %	*Lowest Winning* %
Aberdare	1908/9	5.90	5.90	5.90
Barry	1908/9	16.70	16.70	16.70
Ebbw Vale	1907/8–1911/12	33.10	52.10	18.30
Merthyr Tydfil	1907/8–1910/11	33.00	63.90	11.90
Mid Rhondda	1908/9	30.60	30.60	30.60
Treherbert	1908/9–1909/10	12.50	25.00	0.00

Compiled from a table in Wray Vamphlew, *Pay Up or Play Up*.

EBBW VALE'S NORTHERN UNION RECORD

Season	*Pld.*	*Won*	*Drawn*	*Lost*	*For*	*Agst.*	*Points*	*%*	*Position*
1907-8	30	6	2	22	153	426	14	23.33	26th of 27
1908-9	24	12	1	11	249	269	25	52.08	14th of 31
1909-10	24	9	2	13	156	211	20	41.66	17th of 28
1910-11	30	9	0	21	178	297	18	30.00	25th of 28
1911-12	30	4	3	23	168	520	11	18.33	25th of 27

(Figures compiled from *Tries in the Valleys: A History of Rugby League in Wales*, Peter Lush and Dave Farrar).

The Internationals

Ebbw Vales' Northern Union interlude produced some outstanding players who represented a very successful Welsh Northern Union international team. One of the disincentives to going North before gaining international credentials from one of the home nations was the lack of opportunity that the northern game gave for representative honours. An experimental game was staged at Wigan in 1904 under the proposed unsuccessful rule change that the number of players be reduced to 12. England lost 9-3 to a team called Other Nationalities, which was almost wholly Welsh. The very first full Northern Union international was surprisingly between Wales and New Zealand on 1 January, 1908 at Aberdare. As the result of a last minute try before a crowd of 15,000-20,000 people, Wales go down in the record books as the first Rugby League international side to win a game. The score was 9-8 to Wales. Ebbw Vale was represented on that day by T. E. 'Chick' Jenkins and Oliver Burgham.

Jenkins was a native of Cwm who had gone North to play for Hull. He returned to Wales to play for Ebbw Vale, and put on the full-back Jersey for Wales against the New Zealand touring side. He won seven caps in all, six at full-back and one at centre. He captained Wales twice, in 1910 against England at the Ebbw Vale ground, winning by a resounding 39pts to 18pts, and against Australia at Ebbw Vale losing by a respectable 20pts to 28pts. He remains the only Rugby League player to be selected from a Welsh club for a Great Britain touring side. He toured Australasia in 1910, but was not selected to play in any of the Tests. Burgham played for Wales twice in 1908. He left Ebbw Vale to play for Halifax and gained a test cap in 1911. He is only one of three ex-Ebbw Vale players to have achieved the honour of a Rugby League Test cap, the other two are Tommy Howley in 1924 (6 caps), and Ron Morgan in 1963 (2 caps).

The very first Rugby League international was a close fought match, with the visitors leading 8-3 at half time, and if it were not for Chick Jenkins' fine defensive play the Kiwis would have led by a more significant margin. As the game progressed Wales gained in confidence with some devastating back play which was rewarded in the second half with two tries by D. Jones of Merthyr and H. Francis of Bradford Northern. The *Yorkshire Post* on 2 January, 1908 highlighted Johnny Thomas and Chick Jenkins as the mainstays of the backs with Jenkins playing his best game ever. The Press was genuinely enthusiastic about the Welsh victory, and even the *Western Mail* grudgingly admitted that a win over New Zealand under professional rules was a red letter day for Wales, but went on to say that neither of the teams would have been a match for the almost invincible All

Blacks of 1905. In contrast to other reports the newspaper described the play as decidedly unattractive.

Ebbw Vale gained a third capped player in W. J. Saunders when he entered the field against England at Tonypandy in front of a crowd of 12,000 on Easter Monday 20th April, 1908, which turned out to be a spectacular match and a resounding victory for Wales, running out the winners at 35pts to 18pts. Burgham merited special mention for the stalwart work he did in the pack, scoring the first try in the second half. The Welsh team ran out again the following day to play against Merthyr. The game was described as fierce and fast with Chick Jenkins fielding magnificently and landing a beautiful drop goal. Wales won by the narrowest of margins against an enthusiastic Merthyr side. The score was four goals and three tries (17 points) to two goals and four tries (16 points).

The next two internationals were away to England at Broughton on 28 December 1908, and Wakefield, 4 December, 1909. Only Jack Foley represented Ebbw Vale in these two games which resulted in defeats for the Welsh, 31pts to 7pts and 19pts to 13pts in England's favour. Foley scored a try in the latter. Ebbw Vale was to have been the venue for the Welsh international against the first Australian touring team in 1908-9 but the game was cancelled because of heavy snow. The Welsh League put together a side wholly selected from home clubs to play a hastily arranged match at Merthyr for which caps were not awarded. The Welsh XIII won 14pts to 13pts.

The Bridge End Field got its first spectacle of international rugby league on 9 April, 1910. When England took the field before a disappointing crowd of 4,000. Wales was seeking revenge after two bruising defeats, and was not disappointed. Although trailing at half time Wales outplayed England in every department of the game, resulting in a resounding victory of 39pts to18pts to the home team. Jack Foley and Chick Jenkins were joined by L. J. Llewellyn of Ebbw Vale for his first cap. Llew Llewellyn scored two tries on his debut and with Chick Jenkins scoring two more. The crowd at Ebbw Vale were ecstatic. For his return to international rugby Chick Jenkins was selected at centre and made captain. The *Western Mail* announced that the redoubtable English centre Lomas for once met his match in Jenkins. The victory was well deserved, and but for a few unpopular decisions by the referee the margin would have been even greater. Wales scored nine tries in all against this English team, a record which has never been equalled in either rugby code by Wales against a major side.

England redeemed its tarnished reputation by defeating Wales at Coventry on 10 December, 1910, but of some consolation to Ebbw Vale fans Llewellyn and Foley scored tries in the 39pts-13pts defeat. They were once again joined by Chick Jenkins who returned to his full back position. Four months later on 1 April, 1911 before a lamentably small crowd of 4,000 England consolidated its newly found superiority by achieving its first victory in Wales at the Bridge End Field, Ebbw Vale. Wales put on a lacklustre display with the forwards singled-out for failure to present the backs with opportunities, and Jenkins was criticised for performing way below par at full back. At 27pts to 8pts, the newspapers implied that the score line flattered Wales in this the last encounter between the two teams on Welsh soil until 1926. The same trio of Jenkins, Llewellyn, and Foley once again represented Ebbw Vale, with Llewellyn and Jenkins scoring tries. In the final fixture in Wales during the Northern Union interregnum, Wales redeemed something of its pride holding the Australasia tourists of 1911 to a narrow margin, and although the 'Kangaroos' won by 28pts to 20pts it was generally acknowledged that Wales had the upper hand for more than half the game.

The match was filled with excitement and before a crowd of 7,000 at Ebbw Vale Will Davies, playing on the left wing, scored four tries, and still managed to be on the losing side. Chick Jenkins, who captained the side, and his team mate Bert Jenkins were commended for their fine performances. The captain was joined by two new caps from Ebbw Vale, H. Smith and G. Hitchings, both of whom never played again for Wales. The final international before the last of the Northern Union clubs folded in Wales was an away game against England at Oldham. A dispirited Welsh side including Chick Jenkins and L. J. Llewellyn from the beleaguered Ebbw Vale club lost dismally in a 31pts to 5pts thrashing.

The demise of League in Wales did not cause undue concern in

Waunlwyd Rugby Football Club. Season 1912/13.

the North. Most teams were relieved to be released from the drudge of travelling for fourteen hours overnight to play in Wales. Northern Union was always going to struggle for survival not only in the face of a concerted campaign of vilification by the WFU, but also because of the rise of Association football. It was football in both Merthyr and Ebbw Vale that very quickly began to attract the crowds, and press attention. Welsh Northern Union clubs also had great difficulty in attracting top players who would much prefer to play for the more well established and financially sound clubs in the North of England. The WFU devised a campaign to eradicate Northern Union from Wales which met with little success in the early years. The strategy was revealed in the *Yorkshire Post*, 1 October, 1907. Walter Rees the Secretary of the WFU was reported as saying that the intention was to annihilate the mongrel game in Wales by sending the top coastal teams such as Newport, Cardiff and Swansea to play in the heartlands of professionalism. He claimed that Cardiff versus Merthyr, billed as 'rugby as it should be played', had drawn a much bigger crowd than the Northern Union club against Batley a few days earlier. This was disputed by the correspondent in the *Merthyr Express* who claimed that not only was the gate not smaller, but the game itself was much more exciting. The Merthyr rugby union club also played a much publicised fixture against Newport, and only narrowly lost by a dropped goal, and against Swansea in January 1908 they only managed to draw a crowd of about 500 in comparison with the rival code where Huddersfield drew close on 4,000. In the face of establishment hostility supporters rallied around their professional clubs. Ebbw Vale claimed that Rees's intemperate remarks has served to increase the gate, and 'The Rambler' reporting for the *Merthyr Express* accused Rees of making an 'hysterical outburst'. In an equally hysterical tone the Rambler challenged Newport and Cardiff to play at the Hill Top ground on the same day as an Ebbw Vale fixture, and then they would see who could attract the bigger crowd and produce the better spectacle.

There is evidence that rugby union was being played in Ebbw Vale during the Northern Union period, but 'The Rambler' largely chose to ignore it, and argued that clubs in the surrounding areas would find it very difficult to survive the competition for gates from the professional team. On Monday, 7 October, 1907 the Ebbw Vale Crusaders played a friendly against Tredegar. The report of the match indicates that Ebbw Vale was a well established 'very smart' team which lost 22pts to 3pts. It does appear, however, that Tredegar's gate did suffer form the Northern Union competition. In its first league match against Blaenavon on Saturday 12 October, the Union reporter 'Pererin' complained that 'the attendance made it evident that the Northern Union games are robbing Tredegar of their gates' (*Merthyr Express*, 19 October, 1907).

After 1912 rugby was still played in Ebbw Vale by local teams, such as Waunlwyd Rugby Football Club, the Newtown Rovers and, because of the impossibility of shop workers playing on Saturday, the Ebbw Vale Wednesday XV.

BIBLIOGRAPHY

Newspapers

The Times, The Western Mail, The Merthyr Express, The Cambrian, The Yorkshire Post, Leeds Mercury, Huddersfield Examiner.

Books and Articles

Tony Collins, *Rugby's Great Split: Class and Culture and the Origins of Rugby League Football* (London, Frank Cass).

Robert Gate, *Gone North*, vols. 1 and 2.

'Memories Flood Back as Rugby League Returns' *Argus*, October 9, 1984.

Gareth Williams, *1905 and All That* (Llandysul, Dyfed, Gomer Press, 1991).

Keith Macklin, *The History of Rugby League Football* (London, Stanley Paul, 1994)

'Creston', 'Football', *The Fortnightly Review*, 55 (1894).

N. L. Jackson, 'Professionalism and Sport', *The Fortnightly Review*, 67 (1900).

Anon. 'Sport and Decadence', *The Quarterly Review* 211 (1909).

Ernest Ensor, 'The Football Madness', *The Contemporary Review*, 54 (1898).

Paul Greenhalgh, 'The Work and Play Principle': The Professional Regulations of the Northern Rugby Football Union, 1898-1905', *International Journal of the History of Sport.*

E. H. D. Sewell, 'Rugby Football', *The Fortnightly Review* 85 (1909).

E. H. D. Sewell, 'Rugby Football and the Colonial Tours', *The Fortnightly Review*, 82 (1907).

Hely Hutchinson Almond, 'Football as a Moral Agent', *The Nineteenth Century*, 34 (1893).

J. B. G. Thomas and Rowe Harding, *Rugby in Wales* (Swansea, Christopher Davies, 1970).

Chapter Three

Rugby and the Ebbw Vale Welfare Association

Between the years 1899 and 1912 the population of Ebbw Vale had increased by fifty percent because of the rapid expansion of the steel and allied industries. Trade Unionism became more of a force to be reckoned with and Liberalism became replaced by Labour as the dominant political affiliation. The economic climate between 1905 and 1937 was volatile, with considerable fluctuations in demand and supply. Both the collieries and steel works were subject to frequent closure, sometimes for prolonged periods. Frederick Mills became the General Manager of the Ebbw Vale Steel, Iron and Coal Company in 1899. He was the only resident manager in South Wales at that time and inherited a plant that was largely obsolete, and immediately set about modernising the works which resulted in increased profits and an astronomical rise in share dividends from 17/- to £4-10s-0d. per share.

Mills was later to become the conservative MP for Leyton in 1932. Ebbw Vale, he thought, had been badly hit by free trade. Free Trade opposed trade tariffs which were used to prevent cheap steel imports from the continent. It is ironic that after the closure of the works in 1929 Mills was to witness the adoption of trade tariffs to protect the industry, but much too late for Ebbw Vale.

In 1911 the Ebbw Vale Company closed the works for nine months causing untold hardship and misery. With no unemployment benefit, and only Poor Law relief thousands of families were on the verge of starvation. The Company claimed that unfair competition had forced it to close its gates, but this excuse was met with a great deal of scepticism from the townspeople and the wider community at large. In fact Sir D. A. Thomas the leading South Wales Coal magnate had joined the board in 1910, and immediately made it clear that he was only interested in coal and that he considered the 10% dividend paid by the steel interests as totally inadequate compared with the 15% return on coal. It was Thomas who pressed for the closure of the works in 1911. Demand for Thomas' coal now diminished and his returns fell below 15%, whereupon he argued for re-opening of the works. Under considerable pressure the Company reopened in April 1912, and soon the work was so plentiful that the plant was working around the clock, and the Company invested in a new sheet mill which produced 600 tons a week.

The Return of Rugby Union

After the First World War returning soldiers who had played rugby in the forces, began to organise an Ebbw Vale team. They were not allowed to play on the Bridge End Field because it had been contaminated by professionalism, but close by there was a ground known as Morgan James' Field. He was a local farmer who rented the land from the Ebbw Vale Company, and agreed to allow it to be used for playing rugby. It is the field that the Grammar School was later to lease from the Welfare Association for its rugby matches on condition that it be available for training on Tuesday evenings and for playing rugby after 1-00 p.m. on Saturdays. When Ebbw Vale Youth first began in the 1968-69 season, coached by Terry Cameron, the Grammar School played in the morning, and the Youth team played in the afternoon, with many of the same players until the Grammar School boys were declared ineligible.

In 1918 the ground was unfit for sporting activities because of its unevenness, flooding and a quantity of large dangerous stones raised above the surface, much of it debris from the nearby crusher plant, and the remnants of the old ironworks. Players, after a hard day's work at the colliery or steel works, would take a pick or shovel over to Morgan James' Field to clear it of large boulders and to dig drains from Beaufort Road across to outlets in the River Ebbw.

They succeeded in making the field free of boulders but failed to prevent it from becoming submerged during heavy rain. A team was formed in mid 1919 under the name of the Crusaders. The secretary and founder was Eugene Cross, and the headquarters, known as '10 Downing Street' was in Chick Zerascki's shop underneath the Palace in Church Street. However, as we have already seen, a highly successful team was playing under the name of the Crusaders before the Great War.

Professional rugby players had been allowed to play alongside amateurs while serving in the armed forces, and many were optimistic that they would once again be allowed to play the amateur code, despite having played professionally, when they entered civilian life. Having fought for king and country, they reasonably assumed that the home Unions could not possibly carry on the policies they had followed prior to the outbreak of hostilities. The issue was one that the Welsh Football Union was immediately forced to address because it received applications from returning soldiers to be allowed to play for amateur clubs. There were differing views within the Union, but it was felt that nothing could be done until the International Board came to a policy decision.

When the English and International Unions met there was no room for compromise, and the WFU once again returned to its hard line on the issue of professionalism and the question of allowing former Northern Union players to resume amateur status. At a meeting in Cardiff on 22 January 1919 the WFU tightened its grip making all clubs responsible for ensuring that no professionals played on their grounds. They resolved: 'That no match can now be played on the ground of any Welsh Union Club in which professionals take part'.

It is in this context that Ebbw Vale sought, and surprisingly gained, re-admission to the WFU. Why was Ebbw Vale so favourably treated after having all of its committee and players expelled in 1907? The most important factor was the establishment of the Welfare Association. The Welfare scheme was both ambitious in scope and financially adventurous. Workers were naturally sceptical of such a magnanimous gesture from the managing director of the steel works. Many were critical because of the expense. They argued that if such large sums were to be wasted on recreation and sport, why could not the company contribute to a health care scheme for the workers? The Welfare scheme was established in 1918 by Sir Frederick Mills, who as we saw in the previous chapter had kicked-off for New Zealand against Ebbw Vale at the Bridge End Field. The scheme provided 28 acres of playing fields and two buses to transport players of various sports, including rugby, to and from the games.

It was Mills who arranged a meeting with Horace Lynn, the President of the WFU, to exorcise the ghost of professionalism. The application appeared before the General Committee of the WFU January 6, 1919. It seems to have taken them a little off guard, they were certainly more circumspect than in any other case in which professionalism was involved. In fact the application came from the chairman of the sub-committee of the Ebbw Vale Football Tournament. No mention was made of the club's former status, neither in the application nor in the WFU's response. The WFU committee decided to hold the matter over until the next meeting in order to allow a sub-committee of the representatives of the rugby clubs in the Union to investigate more fully. The matter was once again deferred on April 3, 1919, and when it arose again on May 22 the WFU appointed a Convenor for the special committee, J. Games, and requested a report. The report was tabled on June 19, at a meeting chaired by Horace Lynn. After a long discussion, the details of which are not recorded, the Committee decided to call for further particulars of the Welfare Scheme and for two representatives to attend the following meeting on July 1.

The fact that the WFU entertained the application and went to some lengths to give it thorough consideration is testimony to Horace Lynn's powers of persuasion and how much he was in awe of the powerful industrialist Sir Frederick Mills, who as we saw had kicked-off for New Zealand at the Bridge End Field when Ebbw Vale hosted them in its days of Northern Union rugby. Together Sir Frederick and his Commercial Manager, I. Gibson, made a formidable force. The WFU could not accept the scheme as it stood because it embraced the Ebbw Vale Association Football Club, which was a professional team. Instead of rejecting the application out of hand the WFU took the highly unusual step of resolving to send a carefully phrased letter in which the Welfare Association was told that as it stood the application could not be recommended, but if it could be proved that the rugby club was entirely separate from the Association football club 'the Committee would be prepared to consider sympathetically any application by such Rugby Club for membership'. Lynn must have given Ebbw Vale every reason to believe that the application would be successful because the club was well advanced in completing its arrangements and compiling a fixture list for the 1919-1920 season. The Welfare's response was to give the necessary undertaking, but also effectively to tell the WFU to stop dragging its feet on this issue:

General Offices,
Ebbw Vale,
July 24/1919

Dear Sir,

I have been requested by the Ebbw Vale Rugby Football Club, attached to the Ebbw Vale Company's Recreation Club, to make an application for affiliation to the Welsh Rugby Union, viz – that the club shall be run on pure Amateur lines, separate and distinct from any other sections of the Scheme.

The Accounts will be kept separate and subject to audit and any surplus funds at the close of the season will not be used for the promotion of any professional side of the Recreation Club.

I would be pleased if you could hurry the matter up, as we have made a complete list of fixtures, many with the Welsh and English Clubs.

In the meantime perhaps you could give us provisional sanction to go on.

Yours sincerely,

H. J. Turner

In an uncharacteristic act of conciliation the WFU resolved to accept Ebbw Vale for membership on condition that the club adhere to the terms of the letter sent on 2 July, 'and that the Professional and Transfer Laws are strictly observed'.

Professional Association football was still being played on the Bridge End Field after the collapse of the Northern Union team. Its chairman was John Cameron, vice chairman Cyrus Davies, and secretary D. B. Miles, better known as Glynfab the sports reporter, a non-de-plume that his son Percy was later to adopt. In 1914 the Association Football Club called for tenders to build a new stand. Humphrey's of Knighstbridge won the contract at a price of £1,100. A further £200 was spent in creating further rooms and offices beneath the seating area. The completion of the project had to await the cessation of hostilities in the 1914-18 war. By 1924 small structural alterations were made at a cost of £50, and the whole stand was painted by Mr. H. Reynolds of Ebbw Vale for £127. There was, however, no electrical lighting in the stand or the changing rooms, and despite an application for its installation in 1931 the request had to be deferred because of the dire lack of funds. The Depression cut deep, and even though facilities were being more extensively used because of the almost total male unemployment, at the same time very little was collected through subscriptions to the new Ebbw Vale Welfare Scheme.

Financial Instability

The whole period between the two world wars was marked by financial instability and no club could rely wholly upon gate receipts which fluctuated wildly during the booms and slumps of the trade cycles. Lack of revenue resulted in a vicious circle. Games with English clubs which potentially raised the gate, led to greater expenses for return fixtures. Increasing prices to compensate for falling gates reduced the attendance even further. In October 1927 Aberavon attracted a crowd of less than 200 after raising admission prices to one shilling. It was suggested that if there was not greater support in the town English fixtures would have to be axed. In September 1929, Aberavon Harlequins, one of the major sources of talent flowing through to the senior team, decided to abandon rugby and adopt the association code.

All sorts of schemes were invented for increasing revenue, many of them requiring the approval of the Welsh Rugby Union. In 1927, for example, there was a heated debate over whether greyhound racing should be allowed on rugby grounds. Given the strong Welsh religious non-conformist tradition in South Wales a large section of the community found the idea of gambling morally repugnant. At Ebbw Vale the no gambling clause in the Welfare's constitution would have prevented greyhound racing taking place.

There was also the issue of allowing a professional sport to take place on amateur grounds. Supporters of the idea argued that there was no difference between allowing sheep dog trials on the Arms Park, for which there were money prizes, and allowing 'electric hare' racing to take place. In recognition of the rising costs of maintaining rugby grounds the Welsh Rugby Union acceded to the clubs' demands. The 'Old Stager', writing in the *Football Echo,* September 17, 1927, argued that clubs desperately needed the extra revenue, and that for Cardiff greyhound racing would save the day: 'it is better to have greyhound racing than to lose the Park as a home for amateur sport'. Cardiff even resorted to running two first teams for five seasons from 1926-7. The experiment was a failure because it resulted in a greater percentage of lost games, a poorer standard of rugby, and complaints from the likes of Northampton, Leicester and Aberavon that Cardiff was not fielding its strongest team against them. The scheme became a financial drain rather than a success.

At the end of the 1927-8 season 'Old Stager' complained that over the last few years clubs had been starved of money. Llanelli's success had ensured loyal support and healthy gate receipts, and the only other club that looked as if it was going to turn a deficit into a profit was Pontypool which had invested heavily in its facilities and was now reaping the rewards.

Throughout the latter part of the 1920s and early 1930s attendance was abysmally low at Ebbw Vale. Even on days when big gates might be expected the turn out was disappointingly low. For example, on Christmas Eve, 1927, on the first game of the 1929-30 season, and against Pontypridd on 23 November, 1929 the crowd was described as 'very small'. In January 1932, against Neath, one of the strongest sides in Wales, the attendance was 'not more than a couple of hundred', due partly to the bad weather. Even for the 'international of the hills' on 30th January, 1932 there was a 'rather disappointing crowd'. The 4d admission charge was beyond the means of most men on the dole, and a gate of £5-00 was regarded as a good day's takings. This was not helped by the fact that visiting Welsh clubs were all too frequently turning up late, or not turning up at all. Much to the annoyance of spectators whose loyalty could not always be relied upon if they continued to be inconvenienced. The *Merthyr Express* registered dismay at the attitude of the Welsh Rugby Union to this problem and suggested that if the practice was not curtailed the already unpopular game of rugby in the Northern valleys would become even less popular (16th April, 1927).

Furthermore, the rise in popularity of Association Football and the relative strength of such valley towns as Merthyr and Ebbw Vale in holding their own against, and often bettering such teams as Newport County, Cardiff City and Swansea Town, made rugby a poor second in the competition for support. In May 1925 Glynfab of the *Merthyr Express* was able to argue that 'in most places in South Wales and Monmouthshire where Rugby stood out as the prominent game it has been under a cloud, and even the big towns, such as Cardiff, Swansea, Newport, Llanelly and Neath have not escaped the depression'.

The Welsh Rugby Union, amid much criticism, had adopted the stance of conserving its resources, and was extremely reluctant to finance club deficits if the spectator support was not there. 'Old Stager', in the *Football Echo*, took an uncompromising line on this. He argued that: 'Those who want Rugby, and those who want to play Rugby ought to be prepared to pay for it; and it is only when unexpected circumstances arise that they ought to expect outside assistance'. He moderated his views as more and more clubs threatened to cease operations and accept the inevitable.[1] The 'Valian' in the *Merthyr Express* complained that 'the unfortunate local industrial depression played havoc with the "gates" and the usual "hillside sportsmen" were seen in hundreds viewing games from many points of vantage that unfortunately overlook the Ebbw Vale Sports Ground.' (17th May, 1930). In February, 1931 'Old Stager' lamented the fact that many of the clubs in the valleys were constantly threatened with extinction because of the economic consequences of the Depression. In 1933 and 1939 reference was made to Ebbw Vale's poor financial position as a causal factor in periods of poor form on the field.

Rugby in the valleys was disproportionately badly hit by the Depression for a number of reasons. First, clubs were losing their best players at an alarming rate as they left the district to seek work elsewhere, usually in England where former club mates had settled. Second, those men who were in work, especially in the collieries, found their working hours extended on Saturdays. Representations were made to mine owners, but often to no avail. And, third, the aloofness of the premier clubs in the South denied the unfashionable rugby sides in the valleys fixtures that could attract larger crowds. In this respect, once again Ebbw Vale was recognised as the recipient of countless injustices. The *Football Express* reported on 7 September, 1929 that because of this aloofness 'the Ebbw Vale fixture list is not as attractive as a club of their standing should warrant.' The following week in the course of a report about an excellent clash with Bristol, it was suggested that 'one cannot help thinking, nevertheless, that it is not in the best interests of the game in the valleys of Monmouthshire, where rugby is having a struggle, to find a club like Ebbw Vale with such a feeble fixture list for quite half the season.'

The Welfare Ground

The Bridge End field had long served the purpose of a recreation ground. From the early 1700s large fairs were held on what was

1. Relatively the WRU was more generous than other Unions in acknowledgement of the working-class character of the game in Wales. Between 1920-1933 the WRU supported clubs and junior leagues with £28,000.

Ebbw Vale Rugby Ground, circa 1930.

described as 'the lower part of the land, in the vicinity of Pont-y-Gof'. Fairs were still a commonplace on the ground in the 1890s with the favourite attractions beings Scaretts' Boxing Booth, Ford's Dobbie Horses, and Haggers' Gaff. The fair also included a carousel and accompanying organ music, boats on the River Ebbw, Skittle Alleys and coconut shies. The field had been part of Pont-y-Pudin Farm, in the Earl of Abergavenny's estates. The ground was leased by the Nantyglo and Blaina Company who in turn seem to have leased it on an annual basis to Messers Phillips and Sons Brewers of Newport who held the lease on the Bridge End Inn. The Ebbw Vale Steel, Iron and Coal Company acquired the lease, and its house agent, Mr Henry, had the Old Barn demolished. The area around the field was heavily industrialised. The ground later used for practise, and, second XV and youth games, was a shale deposit for the waste from the mine shaft near Waterwheel Cottage by the playing field. There was a second mine shaft opposite the King's Arms Hotel. The shale from this shaft was deposited on the bank, which is now the site of the terraces on the current ground. During the 1920s the Ebbw Vale Company provided some railway sleepers and iron bars to create make-shift terracing on the shale tips. Members of the football and rugby clubs provided the labour on a voluntary basis.

Developing rugby grounds was an expensive business and all of the major clubs in Wales found it difficult to raise the necessary revenue. After the collapse of the Ebbw Vale Company's Welfare Scheme in 1921 the grounds were leased for 21 years at a cost of 1 shilling per annum, which enabled the new Ebbw Vale Welfare Association to apply for development grants from the Miner's Welfare Fund which granted £5000 in 1924 and £3000 in 1925. In 1924 the wooden posts and colliery rope wires around the rugby ground were removed and replaced by iron fencing. In 1925 the Society of Friends International Voluntary Labour cleared the shale tips from opposite the bowling green, extending the out field of the cricket ground. When in 1937 a fence was erected around the cricket area it was the first time that the whole ground had been enclosed.

With the increased use of the ground reports of the deplorable condition of the playing surface became more frequent. Given that the ground was situated over 900ft above sea level, and that rain fell for over two hundred days of each year, it is not surprising that with poor drainage the playing surface was in a deplorable condition. Wet weather not only affected the gates, but also waterlogged the playing area. The quality of the rugby suffered, the enthusiasm of the players for the game waned, and occasionally matches simply could not be played. On October 22nd 1927, for example, in the middle of dire economic uncertainty, the morning rain waterlogged areas of the pitch, and only a meagre crowd turned out to watch Ebbw Vale, without six of its regular players, lose to Pontypool by 6pts to 3pts. Conditions were so bad on January 28th, 1928 that the game was abandoned after fifteen minutes play with Ebbw Vale leading 5pts to nil against Mountain Ash. Morale was low among the players and on March 10th 1928 Ebbw Vale could only field thirteen men against Pill Harriers.

Despite constant complaints about the over-use of the ground and the damage it was causing, the Ebbw Vale Welfare Association, during the Depression, looked favourably upon almost all applications for the use of the ground because they were usually for charitable

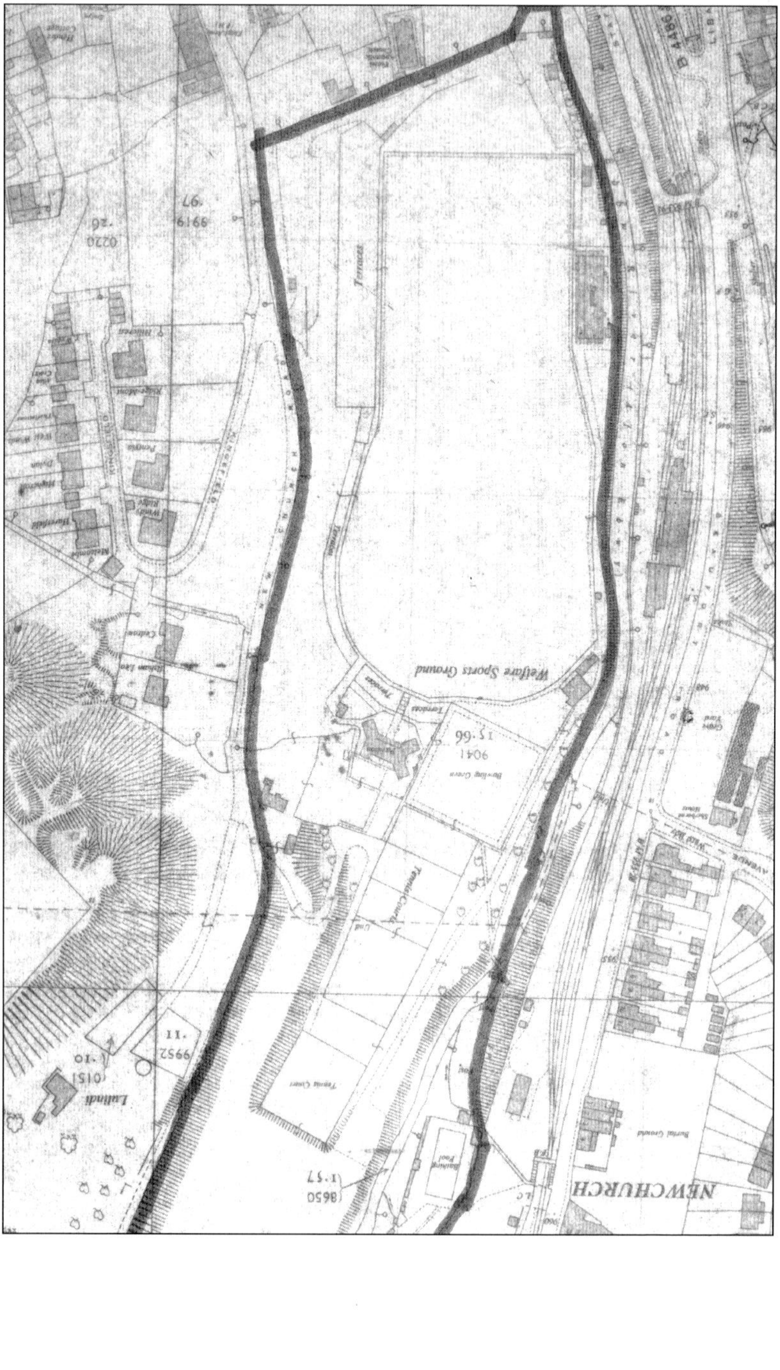

Section of a map of the Welfare playing fields, bowling lawns and tennis courts.

purposes. Over use of the ground did untold damage to the playing surface, which never had a enough time to recover in between events, which ranged from marching bands to horse jumping. In 1932, for example, the soccer club complained about the state of the ground to the Executive Committee, which in turn instructed Alf Morris to give it his immediate attention. The Committee itself, however, was responsible for the state of the pitch because it seemed incapable of refusing requests for its use. In the 1931-32 season there were sixty eight games played on the ground, and both the football and rugby clubs trained there on Tuesday and Thursday evenings. Despite these considerations the Executive Committee approved an application in July, 1935 for the Ebbw Vale Harlequins rugby team to use the ground, changing rooms and showers on one day per week.

The most significant development came after the Second World War. Expensive improvements could not be undertaken while the ground remained the property of The Richard Thomas Company. The Miner's Welfare fund once again contributed generously to the Welfare Association to enable it to purchase the 26 acres of ground it currently leased. The freehold of the property was purchased on 2 June, 1945. In 1948 the Miner's Welfare Fund granted £5000, and a loan of £2000 was raised from the bank to begin the work of re-surfacing. A contractor was hired to level, drain and seed the ground.

The ground was out of commission for a season and a half while the work was carried out. During this time Ebbw Vale played all their home games on neighbouring grounds, particularly Bryn-mawr and Tredegar. Beside the inconvenience, revenues to the club dropped considerably.

The President of the Welsh Rugby Union, Sir David Rocyn Jones, re-opened the Welfare Ground on 3rd September, 1949, by kicking-off at the first game played on the new surface. Before a record crowd the Ebbw Vale Welfare band provided the entertainment before Newbridge ran out onto the field. With the new surface and general improvements around the park, the *Argus* described it as 'one of the best grounds in this part of Monmouthshire'. The *Football Echo* claimed that the ground had never looked better and that

Sir David Rocyn Jones at the re-opening of the Welfare Ground, 1949-50. Eric Finney, captain.

Ebbw Vale had achieved its objective of having one of the best centres for rugby in Monmouthshire. The stand and the dressing rooms had been refurbished, new railings erected around the playing area, and new entrance gates were being built. The following Saturday the *Football Echo* reported the Newbridge game and asserted that 'few clubs in South Wales now have the facilities that Ebbw Vale enjoy', but added what proved to be a prophetic note of caution in claiming that 'some people entertain slight doubt about how the ground itself will stand up to the great amount of use it will be put to.'

The rugby match against Newbridge was not attractive, but both sides provided excitement with spirited performances. The Ebbw Vale pack, led by captain Eric Finney, outplayed Newbridge in the first half, and Jackson the Valian's hooker more than held his own against the formidable Harris in the heels. The pack played magnificently in securing plenty of quick clean ball, only to be let down by the backs who were out-classed by their Newbridge counterparts. The wings, John Pugh and J. B. Williams were starved of the ball, and on the few occasions that it did go out wide, they failed to capitalise. The saving grace was at full-back. Ron Jones fielded and kicked magnificently ensuring that at half-time Ebbw Vale were in front by one penalty goal kicked by Ben Edwards. The second half, however, saw Newbridge's fortunes revive, with most of the play going its way. A try scored from an awkward bounce by Roberts was converted by Cale, edging Newbridge in front by 5pts to 3pts. Ebbw Vale responded with vigour and crossed the line, only to be called back for an infringement. In the dying moments of the game Newbridge consolidated its position with a fine dropped goal from Norman. It was disappointing for Ebbw Vale to lose its first game on the newly reopened ground, and while Newbridge deserved the win, it did not deserve to do so by such a margin.

By the end of the season serious problems with the drainage and playing surface had become evident. Repairs had to await the fulfilment of obligations to stage other sporting events. Emergency repairs were made in June and part of the surface was completely re-laid. Heavy rain over the summer enabled the turf to knit perfectly. At the start of the 1950-51 season it was reported that the ground was looking well, and had been given every chance to repair itself by holding the trials at Cwm and the Top Field. By Christmas the old problems were once again evident despite a more cautious approach to its use. Ebbw Vale School Boys association football, for example, was left homeless when it was denied further use of the ground. During periods of rain the surface gave cause for concern and generated damaging rumours about the possibility of play. On December 9, 1950 Ebbw Vale played Penygraig on a ground that was 'on the heavy side', but suitable for play. The gate was affected, however, by rumours that the match would have to be postponed. The *Football Echo* commented that while the drainage had improved the portion of the surface that had not been re-laid was cause for concern, and was not getting a fair chance to heal because of the constant battering it got from rugby and association football games.

By February 1951 it was evident that further major repairs would have to be undertaken and it was decided that from the end of April the ground would be unavailable until the end of September. March was the wettest month since records began, and there was not a single day on which rain did not fall. Ebbw Vale rugby was not able to fulfil any of its home fixtures over the Easter holiday period because: 'The home ground was in a deplorable state, and the soccer game should never have been played there on Easter Monday. It was waterlogged and had been churned up into a sea of mud' (*South Wales Echo*, 31st March, 1951). By the middle of April it was announced that it was unlikely that anymore games could be played on the ground that season. The Brynmawr and Abertillery grounds were not in a condition to accommodate extra play, but Risca held out a helping hand by allowing use of its ground.

The attempt to solve the drainage problem, then, proved to be a complete failure after only two seasons. Neither the rugby nor football sections could afford extensive repairs. The Football Club declared that it had no funds to put into the pool, and the Rugby Club, similarly pleading poverty, maintained that it could not shoulder the financial burden. The Welfare Association itself refused to entertain the idea of taking out a bank loan and would not increase its agreed contribution of £150.

After just one season of first class rugby Ebbw Vale was once again faced with extinction. Because of the extreme seriousness of the situation both codes called upon the Trustees of the Welfare Association to relay the pitch by using voluntary labour. It was decided that the playing surface would have to be raised to the level of the cricket pitch. The foundation of the new playing surface was to be a base of crushed slag and bricks from the blast furnaces, on top of which was placed a layer of ash from Abercarn on which to lay the drainage pipes, which were covered with soil and turf from farms at Victoria and Waunlwyd.

Prior to the start of the new season alarm bells began to ring. The ground was not going to be ready. The headline in the *Football Echo and Express* for 18th August 1951 read: 'REVIEW OF CLUB PROSPECTS FOR 1951-2 – EBBW VALE FACE DISASTER'. The article talks of an excellent fixture list for the season, the best in the whole history of the club, but claimed that no one seemed to know where and how Ebbw Vale could fulfil the games because there were no grounds available in the vicinity.

The Welfare Association sought expert advice on the condition of the playing surface and employed G. H. Purvis, Principal of Usk Agricultural College. He inspected the ground in August, recommended certain remedial work and the use of fertilisers and scheduled his next inspection for 26 September. Following this decision rumours spread that the Rugby Club was about to throw in the towel. They were so prevalent that the Committee issued a statement assuring fans that whatever happened the fixtures would be fulfilled. There was concern that season ticket holders who paid by subscription would not get value for money. Ebbw Vale made arrangements with some clubs to play their home matches away and to allow season ticket holders free admission. Others were played in Cwm and Abertillery. The second inspection saw improvement in the condition of the ground but Mr Purvis deferred a decision on when it would be fit to play. Despite the difficulties Ebbw Vale opened the account in style by winning all nine of the early games before the ground was fit to use. The opposition included some very strong sides, including Wolverhampton and Nuneaton. The strength of the team was acknowledged by having five of its players picked for Monmouthshire, the highest number ever to come from Ebbw Vale. The players were Ernie Lewis, Graham Powell, J. E. Williams, Eric Finney, and Islwyn Williams.

The first game was played on the new surface on 3 November, 1951 against Abercarn. A deluge of rain fell in the few days before the match was due and the Ebbw Vale officials decided to halt the production of the match programme on the Friday as a precaution. On Saturday morning there was no sign of the ground retaining the water and the drainage seemed to be working excellently. By February it was evident that the ground had come through the worst of conditions and the *Football Echo and Express* declared that 'The ground is standing up to all demands and the new drainage which is operating so successfully is keeping the ground quite dry.' On the 29th March 1952 the same paper wrote: 'There is no doubt, at the present moment, when grounds are in none too good condition, the Ebbw Vale playing area is easily the best in South Wales.' A week later optimism turned to pessimism. The fixture with Ponty-

The new terraces replacing the railway sleepers in 1952.

pridd had to be cancelled because the ground was too hard. The drainage was so effective that it was retaining no moisture. What would happen to the ground in long hot spells? Would the surface dry up and crack?

In order to facilitate an increase in revenue an appeal was made to raise the £650 shortfall for the repairs. There was £700 in the pot. But the cost of putting the ground right even with all the voluntary labour was £1,350. The no gambling clause was deleted from the rules and a weekly tote instituted at the suggestion of Selwyn Davies, the secretary of the Cricket Club, and administered by Jack Cope of the Wages Department in the Ebbw Vale Company, and assisted by Dave Leyshon, who later became the treasurer of the Welfare Association. The income generated was sufficient to embark upon further ground improvements. George Albert Brown was contracted to build new terraces to accommodate 12,000 people. The 26 terraces were completed in 1952.

The Welfare Scheme

The Welfare scheme that Sir Frederick initiated in 1918 was ambitious in scope comprising 25.8 acres of land, including Pant-y-Forest which was 5.662 acres. The income from all of the sections including rugby, but excluding Association football, was paid into the Welfare fund. All expenses were then drawn upon the common fund. The scheme was established on the back of a highly successful post war economy. Production at the collieries rose to record levels, enabling some colliers to earn £20 a week, a sum that led to headlines in the *Times*. Output in the works continued to grow and the Welfare scheme, the only one of its kind in South Wales, not only provided sporting facilities, but also built houses in Victoria and a model hostel able to house three hundred men, but the unmarried youth of Ebbw Vale could not be enticed into it.

In the two years following the peak of the boom and record prices for steel and coal in December 1920 there was a 60% fall in demand. As Arthur Gray-Jones remarks: 'The British coal industry went through crisis after crisis from 1920 onwards, every one of which sharply affected the steel industry, dependent on coal and coke for fuel.'[2] The income paid into the Welfare scheme became insufficient to sustain the extent of activities and the Company Scheme soon found itself in financial difficulties.

A meeting was held at the General Offices on Friday, 19th January, 1923 to discuss the crisis. The chairman of the welfare committee, Dr W. S. Elworthy announced that the Directors of the Company had decided that the scheme should cease, but hoped that it could be continued in some form by another body. The Secretary of the Committee read a statement from the Directors which indicated that an annual donation of £100 would be made available towards the running costs of the new scheme. They also offered to rent the sports grounds at an annual fee of 1/0d. After discussing the matter it was decided that the Secretary should make enquires in order to find out whether the Miners' Settlement Committee was willing to contribute towards the costs, in addition to its grant for the development of the Sports Ground. They further wanted to know whether the soccer club intended to play soccer in Ebbw Vale the next season. The Betterment Fund did not feel able to contribute anything further, but the soccer club responded in the affirmative.

2. Arthur Gray-Jones, *A History of Ebbw Vale* (Risca, The Starling Press, 1970), 193-4.

There was nevertheless an impetus in the town to continue the Welfare Scheme and a joint committee of the proposed new Welfare Association and the Football club met in order to agree terms. It resolved that it would do all in its power to inaugurate a new Welfare Scheme with a target membership of 3,000 paying a weekly subscription of two pence. This target was set by the Ebbw Vale Company as a condition of handing over the playing fields and facilities. In an agreement with the football club the Ebbw Vale Company undertook to reduce the annual rent from £100 to £40, and to relieve the club of other expenses such as the grounds man's wages, rates and taxes. A meeting was held at Christ Church Hall on Thursday 10th May, 1923 to institute a new scheme at a cost to members of two pence per week, or eight shillings per annum. One of the main obstacles to the success of the scheme was the requirement by the Inland Revenue that each membership card had to carry a 4d stamp duty. After sustained representations the tax was reduced to 3d. The contractor who built the Catholic Church in Ebbw Vale, Foster and Hill, gave the scheme a great impetus by agreeing to deduct subscriptions directly from the wages of its employees.

It was acknowledged that the establishment of a welfare scheme would require the cooperation of the townspeople. At first there were only 145 members, and it became imperative to launch a recruitment drive. A hundred posters were printed explaining the rules and objectives of the association, and local dignitaries were approached to support the scheme which now comprised six trustees and sectional representation from the affiliated sports. Rugby and football had two representatives on the committee, while cricket, tennis, schoolboys football, quoits, bowls, angling, gymnastics, and athletics all had one each. The Association was of much broader scope than sport and encompassed the Brass and Orchestral bands who also had one representative each. A wide variety of further applications were received and approved including proposals to establish Hockey and Piscatoria sections. In 1925 the Fur and Feather Society was accepted as a section on condition that it incorporate the Homing Pigeon Society. In the 1930s a baseball league was established, but was not represented on the committee.

The Ebbw Vale Company was also invited to be represented, but declined on the grounds that it would not in the short term be in the interests of the scheme. In June of 1934, however, the rules of the scheme were amended to provided for two representatives from the Ebbw Vale Company.

The scheme was not particularly attractive to small local employers and their employees because of the long hours worked. With only Wednesday afternoon free there was little leisure time to take advantage of the outdoor facilities provided by the Association. The exception was the rugby team formed by shop employees which played on Wednesday afternoons. The team became members of the association and played their home matches on the 'top field' at Hill-top. By June 11, 1923 membership had grown to 312, and by July it had reached 675, and in September it was 1,374, still well below the target of 3,000 estimated to make the scheme viable. By 1925 there were less than 2,000 members, but nearly every organisation in town demanded to use the facilities of the Welfare Association.

The meeting of the Association held on Friday, 14 September, 1923 appointed the trustees and officers of the scheme, and a week later they voted to allot themselves special admissions tickets to allow free entry into all events at the Sports Ground. The Patrons were the Chairman and Directors of the Ebbw Vale Steel, Iron and Coal Company Limited, and the president was Evan Davies M.P. The Executive Committee comprised David Evans J.P. (chairman), Mr A. E. J. Mees (Treasurer), Mr. T. M. Henry (Secretary) and Messrs. David Evans J.P., Llewellyn Carter, George Morris, Jack Griffith, Cyrus Davies and Dr. Elsworthy, all trustees. George Morris resigned shortly after on being appointed to the position of Labour Party Organiser for South Wales. He had been an Executive Committee member of B.I.S.A.T.A. and leader of the Steelworkers.

Employees

Under the original welfare scheme the grounds man was a cricketer, Mr. Gibson, who was on the Company payroll, and the cricket captain was the general manager of the Ebbw Vale Company, Robert Graham. With the demise of the scheme the Company withdrew the services of Mr Gibson and the new Welfare Scheme secured the services of Alf Davies. The meeting of 14th September 1923 reported that the grounds man of the Sports Field at Bridge End would be paid £3-00, and that he and his wife were to run the canteen independently for a year in the first instance. They provided after match teas for 6d and 9d per person.

Alf was provided with a Spartan compliment of machinery consisting of a mare called Betty, who mysteriously seemed to be in foal every year. The mare pulled a two wheeled flat bottomed cart, with an extra heavy roller for the cricket pitch, and a heavy roller for the rugby ground. In addition, he had a grass cutting machine, a couple of forks to pierce the ground, a spade, and a bar used to dig holes. Alf's wife acted as his labourer in tending to the playing fields, bowling green and tennis courts. The red ash used on the tennis courts was brought down from the tips by Alf pushing the cart, after Betty had loaded it inside the shaft. The courts were sprinkled with the fine ash and then rolled, but on fine windy days much of the ash would be lost, and when blowing in a northern direction it would settle on the bowling greens and on the whites of the players. In a letter to the Executive Committee a bowls section secretary complained that 'we all looked like red Indians and the green was not green anymore'. Eventually a new surface was provided by En tou Carr at a cost of £1,250, but despite it being dust free players thought the surface much worse than the ash and numbers using the facility declined. In 1924, following the successful application for grants of £5,000 and £3,000 the Drill Hall was purchased at a cost of £4,000, and Waterwheel cottage at the Bridge End Field was purchased for the grounds man for £300.

By 1929, prior to the closure of the Ebbw Vale Works, the head grounds man was paid £4-0s-0p per week, for unlimited hours. As a consequence of the Depression and the imperative need for the Welfare Association to cut costs, Alf Davies's wages were reduced to £3-10s-0d. As a concession it was proposed that his hours be limited to 48 per week. He accepted the wage cut, but preferred to continue working unlimited hours. In 1935, nevertheless, he requested an additional fortnight leave, making a total of four weeks, in order to visit the Canary Islands.

The Welfare Hall was an amenity provided by the Welfare Association which was largely used for weekly dances organised by the various sections. There was a caretaker husband and wife who received a salary of £2.10s.0p and free accommodation. Their income was supplemented with the receipts from the cloakroom, which sometimes amounted to 13 shillings. In 1927 the Welfare Committee decided that this was much to generous and decided that the couple could retain the first 7s/6p., and that the rest should go to the section promoting the event. The Hall gradually became the venue for the gymnastics section and the sports facility for the Technical School.

Extended Activities

The Welfare scheme extended its activities into creating children's playgrounds, but found that the cost was too heavy for the finances to bear. It delegated responsibility to the communities, and then Ebbw Vale Urban District Council stepped-in and assumed control. During the general strike of 1926 the Welfare Association sought to provide relief for poverty stricken families, and despite the fact that very little income was accruing from the use of its facilities, they were nevertheless used more heavily than ever before because people had more time on their hands. The situation was exacerbated by the Wall Street Crash and the onset of the Depression.

The district surrounding Ebbw Vale experienced a long and severe depression from 1920 to 1936, and the closure of the Steel Works in 1929 was a consequence rather than a cause of adverse economic conditions. From 1921 there was a gradual erosion of working conditions, including local allowances and special payments for working in abnormal conditions. Miners became militant in the face of the abandonment of a national wage scheme in favour of local bargaining. Both the Steel Works and the collieries lay silent for six months of 1921, and profits rapidly became converted to heavy losses. By the beginning of 1922 wages in the collieries had been cut by half. During continued industrial unrest, and the uncertainty of supply of coal for coke to run the blast furnaces Frederick Mills closed the Steel works in September 1922, blaming Evan Davies the local MP for fuelling unrest. The collieries agreed to accept a trial compromise for three months and resumed work in October, 1922, but the Steel Works remained closed until May, 1923. By 1925 the steelworks was operating at 75% capacity, and the collieries worked intermittently. Under pressure from the Miners' Federation which was resisting further demands for wage cuts and an increase in working hours the Government capitulated and provided a subsidy, but also set up a Commission to look into the problems of the industry. The Samuel Report of 1926 recommended ending the subsidy, extending working hours and wage differentials by district. The miners immediately responded and were backed by the railwaymen and transport workers in the General Strike of 4th-13th May. With the collieries and steelworks already lying idle the General Strike was hardly noticeable in Ebbw Vale. The Miners' strike continued until the end of November, and the steel works remained closed until February 1927, causing immense suffering for the local community, alleviated only by the resolve of the men and the energy of local relief committees. Relief was administered by local Boards of Guardians which Neville Chamberlain thought much too generous, and replaced them with Commissioners. W. B. Dixon the chairman of the Commissioners for Bedwellty became notorious for his severity, a reputation difficult to acquire in already severe conditions.

On top of the hardship came the second major pit disaster in the history of the town. In 1871 nineteen men had died, a number eclipsed by the enormity of the Marine Colliery Disaster of 1927 in which fifty-two men were killed. At 6.00am on 1st March there was a huge gas explosion in pit number one. The cause appears to have been a rise in the level of gas in the Black Vein seam above the safety level of 2½%. It is likely that the wire cable pulling the coal trams struck a stone and caused a spark to ignite the gas. The explosion

Crowds around the Marine Colliery out buildings awaiting news.

shook the village of Cwm, and people immediately ran to the pit head. There was no hysteria, just silent, sombre expectancy. At first only men, followed by the wives, mothers and daughters, waited for news. It was mid afternoon before the first bodies were brought to the surface, the rescuers having to overcome the almost insurmountable hurdles of poisonous gas and collapsed workings. Some of the bodies were so badly burnt from the explosion that they were unrecognisable. A doctor opened a vein in the arm of each victim releasing a trickle of thin light pink blood, a clear indication of carbon monoxide poisoning.

The Ebbw Vale casualties were buried next to the victims of the 1871 disaster in the Cemetery opposite the site of the present Comprehensive School and Further Education College. Thousands of mourners littered the slopes to watch nine hundred miners, physically

"A DARK ST. DAVID'S DAY."

William Penny, labourer, 103, Canning-street, Cwm.
David Evans, labourer, Upper Gelli, Llanelly Hill, Brynmawr.
Edward Mason, labourer, 5, Railway-view, Cwm.
William Warren, assistant-collier, 25, Curre-street, Cwm.
John Clarke, collier, Mill-terrace, Cwm.
Trevor Matthews, collier, 43, Marine-street, Cwm.
Herbert Matthews, collier, 13, Park-view, Waunlwyd.
Walter Shellard, collier, 6, Mill-terrace, Cwm.
William Jones, collier, 32, Council-street, Ebbw Vale.
Alf. Griffiths, collier, 36, Canning-street, Cwm.
Joseph Chappell, assistant-collier, 42, William-street, Cwm.
Ben Stibbs, assistant-collier, 52, Stanfield-street, Cwm.
John Miles, collier, 71, Canning-street, Cwm.
Charles Monaghan, labourer, 74, Canning-street, Cwm.
William Crowley, labourer, 8, Rees-street, Ebbw Vale.
Fred Trowbridge, labourer, 12, Duffryn-road, Waunlwyd.
Harry Brain, labourer, 104, Marine-street, Cwm.
Wilfred Probert, labourer, 29, Station-terrace, Cwm.
Ellis Williams, examiner, 73, Marine-street, Cwm.
Llew. Jenkins, labourer, 24, Station-terrace, Cwm.
Fred Green, repairer, 48, Canning-street, Cwm.
R[illegible] Davies, labourer, 43, Western-terrace, Ebbw Vale.
Jim V[illegible]ghan, labourer, 53, Woodland Village, Steel Works, Ebbw Vale.
Walter Mathlin, assistant-labourer, 114, King-street, Cwm
Tom Lewis, engineman, 8, Station-road, Waunlwyd.
Tom Tarr, labourer, 2, Duffryn-villas, Cwm.
John Hobbs, labourer, Duffryn-villas, Cwm.
William Dudley, labourer, The Huts, Beaufort.
John Rogers, jun., labourer, 18, The Huts, Cwm.
Samuel Harbin, Stuart-street, Cwm.

H. W. Southey & Sons, Ltd., Merthyr.

In Memoriam.

In Loving Memory

— OF THE —

52 MINERS

— WHO —

Lost their lives in the terrible colliery explosion

— AT THE —

MARINE COLLIERY, CWM, EBBW VALE.

MARCH 1ST, 1927.

The printed commemoration card listing the names and addresses of those killed.

Messages of Sympathy received from all parts of the World.

A sudden change : at God's command they fell ;
They had no chance to bid their friends farewell.
Swift came the blast, without a warning given,
And bid them haste to meet their God in Heaven.

"Boast not thyself of to-morrow ; for thou knowest not what a day may bring forth."

Names of the Victims.

Bert Button, collier, 22, Canning-street, Cwm (single).
Tom Morris, collier, 4, King-street, Cwm (single).
William Pickford, assistant-collier, 5, Osborne-road, Brynmawr (single).
W. G. Davies labourer, 9, School-terrace, Cwm (married).
Robert Prester, haulier, 242, Marine-street, Cwm (single).
Harold Reed, fitter, 224, Marine-street, Cwm.
Gordon Riddock, labourer, 187, Marine-street, Cwm.
Tom Gatehouse, labourer, 191, Marine-street, Cwm.
Albert Wright, labourer, 2, Waen Goch, Beaufort.
Tom Morris, haulier, 108, Beaufort Hill, Beaufort.
Charles Lee, labourer, 123, Marine-street, Cwm.
Richard Monaghan, collier, 74, Canning-street, Cwm.
Arthur Medland, assistant-collier, 93, Curre-street, Cwm.
William Matthews, overman, Kitchener-terrace, Cwm.
John Rogers, examiner, Railway-view, Cwm.
Sidney Hill, repairer, 3, Steward-street, Cwm.
Charles Green, repairer 85, Lilian-grove, Ebbw Vale.
William Bryant, repairer, 2, New Cwm-terrace, Cwm.
Ted Wilcox, ropeman, 25, Crosscombe-terrace, Cwm.
Wilfred Button engineman, 22, Canning-street, Cwm.
Richard Nation, haulier, 77, Emlyn-avenue, Ebbw Vale.
Charles Cox, haulier, 122, King-street, Cwm.

weakened from months of deprivation, but unbowed in spirit, precede the funeral cortège. At Cwm the dead were buried in one huge rectangular grave before a crowd of fifty thousand people, who stood in silence as the large procession made its way slowly to Cwm Cemetery, accompanied by funeral marches played by three brass bands. A distress fund was established for the widows of the victims, and funds poured in from all over the country.

The implications of the disaster had far wider significance for the nation as a whole. Prior to the disaster miners were vilified in the press for being unpatriotic in refusing to accept without a fight the continuous erosion of their working conditions and wages. They were admonished by the press for not facing-up to the hard reality of the economic conditions. After the disaster something like national guilt descended, and the press changed its focus to the danger and hardship of working underground. The feeling now conveyed was that miners had been badly treated and deserved more for the risks they daily faced. Such a turn around strengthened the resolve of the miners.

1928-29 saw increased investment in the steel works, and levels of production that matched those of 1920. Even though the company made losses that year, there was cause for optimism. However, the rumours of the closure of the Ebbw Vale Company proved to be uncomfortably accurate. The Chairman of the Company, Sir Frederick Mills, announced to the town in late 1929 that statutory notice of redundancy was being served on all of the employees of the Works, which inaugurated the severest period of depression that Ebbw Vale had ever known, producing unremitting hardship through the years up to 1936. The Company had not made a profit since 1923. Thousands of men were forced to leave home and seek work in England or face almost certain starvation at home. The Welfare Association made a heroic contribution to maintaining morale, despite the fact that its income was less than 30 shillings a week from the few people still working, and that debts were accruing at an alarming rate.

During the long period of severe unemployment which followed, the sports ground and Welfare Hall made vital contributions to the life of the community. In addition, various schemes were proposed and approved by the Welfare Association Executive Committee on the understanding that no funds were being committed. Schemes were proposed to build an ornamental fish pond and a 220yd cinder track, but the most adventurous was the idea to construct a swimming baths with changing rooms.

After the death of an Ebbw Vale Grammar School boy by drowning in a local pond Eugene Cross proposed the building of a Lido. It was the responsibility of the initiators of the schemes to recruit voluntary labour and to raise the necessary funds. F. G. H. Cooper who had at one time chaired the Welfare Committee donated the first £100 for materials, and Isaac Caswell the contractor and coal merchant provided lorries to transport sand from the filtration reservoir and chippings from the Ebbw Vale Company's crushers. He also provided several tons of cement free of charge. The Lido was to be 90ft long and 38ft wide, with a depth ranging from 3ft at the shallow end to 6ft at the deep end. The pool would hold 100,000 gallons of crystal clear water from the 'Tom Jones' Level three hundred yards to the North of the Lido. The cost of the water was £5-00 per annum. Charles Heal, an unemployed Civil Engineer used borrowed instruments to lay out the levels and dimensions, while Jack Bush, a carpenter and joiner, utilised any piece of wood that could be appropriated to build the shuttering in between training to improve his speed for the 'Powderhall' sprinting competition. He would sprint from the Welfare in his running spikes and shorts, slip on his working boots and prepare the shuttering for the men to pour the concrete. All the concrete was mixed by hand, and no mechanical aids were used except for the excavation of the river bed.

The first sod was cut by Eugene Cross in April, 1930 and the shell was completed by August. Work was carried out by an army of volunteers who gave their time and energy tirelessly for nothing more than a few Woodbines a day, for which 7 shillings was allocated daily to purchase a box. The completed baths cost under £1000, of which £750 was donated by the Miners' Welfare Scheme.

Even though the number of volunteers dropped because of the continuous exodus of men from the area improvements to the baths continued to be made. Initially the water was freezing cold, relying upon the sun to make it tolerable, until the purchase of a second-hand boiler for £38 from the Stow Hill baths, Newport. Coke was cheap and in plentiful supply. Volunteers stoked the boiler and kept the temperature at a constant 70°. The installation of electricity brought with it coloured lighting and a floodlight which enabled swimming to continue way past dark. One of the most popular attractions of the baths was the midnight swimming sessions and galas attended by young and old alike. Its popularity was partly due to the fact that mixed swimming was a feature of the baths from the outset. It also provided an essential service to the schools in allowing swimming lessons during week days. David Lewis, 'Spargo' was appointed the pool superintendent, for which he gave his services free of charge. A swimming coach was appointed to give lessons to school children, and his wages were paid out of the 1d cost per pupil per half hour session. The money was paid by the Local Authority. This gave schools the impetus to form swimming teams and organise competitions, under the leadership of Mr. MacCarthy, the head of the Roman Catholic School. The winners of the competition were rewarded with the Cyrus G. Davies Shield. The schools that competed were Rassau, Beaufort Hill, All Saints, Willowtown, Pontygof, Briery Hill, Waunlwyd, Victoria, Cwm Duffryn and Cwmrhydderch. In addition the Welfare Swimming Club was established and a water polo team instituted, with the most popular fixture against the accomplished Abertillery team.

Even though the Depression showed no signs of abating tenders were called for the erection of the Cricket and Bowls Pavilion. It was built with the aid of a £1,900 grant from the Miners' Welfare Fund. Because of the severe shortage of work, competition for the job was fierce, attracting tenders from 12 contractors in South East Wales. The highest was from J. E. Jones of Pontllanfraith at £2,150-9s-0d, and the lowest Frank Hann of Ebbw Vale £1,793-10s-6d. The successful contractor was William Miles and Son, who tendered a price of £1,832, excluding landscaping, with plumbing undertaken by W. Jones, and electrics by Gibson's of Caerphilly. The pavilion was officially opened in 1933 by Sir John Beynon, who was chairman of the Ebbw Vale Steel, Iron and Coal Company.

Revival of Fortunes: Richard Thomas & Co.

In 1935 rumours circulated that the Iron and Steel works, along with a number of collieries, had been purchased with a view to resuming production. A great deal of work was done behind the scenes by Aneurin Bevan and Ernest Bevin to persuade Sir William Firth to site his proposed American style steel works at Ebbw Vale, primarily to alleviate the more than 50% unemployment rate. Firth had become chairman of Richard Thomas & Co. in 1931 on the retirement of Henry Bond. He was an aggressive investor and embarked upon a programme of expansion and mergers. By 1936 Richard Thomas & Co. was a major player in the steel industry. Besides eight collieries and eight brickworks it owned eight steel works, eight rolling mills, two hundred and seven tinplate mills and forty seven sheet mills. Firth was initially attracted to Redbourne as the location of his major venture, but as a result of considerable government pressure, probably including direct intervention from the Prime Minister Stanley Baldwin, and certainly government finance, Ebbw Vale was purchased from Sir John Beynon, the chairman of the Ebbw Vale Company and president of the Welfare Association. The decision was not popular with Firth's own board and his assistant managing director, A. W. Dick, felt strongly enough to resign over the issue. A glimpse of Firth's uncompromising and determined character is evident from a letter which Firth wrote to Dick: 'Get the following thought clearly into your head – that I have worked all my life building up the Grovesend to what it is today and getting Richard Thomas to where it is today, and that no opposition from anyone will weaken my determination to go on working the way I think best.'[3]

At a meeting in Ebbw Vale House, at 5-00pm on Friday, 28th February, 1936 Sir William Firth informed representatives of the community and trades unions that the Richard Thomas Company intended to build modern Hot Strip and Cold Reduction mills on the site of the old works. Robert McAlpine Contractors arrived on

3. Cited in David Wainwright, *Men of Steel: A History of Richard Thomas and His Family* (London, Quiller, 1986), 88.

site on 13 April 1936, and on 28th October, 1938 the first coil was rolled at the Hot Strip Mill, followed on 5th November by the first tinplate rolled on the Five Stand. The 3 Stand came into operation three weeks later. The *Investors' Chronicle* of 24, April 1939 described the process at Ebbw Vale as 'a marvel of ingenuity and efficiency'. 97.8% of the workforce was locally trained. This, however, did not occur immediately, and unemployment in the town went up on the opening of the new works before it came down again.

Firth's scheme for a fully integrated American style plant was extremely ambitious and ran into financial difficulties before it was completed. At this point the industry and the banks combined against him and forced a restructuring of the Board in return for finance. The controlling consortium, set up by the Bank of England and the Securities Management Trust, deposed Firth on 15 April, 1940. He was replaced by Ernest Lever from the Prudential. Firth was vehemently opposed to the company's decision to merge with Baldwins in 1944 on the grounds that Richard Thomas & Co. would be purchasing for five and half million pounds obsolete sheet mills and two collieries that were not needed. On losing the battle Firth took a retirement package and moved to South Africa.

Sir William Firth was a generous supporter of the Welfare Scheme. Along with the personal commitment of the General Manager the Welfare Scheme once again flourished. In 1938 the Welfare Association held a fete in order to raise funds to clear its debt of £300. The fete was opened by John D. Firth who pledged to make up the difference between the proceeds and the balance of the debt. The Richard Thomas Board provided an annual grant of £500 which ceased with the departure of Sir William and the arrival of Richard Thomas and Baldwins. The new company, however, continued to be generous in its provision of material aid. The Sir William Firth memorial gates still stand at the entrance to the Welfare Ground, and were unveiled by Aneurin Bevan, who was Firth's successor as president of the Welfare Association, and had been one of the principal lobbyists for attracting the Richard Thomas company to Ebbw Vale.

Aneurin Bevan in 1959 at the opening of the Sir William Firth Gates with Eugene Cross and his wife to the right.

BIBLIOGRAPHY

Newspapers

Gwent Gazette, South Wales Argus, Western Mail, The Football Echo.

Books and Articles

Glynfab, 'Ebbw Vale Welfare Association', (1968). Produced to commemorate the fiftieth anniversary of the founding of the scheme in 1918. A Celebration Dinner was held at the Welfare Hall, 30 October, 1968.

Eugene Cross, 'The History of The Ebbw Vale Welfare Association 1918-1970'. Unpublished typescript and handwritten account of the Association. Held in the archives of EVRFC. The account is chronological and based on the minutes of the Ebbw Vale Welfare Association.

Anon, 'Ebbw Vale Welfare Association: A Brief History', (1973). Produced to celebrate fifty years of the newly constituted welfare scheme 1923-1973. Celebration Dinner held at the Welfare Hall, 26 October, 1973.

David Wainwright, *Men of Steel: A History of Richard Thomas and his Family* (London, Quiller, 1986).

Chapter Four

Wearing Down the Sceptics

In 1950 Emrys Evans wrote a short book which detailed the histories of all of the main rugby clubs in Wales. The most important clubs had two to three pages devoted to them. They were Cardiff, Newport, Swansea, Llanelli, Neath and Aberavon. Next in the order of importance came Bridgend, Newbridge, Penarth, Glamorgan Wanderers, Abertillery and Cross Keys. Behind them came Maesteg, Abercarn, Pontypool, Pontypridd and Briton Ferry with half a page each. Five clubs merited a paragraph: Blackwood, Blaenavon, Caerleon, Llangwm and Penclawdd. Ebbw Vale does not figure at all despite its impressive post-war success and elevation to first class status in the season in which the book was published. This chapter traces the fortunes of Ebbw Vale Rugby Football Club from 1919 to its transformation into one of the most powerful and impressive clubs in Britain. It is a story of the struggle for recognition in a constant battle against the indifference of the WRU and the aloofness of the southern clubs.

The Ghost of Rugby League

We have already seen how Ebbw Vale exorcised the ghost of professionalism in 1919 and became re-admitted into the Welsh Rugby Union. The ghost, however, came back to haunt the club on more than one occasion. At the General Committee Meeting of the WFU (gradually coming to be known as the WRU), 22 August, 1919, it was noted that stories had appeared in the Press which linked Ebbw Vale to an application to re-join the Northern Union. The members were incensed and directed the Secretary to write to the Ebbw Vale club demanding an explanation. A letter was sent on 23 August in which the Officials of Ebbw Vale were reminded of the assurances that they had given about their intentions regarding amateur status. N. J. Turner, the club secretary, was quick to reply. In a letter dated August 28, 1919, he denied that anyone associated with the club had made an application for affiliation to the Northern Union. As a result of his investigations he was able to report that the secretary of the dissolved Northern Union company had in fact made overtures on his own behalf, and that the present rugby club could not be held responsible for his actions. The explanation was sufficient to satisfy the ruling body.

Given that Ebbw Vale Northern Union promoted a medal competition in the town there was still ambiguity over the eligibility of players who had participated in amateur games under Northern Union rules. Ebbw Vale Crusaders, the team that Eugene Cross helped to re-form after the First World War, was faced with the dilemma in 1920 of wanting to field Tom Jenkins of Cwm who had once played for the 'Shopper's Cracks' in the medal competition. The Crusaders sought clarification from the WFU which was sympathetic. The secretary of the WFU was directed to make further enquiries to ensure that payments were not made, and pending a satisfactory outcome, Jenkins would be allowed to take part in the amateur Union game.

The Crusaders were more circumspect about not wanting to run foul of the WFU than Ebbw Vale rugby club. In 1924 it was decided formally to appoint a trainer under the auspices of the Welfare Association that superseded the welfare scheme of the Ebbw Vale Company. Mog Price had trained the team from its readmission to the WFU. There were two applicants, Tom Fisher and Mog Price. The latter was appointed, either in ignorance, or blatant disregard, of the fact that he had been the trainer of the Ebbw Vale Northern Union side. Team photographs show that Mog Price was the trainer from 1919, and that his appointment merely confirmed his position. Morgan Price was a blacksmith by trade who gave over fifty years service to the club as a player, committeeman and Trainer. He kept strict discipline in the dressing room, and looked after the kit, which was not in abundant supply, better than he would the crown jewels.

In 1926, the year of the General Strike, the WFU and Ebbw Vale Rugby Club once again found themselves embroiled in a controversy involving Northern Union rugby football, which was now officially named Rugby League. The Ebbw Vale Welfare Association was anxious to raise funds to pay off the debt of the War Memorial and came up with a scheme which would involve both Union and Rugby League international sides playing on the Welfare Ground. The rugby club wrote to the WFU requesting a charity fixture on 1 May between a Welsh fifteen and Ebbw Vale. The WFU responded by approving the request but demanding an assurance that professional rugby would not be played on the Welfare Ground and reminded the club of the rule of immediate suspension if professional rugby football was played on the grounds of affiliated clubs. On 16th April both D. A. Jones, the Secretary of Ebbw Vale Rugby Club, and Tudor M. Henry, Hon. Sec. of the Welfare Association Committee independently wrote to the WFU. Jones contended that the Welfare Committee had now been fully appraised of the conditional nature of the offer of a Welsh international fifteen, and that the idea of a Rugby League game had been dropped.

Henry wrote apologetically contending that the Welfare at no time realised that it was jeopardising the position of the rugby club and had without delay dropped the idea. He explained that the object of the professional match was to raise funds and not to introduce rugby league into the area. The WFU accepted the assurances and authorised further preparations for the international side to play at Ebbw Vale. It was decided that the Union cover all the expenses of the Welsh side including tea at Ebbw Vale. Players who required scarlet shirts would have them provided, and those players who had already played for Wales could wear the shirt they had. The selectors chose a strong team, including the legendary Cardiff pair R. A. Cornish and 'Bobby' Delahay. Cornish was a versatile and gifted player who also played soccer for Cardiff Corinthians. He captained Cardiff in the1922-23 season, and played 10 times for Wales. He went on to become chairman of the Welsh selectors and died at the age of 51 in 1948. Delahay was a builder from Bridgend and played 148 games for Cardiff, captaining the side in 1927-28. He won 18 caps for Wales at scrum half, fly-half, and centre.

The match was eagerly anticipated, but turned out to be a great disappointment. There were less than 2,000 there to watch it, and nearly half of the current internationals selected to play withdrew. The team was to have had all the current international side, but only eight turned up. To add to the disappointment it had rained all morning and the ground was once again knee deep in mud. The *Merthyr Express* report on the game was quite scathing in its criticism of the WFU, questioning its motives for staging the game. It was not a magnanimous gesture to help the War Memorial Committee, but a propaganda exercise to promote the amateur game over the professional. It was the view of the author that the exercise had backfired.

On 19th May, 1926 Ebbw Vale Rugby Football Club wrote to the WFU thanking it for allowing an international side to play at Ebbw Vale on 1st May. The gate receipts allowed the War Memorial Committee to reduce its overdraft by approximately £120, far short of the £600 owing. After having assurances from the Welfare Association and the rugby club, the WFU must have felt reasonably confident that it had eliminated ideas of Rugby League from Ebbw Vale altogether. Nothing could be further from the truth. A Rugby League game between Monmouthshire and Glamorganshire was played on 2nd May, 1927.

This game came about in the context of a concerted effort by the Rugby League authorities to re-establish rugby league in Wales, building upon the foothold gained at Pontypridd. There were also plans to inaugurate an amateur rugby league in South Wales. The controversy surrounding the game at Ebbw Vale has been variously documented, but its true character has never been revealed. It is usually suggested that the decision was made by the Welfare Committee, on which the rugby club had only two members who were outvoted. Given that Ebbw Vale did not own the ground it would be unreasonable for the WFU to enforce its policy of suspending any club that allowed Rugby League to be played on its ground. The Rugby Union is usually congratulated for seeing reason and backing down.[1]

1. Peter Lush and Dave Farrar, eds. *Tries for Wales* (London, League Publications, 1998), 61-2 and David Smith and Gareth Williams, *Fields of Praise* (Cardiff, Wales University Press, 1980), 227.

This version of events ignores the fact that the WRU had been given assurances the previous season and had every right to feel aggrieved with both the Welfare Association and Ebbw Vale Rugby Club. The Club, however, was blameless, and D. A. Jones thought the WRU justifiably angry at the Welfare Committee. Jones himself pointed out in an interview in the *Western Mail*, April 9, 1927, that the Welfare Scheme had accepted the conditions of the WRU when Ebbw Vale was re-admitted in 1919. It was not, of course the same Welfare Scheme, and the Ebbw Vale Welfare Association obviously did not feel itself bound by the undertakings of its predecessor.

Ebbw Vale RFC took out an injunction against the Welfare Association to prevent the game. Mr H. Johnson for the Welfare Association argued that the playing fields were owned by the Ebbw Vale Iron and Steel Company, to which a nominal rent was paid. Considerable expense had already been incurred in advertising the match and the Rugby Club had no right to attempt to ban it. The application was refused. Even though Ebbw Vale Rugby Club resorted to the law to prevent the game the WRU still persisted in its stubborn attitude. The irony of the situation was that the man after whom the rugby ground is now named, Eugene Cross, was largely responsible for the debacle, and was disowned by the rugby club committee on which he held a seat. Mr. Cross's own account of the history of the Welfare Association is curiously silent on this whole episode.

The main problem was that Eugene Cross was one of the instigators of the proposed rugby league match and was among the group who travelled to Pontypridd to discuss arrangements. This was much to the annoyance of D. A. Jones, the Secretary of the rugby club who entered into a secret correspondence with the WRU. In a letter of November 27, following one that he had written on 24th November, Mr Jones informed the Union that he had now become aware that the 'Ebbw Vale General Distress Fund, of which Mr. Cross is a very active member, approached the Pontypridd Rugby League Club'. He was not prepared to divulge at this time whether Mr Cross was present in the delegation that went to Pontypridd. Jones maintains that there was an almighty row between him and the Welfare Association. He dissociated himself completely from the actions of the Association, and a meeting of the Rugby Club Committee, from which Mr. Cross was absent, fully backed Jones. He concludes his letter by saying that: 'If Mr. Cross as a member of this Club has done anything to bring this match about, then as far as I am concerned he no longer sits on the Rugby Committee, nor will he be allowed to take an active part in the Rugby game and I trust I shall get your co-operation in bringing this about.' On December 2nd 1926 Jones wrote to the WRU informing it that Mr. Cross had indeed been a member of the delegation to Pontypridd, and that the Chairman of the rugby club had intervened in a meeting to prevent it being recorded in the minutes. Jones suggested that the WRU request the minute book, and supplied a draft letter that could be used as a template. The minute book was requested on 11th December and an emergency meeting was held in the Queen's Hotel, Cardiff 28th December. The minutes show that D. A. Jones interrogated Eugene Cross about his role in the proposed rugby league game, but that the Chairman intervened and said that he would ask Mr. Cross privately. The Secretary of the WRU, Walter E. Rees, demanded an answer to the question by 6th January, but does not appear to have received one. Instead, letters were sent in March by the Welfare Association and the Miners' Welfare Fund urging the Union to acknowledge that the proposed league match had nothing whatsoever to do with the Ebbw Vale RFC, and was vehemently opposed by its committee. These pleas were rejected and the decision stood that the Ebbw Vale Club would be suspended if the game went ahead. After the game had been played Ebbw Vale begged to be allowed to send a delegation, to which a meeting of the General Committee conceded on 19th May. On June 2nd the delegation placed a written application for reinstatement before the General Committee. After a long discussion it was resolved 'That the Ebbw Vale Club be re-instated, subject to a satisfactory undertaking being given by the responsible officers of the Welfare Committee to the effect that no Professional Rugby be played upon the Ground in future'. The rugby club took legal proceedings against the Welfare Association to secure such an assurance. The WRU agreed to pay the costs of £89-4-0, while maintaining that it did not regard this as

W.R.U.'S FIRM STAND.

DECISION REGARDING THE RUGBY LEAGUE RE-AFFIRMED.

By "OBSERVER."

For nearly three hours on Thursday the Welsh Football Union General Committee discussed two subjects—the slight alterations to the laws which will be adopted by the International Board at a meeting next month, and the Rugby League game which will be played at Ebbw Vale on May 2. The latter subject occupied most of the time, and I am afraid the Welsh Union members will find themselves up against a brick wall if they attempt to make the match at Ebbw Vale a "test case" in forbidding professional games on grounds used by amateurs.

Many Welsh Union clubs play at home on grounds loaned by a local landowner, and if the latter wishes he may at any time hand the ground over to the Rugby League. The Ebbw Vale Rugby team play on the Welfare committee's ground and have no more to do with the control of sport there than the Welsh Union or the Rugby League.

If the Welsh Union rigidly adhere to their resolution passed last year, then the only thing to save Ebbw Vale for amateurism is for them to notify the governing body prior to the Rugby League game that they are moving their quarters. If they leave their present ground they will make a very welcome present to professional Rugby, for the Northern Union—as it is erroneously referred to by the Welsh Union—will gladly step in to establish another fort in South Wales.

PLIGHT OF WELSH UNION CLUBS.

While I do not look with alarm upon the attempt of the Rugby League to conquer South Wales, I think the Welsh Union members are not acting wisely in bringing matters to a head at Ebbw Vale. The long-drawn-out trade dispute ended in many clubs being on the verge of bankruptcy, and it has been a hard struggle to keep the game going. "Gates" have not been as good as they should be during the last couple of months, and harassed officials are seeking loop-holes to escape financial disaster. A thrust from the prong of the Welsh Union such as Ebbw Vale is threatened with may lead to a despairing club seeking a change of fortune under a new régime.

There are many second-class clubs in South Wales almost at the end of their tether, and I hope the Welsh Union will help them before it is too late. Clubs like Ebbw Vale do not need a threat to keep the amateur Rugby flag flying—but assistance. I know the officials of Ebbw Vale are as keen on Welsh Union Rugby as the big clubs, and it is not they who should be threatened, but the people who run the Welfare Association at Ebbw Vale.

As a matter of fact, there are many grounds in Wales which will shortly come under the ban of the Welsh Union if they persist in their present policy. Amateur Rugby clubs playing on "Welfare" grounds will be told that they must stand aside on certain days for professional matches, and, being only represented by one sport of many on the committee, will find themselves automatically suspended through no fault of their own.

SYMPATHY WITH WELFARE COMMITTEE.

The game which has incurred the wrath of the Welsh Union is for the Ebbw Vale War Memorial. A year ago a similar match was proposed and sanctioned by the Ebbw Vale Welfare Council, but the latter gave way when the Welsh Union decided to send an international side to the town. Unfortunately, the Welsh Union at the same time decided to suspend clubs which, whether they had control or not over their grounds, harboured a professional Rugby game.

I think the wording of this was very unfortunate. For instance, there are hundreds of Welsh clubs playing on farmers' fields, and at any moment Rugby League teams may rent the playing pitch for even one afternoon, and thus stop for ever the activities of those who desire to remain amateurs.

The fact will not be lost sight of that the Rugby League game at Ebbw Vale is for the local War Memorial Fund, and thus the sympathy of the district will be with the Welfare Committee.

THE OFFICIAL REPORT.

"A report was received from the International Board in connection with the recent meeting of that body, stating that minor alterations of the laws of the game were suggested which would not be finally decided upon until the special meeting of the board in May.

"Correspondence was read from the Ebbw Vale Club relating to the playing of the Northern Union match on May 2, and the meeting re-affirmed the decision arrived at on April 22, 1926, when every club in the Union was notified by circular that in the event of professional Rugby football being played on the ground of any club affiliated to the Union that club would at once be suspended."

An article from the Western Mail, *April 8, 1927.*

a precedent, nor did it imply that the Union felt an obligation in this matter.

Throughout the dispute the Welsh press had little sympathy with the WRU. It was argued that clubs like Ebbw Vale needed encouragement rather than threats. The economic depression and the trade disputes surrounding the General Strike were affecting the gates of all clubs, and the actions of the WRU were likely to drive the more financially insecure into professionalism in order to become viable. The WRU was criticised for not acknowledging that most clubs had no control over their grounds. Many second class teams played on Welfare grounds or fields owned by farmers and decisions regarding the use of the facilities was out of the hands of the rugby club officials. The Ebbw Vale Welfare Association could not see any difference in principle between a professional rugby match and professional soccer and cricket matches taking place on the same ground. At Ebbw Vale soccer and cricket was professional and played at the Welfare Ground in the full knowledge of the WRU. The fact that the proposed game was in aid of the War Memorial was bound to attract the sympathy of the local community.

It is unclear what if any disciplinary action was taken against Eugene Cross by the Rugby Club Committee, but what is clear is that Mr Cross could not have been ignorant of the assurances given to the WRU by the Welfare Association the previous year, nor could he have been oblivious to the fact that his actions jeopardised the affiliation of Ebbw Vale Rugby Football Club to the Welsh Rugby Union. In fact, his actions led to the suspension of the club, and his indiscretion was covered up by the Chairman, much to the anger of the Secretary. A final irony in the saga is the fact that by the next time rugby league was played at Ebbw Vale in the 1980s the Welfare Ground had been renamed Eugene Cross Park.

Newport Encounters

Despite being re-admitted into the amateur Union in 1919 Ebbw Vale continued to be plagued by the old problem of being unable to attract the fashionable clubs across the southern belt of Wales to travel to the wilds of the hills. The fixtures secretary was in contact with the leading English clubs but was unsure whether commitments could be made without first being affiliated to the English Union. In 1920, in a desperate attempt to improve the fixture list, the club devised a plan to apply for affiliation to the Rugby Football Union. D. A. James wrote to the WRU explaining the Ebbw Vale predicament. He maintained that: 'I have tried in vain to obtain fixtures from the leading Welsh Clubs, but they do not seem inclined to recognise us just at present, although Newport have been kind enough to offer us a date for next season. I shall be glad to know, if you have any objections to my applying to Mr. Marriot Twickenham to become affiliated to their Union?' The matter was discussed by the General Committee Meeting of the WRU 20th May, 1920, which resolved to refuse the request and to write to the Rugby Union asking it to defer any such application. The WRU did nothing, however, to put pressure on Welsh clubs to establish fixtures with Ebbw Vale. Throughout the inter-war period Ebbw Vale continued to have difficulties in confirming a strong fixture list.

Newport initially established fixtures with Ebbw Vale following re-admission to the Union, at first playing only a home game in 1920-21. Ebbw Vale was an attractive fixture because of the tremendously successful 1919-20 campaign in which the last two games of the season decided the league championship. The fight for top place was between Ebbw Vale, Tredegar and Talywain. The season started with a series of uneven performances with the Valians going down to Blaina, and Talywain, before rallying to beat Cardiff Grange, only to lose to Tredegar, draw with Risca and suffer another defeat against Abertillery on 15th October 1919 after a dropped goal by Dr Fahmey secured four points for the win. Ebbw Vale then became more focused and played the sort of rugby for which it had become famous in the 1890s. On 24th January, 1920 the Football Echo reported that: 'Rugbyites have something to be proud of at the continual success of the local team. Their last defeat was registered as far back as October 15, and since they have consecutive wins in their favour (14 matches away from home).' This run of success included revenge against Abertillery by 11pts to nil. The fourteenth of these matches resulted in a humiliating defeat for Cardiff University which conceded twelve tries. Five of the tries were scored in the first half, but none converted, and of the seven scored in the second half only two went over the cross bar. Ebbw outclassed a plucky student side with Harry Thomas, the Welsh reserve winger producing a marvellous display of skills. The score of 40pts to nil was almost unprecedented, but was surpassed on 3rd April when London Scottish succumbed by 43pts to nil. The Valians also crushed Lydney by 26pts to nil, Penylan by 23pts to nil, and Mountain Ash 24pts to 3pts. Reports of the Mountain Ash game lamented that the visitors were lucky to get away with only a 21pt margin. The weakest part of the Ebbw Vale game was in the kicking department with only two of the seven tries being converted.

The championship for Ebbw Vale hung on the penultimate game of the season, and what made it more exciting was the fact that it was also the clash with Tredegar, the 'international of the hills'. If Ebbw Vale won, the championship would be hers, but if Tredegar won the likelihood was that Talywain would take the prize.

A record gate from all parts of Monmouthshire assembled to see the clash of the season. Both sides intensified their training regimes, and both were at full strength. They fought like demons, conceding nothing to each other. At the end it was disappointment for Ebbw Vale in only managing to hold on to a nil-nil draw. In drawing, however, there was still hope, but once again the result rested upon the outcome of a heated rivalry. In the last game of the season on 1st May, 1920 Ebbw Vale played Abertillery, and to its bitter disappointment again managed only a nil nil draw. The championship was lost and Talywain took the crown. To come second in the Monmouthshire League after such turbulent times in the first twenty years of the twentieth century was a remarkable achievement.

In the 1921-22 season Ebbw Vale opened with a nil nil draw against the Monmouthshire League champions. The Iron and Steelworks town was acknowledged to be one of the strongest sides in the Monmouthshire League, though 'not as clever' as the previous season (*South Wales Argus*, January 17, 1921). The first of the Newport clashes

Ebbw Vale RFC 1919-20 captained by Mike Hurley.

was played at Rodney Parade 15 January. The colours of both teams were black and amber, so in the first encounter Ebbw Vale turned out in dark blue shirts against a considerably weakened Newport, or the Usksiders as they were known. Newport had six men on duty for Wales at Twickenham, a seventh on the bench for England, and an eighth earning a cap for Ireland. Ebbw Vale also took the field without some of its key men, Fisher and Edwards were absent from the forwards, and Hopkins from the backs.

For the first ten minutes Ebbw Vale dominated and pressed Newport hard in the home 25. If it had not been for the superb defending of Harold Birt and Fred Davies the Valians would have crossed the line. Suddenly, Newport turned the game around with an heroic dash up the wing by Owen who was valiantly brought down in the 25 by Vale's fullback Enoch Jones. The fight back was continued with an inspired performance from Tommy Vile who had been brought in to fill the gap made by Jack Wetter the Welsh captain. At outside half Vile surprised everyone with his quick thinking and agility. Although he was an ex-captain of Newport and

Welsh international he had not played first class rugby for years. He easily outclassed the Cowell brothers of Ebbw Vale at half-back. Ebbw Vale was forced into conceding a penalty which Fred Birt capitalised upon with a wonderful kick. Towards the end of the first half Newport mounted a concerted attack which culminated in a fine unconverted try by Tom Jones. Newport consolidated its position with some hard work early in the first half which was rewarded with a sprint down the wing by Rees, resulting in an unconverted try. Ebbw Vale mounted an impressive revival with Lawrence, James, Charles, Jones and Williams all falling narrowly short of the line, but Newport re-grouped and smothered the Vale attack. In the final minutes of the game Fred Birt frustrated a clever dribbling movement by the visiting forwards, who throughout the game had the better of their Newport counterparts. It was the inspired performance of the Newport backs, particularly Birt and Vile who won the game for the Usksiders by 9pts to nil.

The second of the Newport clashes came in the following season, over the Christmas period. On a Rodney Parade damaged from previous games, wet from the heavy rain, but drying out as a strong breeze blew over the surface, helped by tons of sand scattered in

Ebbw Vale RFC 1920-21 captained by Joe Lawrence.

front of the stand to firm-up the boggy part of the field. In this encounter Newport put out as strong a team as it could. Ebbw Vale played a hard first half, allowing the home side very little scope to break away. The Valians were a strong, fit and finely toned side which kept Newport on its toes throughout, but at the end of the day the home forwards had the edge. At half-time the score was 10pts to nil, and extended to 26pts by the sound of the final whistle.

In 1923-24 Newport played Ebbw Vale at home and away, winning both games. Saturday, 8th December saw Newport visit Ebbw Vale for an official fixture for the first time. The two previous occasions had been away. It was an historic occasion, and although the weather was miserable, the crowds turned out in record numbers to welcome the visitors. In a hotly contested game Newport came out the winners by 8pts to 3pts. The return game came on 19th April 1924. Ebbw Vale came out looking as if the players would run Newport all the way. The Valians were on top during the first half, but failed to score. Some brilliant defending also prevented Newport from scoring. In the second half the speed and finish of the home side came to the surface, and the Valians were well beaten. Overall the game was unattractive and unexciting. There was very little adventure in the back play, and far too much reckless passing among the Newport forwards. While Ebbw Vale was strong in defence, the players showed very little initiative and never posed a serious threat. The Vale went down by 10pts to nil at Newport. After scoring only 3pts against Newport in four games the fixture ceased. Ebbw Vale had not made the cut as far as Newport was concerned, and remained a second class side unable to match the first class clubs of the South.

From 1930-1 Newport established a pattern of beginning each season with a game against the Monmouthshire League, impressively winning every meeting until the annual encounter finished in 1936-7. Ebbw Vale once again resumed hostilities against Newport in the 1939-40 season, but lost both home and away, 8pts to 6pts at the Welfare Ground, and 16pts to 8pts at Rodney Parade.

When normal fixtures resumed at the end of the War Newport could find no place in its official schedule for Ebbw Vale, despite the valiant efforts of the men from the hills throughout the War.

Unofficial Welsh Champions 1953-54. Big Ben Edwards is seated in the centre of the third row with Eric Finney immediately above him.

There was a friendly game on 21st September, 1949 which is not recorded in Newport's fixture lists. Newport was suffering from a number of injuries and sent a team to Ebbw Vale that was under strength and unrepresentative. It was not until the 1953-4 season that the two Gwent clubs began to meet again on a regular basis. By this time Ebbw Vale was not only a recognised first class team, but had also topped the unofficial merit table. The Vale team travelled to Newport on 12 December, 1953, taking with them as captain 'Big Ben' Edwards, formerly a regular at Rodney Parade in the black and amber shirt. Edwards had started playing for Newport in the 1947-8 season, but his exceptional talent as a goal kicker was not discovered until later. In the 1950-51 season Ben Edwards set the Newport scoring record, 159 points which he achieved by kicking twenty-five penalties and forty-two conversions.

Edwards was responsible for the Rugby Union's short-lived ruling that no objects or earth could be used to tee-up the ball for place kicks. This ruling followed a bizarre report in a West Country newspaper after Newport played Exeter away from home. It had been a particularly dry season, making the ball difficult to place. Ben Edwards bought some plasticine from a local shop and gave it to the full-back Bob Hughes for safe keeping during the game. When Edwards took his first kick, which missed the goal, he called for the plasticine and used it as a tee. The referee, Les Evans, refused to allow it to be used a second time. The local paper reported this incident by suggesting that Ben Edwards had borrowed the full-back's teeth to use as a tee!

Edwards joined Ebbw Vale in the 1952-3 season, leaving Newport with a gaping hole in the kicking department which it failed to fill. Newport's fortunes during the 1953-4 season were at a post war low when Ebbw Vale turned up at Rodney Parade. This was the season that Ebbw Vale was to become the unofficial Welsh champions for the second time.

The Ebbw Vale team that played against Newport was I. Shee; D. Richards; J. Williams; K. Bevan; J. Pugh; G. Evans; I. Evans; L. Coldrick; A Jackson; R. Cameron, L. Harries; B. Edwards (capt.) H. Mathews; E. Finney and G. Griffiths. Ebbw Vale had a storming start to the game, winning a line-out and three set scrums yards from the Newport line in the first few minutes. Only desperate smothering tactics prevented the valley men from scoring. The hearts of Newport players sank when a penalty was conceded twenty-five yards from the posts. Big Ben Edwards stepped-up to execute the kick, but uncharacteristically sliced it to the side of the goal. Another incident in which the Ebbw Vale wing Ken Jones was ankle tapped gave Edwards a chance from the half way line, but the distance was just too far. It was third time lucky for Big Ben when Newport conceded another penalty thirty yards from its line. Newport mounted a vigorous attack but failed with a penalty and dropped goal within two minutes. A handling error lost Newport the initiative and Eric Finney led a forward rush, taking Vale within the Newport twenty-five. Malcolm Lewis was taken to hospital with a suspected broken leg and Newport had to make some tactical changes, putting Ken Jones in the centre and bringing Ian McJennett from lock to the wing. Ebbw Vale led at the interval by 3pts to nil. With only fourteen men, Newport put up a credible show in the second half, but was always up against it. After some vigorous defending in the Newport half the ball went loose and was scooped up by J. B. Williams who sprinted twenty-five yards to the line. Edwards converted. Shortly after K. Bevan increased the points margin with a dropped goal, and Newport replied with a converted try. Ebbw Vale kept the pressure on right until the end, and a few minutes before the final whistle D. Richards scored a try near the corner resulting from a skirmish almost on the Newport line. Ben Edwards made a magnificent kick from the touch line to complete the scoring. Ebbw Vale won 16pts to 5pts. The *Football Echo* for 12th December commented that: 'The Ebbw Vale forwards and their backs were quicker on the ball in this thrill packed game and the valley men thoroughly deserved to win'.

The Depression Years

We saw in the last chapter how seriously Ebbw Vale was affected by the economic fluctuations of the 1920s, which became exacerbated by the closure of the Steel Works in 1928. Most clubs in South Wales found it difficult to sustain a reasonable level of crowd support because even with low entrance charges unemployed men having to rely upon Poor Relief could not afford them. There was a noticeable increase in the number of people watching games from vantage points outside the ground. Two additional factors served to exacerbate an already difficult situation. Association Football had taken a hold on the valleys in the years after the First World War and Ebbw Vale became one of the leading clubs in Wales playing in the same league as Swansea Town and Newport Town, and collecting plenty of silver along the way. Merthyr also had a very strong Association football team and loyalties were being stretched between the two codes. Rugby did not do itself any favours by allowing to develop a fairly lax attitude towards punctuality. Crowds were often kept waiting for the visiting team to arrive. This became such a problem at Ebbw Vale that the Committee tabled a motion at the WRU General Meeting to introduce punishments for late arrival, but was defeated on the grounds that the men were amateurs and the introduction of such a rule smacked of professionalism.

During the early 1920s Ebbw Vale was able to field a powerful team and began to recover some of the reputation it had had in 1890s. Even formidable opponents such as Mountain Ash, endearingly known as 'The Old Firm', were in trepidation over visits from the Valians. Following the First World War Mountain Ash failed to beat Ebbw Vale nine times in succession, on the ninth in November 1923 it drew 3pts all, but finally succeeded on 16 February, 1924 in overcoming Ebbw Vale by 6pts to nil. Ebbw Vale was capable not only of beating local opposition, which it often did with ease, but also some quite strong English sides. At the end of the 1922-23 season, with Enoch Jones at full-back and Joe Lawrence leading the forwards Ebbw Vale easily beat Rhymney and Blaina, but also took on 'Rugby – a smart English combination with a high reputation'. Jack Price was the man of the match in the three quarter line, producing some scintillating moves which he turned into four tries, thoroughly demoralising the opposition. During this season Ebbw Vale held its ground record, although it looked distinctively at risk against Crumlin and Pill Harriers in the last two games of the campaign. On a ground that was 'in a very bad state' Crumlin went into the lead, but the score line was equalised by Enoch Jones, whose 'star performance' prevented a menacing Crumlin side from putting more points on the board. After composing themselves in the latter part of the game Ebbw Vale scored again to win 6pts to 3pts. It was once again Enoch Jones, the most reliable back in Monmouthshire, who won the day with a penalty goal against the 'famous Pill Harriers'.

The blow of having Newport pull out of the fixture list after 1923-24 was compensated by being able to attract the famous Neath and Bridgend sides, and retain the Aberavon encounter, while adding some top English opposition in Nuneaton, Bedford, and Northampton, thus confirming the general opinion that the men from Ebbw Vale were a class above the local opposition, especially the likes of Brynmawr, Rhymney and Blaina. The previous season had started off on a shaky footing for Ebbw Vale because the forwards did not knit together as a unit. There were grave worries that the Valians would slip from the top rank in Monmouthshire if the forwards did not improve. Against Blaina, for instance, Ebbw Vale was considered lucky to win as a result of a nice pass from Kerton to Police Constable Cleaves who crossed the line to give Enoch Jones an easy conversion. There was a marked contrast between the first and second halves of the season. Up to Boxing Day Ebbw played 18 games, winning only four, but had drawn 8. A respectable, but not an impressive record. In the remaining 23 games the Valians hit better form, winning 15 and drawing 1. These included some very tough games at the end of the season against Abertillery, Pontypridd and Aberavon. Against Abertillery the score was 8pts to nil, and was taken as a test of the character and strength of the Ebbw Vale side. Abertillery was regarded as ranking among the first class clubs in Wales and had beaten some of the best that season. In winning this match Ebbw Vale confirmed that it too deserved to be ranked among the premier clubs in Wales.

The 1925-26 season confirmed Ebbw Vale's claim to be a first class side when it retained its home record throughout the season, despite its severe financial difficulties, and despite the fact that two of its hardest games came at the end. Ebbw Vale consolidated its claim to first class status when it took on Bridgend and Neath. On 18th April 1925 Bridgend visited Ebbw Vale for the first time and fielded its strongest team, including its three international players. Ebbw Vale's 14pts to nil victory was described as 'a remarkable triumph.' Ebbw Vale managed to neutralise the Bridgend internationals throughout the game, in particular Cyril Thomas 'was kept too cramped to be effective'.

On the eve of the last game of the season Ebbw Vale could look back with pride on one of their most successful campaigns ever. In the previous few weeks they had beaten some daunting opposition in Aberavon, Cross Keys, Resolven, Pontypridd and Pontypool. Neath had beaten the Valians narrowly by 8pts to 3pts, and in the final game of the season Ebbw Vale were out for revenge. A record crowd turned-out to see, and gave a rousing cheer to, the Neath all blacks on their first visit to Ebbw Vale. 'Glynfab', reporting in the *Merthyr Express*, 9th May, 1925, argued that the game was:

> 'one of the best of the season, and as we had an opportunity of witnessing a serious display by a first-class side it is surprising what little difference there is after all between that and the play of a side that is scheduled as a second-class team. Clearly on the run of play for the whole period of the game, Ebbw Vale were the better side, and the superiority was not shown at the expense of orthodox football, as is often the case when teams of a different class meet. But Ebbw Vale set up a high standard of football that would be difficult to beat by the best of the first class clubs'.

Ebbw Vale was gaining a reputation for fast, open attractive rugby, and had the measure of most sides when it stuck to its own style of play. Occasionally when it encountered a different style of play Ebbw Vale would respond in kind, but often to its detriment. The reputation that Pontypool had in the 1970s for ten man rugby was forged very early in its history. When Ebbw Vale encountered Pontypool in January 1926, for example, it was reported that if close play was to be the ruling factor then the result would be a very close call because it was a style of play for which Pontypool was famous, while on the other hand 'Ebbw Vale are noted for open work, and have brought off some wonderful performances through this policy' (*Merthyr Express*, 26th January, 1926). Ebbw Vale was criticised for adopting the Pontypool style of play and making the result a much closer call than it needed to be. Even in taking Pontypool on at its own game Ebbw Vale had them 'beaten to a frazzle', with the incredibly versatile veteran Joe Lawrence coming out of the pack to play full-back and putting on a very 'classy display'.

Under Tom Kerton as captain morale was high when the real test of status came the following season in a return match with Neath. The Valians had lost away to Neath, but were confident of being victorious at home. Neath played very attractive open rugby, using the backs effectively to mount attack after attack, but every time Ebbw Vale's defence was impregnable. The forwards played a devastating game, making every tackle count, and feeding clean effective ball to the backs who were able to capitalise. Bird, from Abertillery, scored no less than five tries, ably assisted by Bantam Jones, Kerton and Roberts, who all put in class performances. In beating Neath 20pts to 9pts, Ebbw Vale was able to strengthen its Welsh fixture list further, but the heavy costs of travelling to England forced the Committee to cut back on the 'foreign' opposition. One of the great coups was that of adding Cardiff for the first time in the 1926-7 programme, a coup that was somewhat diminished with the realisation that it was Cardiff's 'other' first team that Ebbw Vale played.

The morale of the team was sustained, even through the most adverse seasons, during the late 1920s and early 1930s by Tom Kerton, Dai Regan Jones and Albert Kerton, all of whom captained the side. Tom Kerton again from 1928-29, Dai Jones from 1929-31 and 1933-36, punctuated by Albert Kerton 1931-33. Before small crowds the teams of the Depression years fought hard to maintain respectable records, despite the fact that morale and confidence was severely dented by the indignity of soup kitchens and means tested Poor Relief. At the start of the 1927-28 season Ebbw Vale got off to a lack lustre start in going down to Aberavon, but turned the situation around by drawing with Abercarn and beating Stroud by 3pts to nil. The season was somewhat like a roller coaster because the following game against Pontypool resulted in one of Ebbw Vale's greatest defeats, going down 26pts to 3pts. Throughout the season the highs and lows were repeated, but Ebbw Vale never lost heart and finished with a creditable tally of successes, without being able to call it a distinguished record. Newspaper reports during the latter part of the 1920s talk of circumstances conspiring to cripple the once virile club, but suggest that with a young and enthusiastic team, and a determined committee the valley team was optimistic that its prospects were bright. Rugby at the Ebbw Vale Grammar School was proving to be a life-line in channelling new blood through to the senior team at times when players were being lost in the search for work outside the area.

Ebbw Vale was even capable of turning on a display that was reminiscent of its former glory as the champions of the hills. Ebbw Vale could certainly beat the likes of Crumlin convincingly, as it did in September, 1929, only to crumble before tougher opposition such as Pill Harriers. Occasionally, however, when faced with a team such as the powerful Bristol XV Ebbw Vale could put on a display second to none. In what was described as a hard tussle which took place on 29th September, 1929, the *Football Echo* carried the headline: 'Best in Welsh Rugby – Tasted by Crowd in Ebbw Vale Fare' (5th October, 1929). The correspondent revelled in the display of rugby which Ebbw Vale won by 9pts to 6 pts, adding that if only the same standard could be maintained, what a glorious season the Monmouthshire side could anticipate. The game proved to him two things: 'that rugby has not lost its hold on the crowd, who are still ready to be thrilled with bright open football: and that in the Ebbw Vale side, a team of youngsters, there is the ability to rise to the occasion'. After some indifferent performances before Christmas against Pontypridd and Pontypool, and a draw with Mountain Ash, the latter part of the season picked-up considerably for the club to make an announcement: 'The committee desire the Rugby loving public to know through the medium of the *Merthyr Express* that

Ebbw Vale Rugby Football Club 1929-30. Dai Regan Jones, captain.

since January 4, 1930, 18 matches have been played, 14 won, 2 lost, and two drawn. 144pts for and 55pts against'.

Such optimism was short lived with an immediate return to quite uneven play throughout the next few seasons, sometimes excelling, while at others drawing with or going-down by narrow margins to teams of which Ebbw Vale should have had the measure, such as Abergavenny, Blaina, Blaenavon, Mountain Ash and a much diminished Tredegar. The Valians were still capable of surprising the opposition, as they did, for example, at Neath in January 1931 where the All Blacks were momentarily unhinged by the determined Ebbw Vale youngsters. Neath managed to scrape a victory by 6pts to nil. The following January Ebbw Vale gave Neath an even greater fright. In rising to the occasion of fulfilling one of the strongest fixtures on its list Ebbw Vale held Neath to a one point margin, 8pts to 9pts in conditions that deterred most followers from coming out in support.

1933 saw both the rugby and association Ebbw Vale teams languishing at the bottom of their respective leagues, mainly due to lack of financial support. The soccer team's fall from grace was even greater than that of the rugby club. In the previous few seasons it had headed the table in the Southern League and Welsh League, and won the Welsh cup in a memorable game against Swansea Town. Ebbw Vale's rugby record in 1932-33 was so abysmal that hardly any mention of its efforts merited reporting. Both codes managed to redeem themselves from total embarrassment by unexpectedly doing well in competitions. The rugby team reached the final of the Ben Francis Cup. It was played at Brynmawr Recreation Ground and Blaina were bidding to win the cup for the fifth time, the fourth in succession. On such form Blaina was the favourite and before three thousand spectators put up a valiant effort. Reduced at one time to thirteen men Blaina battled courageously but was defeated 'in one of the prettiest movements of the game' which resulted in a try scored by E. Nichols of Ebbw Vale. The Soccer club defeated Newport County in the semi-final of the Monmouthshire Challenge Cup and went on to defeat Lovell's in the final at Tredegar.

Ebbw Vale's financial position worsened in the mid-'thirties to the extent that other valleys clubs combined to form a team in order to raise funds for the poverty stricken Valians. Even though it was an entertaining game with bright open rugby as its main feature, the fact that the match was played on Monday deterred many from attending. A disappointing, and disappointed, crowd saw Ebbw Vale go down to the Joint XV by 14pts. to 9pts. Very few of Ebbw Vale's matches were reported in the *Merthyr Express* for the seasons 1933-34 and 1934-35, but there is evidence of some improvement in the play, although the performance is patchy. At the end of the 1933-34 season Ebbw Vale was still capable of being described as 'one of the best teams in the Monmouthshire valleys' (*Merthyr Express*, 21st April, 1934), but with little justification. There were few sign over the next two seasons of any revival in fortunes. With the *Merthyr Express* almost ignoring Ebbw Vale's record we find in the *Football Echo* that results of many games are published, but few match reports. An indication of Ebbw Vale's record can be gleaned from the eighteen results recorded for 1935-6. Of these 11 were lost, 5 won and two drawn. The Ebbw Vale Association Football team remained uninspiring. At the end of the 1933-34 season at the top of the Welsh League Swansea Town left its nearest rival Barry Town out of sight with 46pts. Barry had only 33pts. Ebbw Vale, however, was third from the bottom of the League with 17pts.

As Ebbw Vale's economic prospects grew, and speculation about the building of a new steel plant engendered greater optimism, the fortunes of Ebbw Vale Rugby Football Club began to turn as the enterprising committee sought to put new vigour in a team that had not inspired confidence for some time. This turn in form coincided with the captaincy of Wally Talbot. Throughout the 1936-7 season the *Western Mail* expressed surprise at the great progress being made in rugby at Ebbw Vale. Phrases such as 'playing pretty football', 'remarkable stride', 'splendid advance', 'brilliant play', 'bright exhibition' and 'great improvement' became standard in the reporting of games as Ebbw Vale broke record after record and gained considerably in confidence. In February, 1938 Ebbw Vale took away the ground record of the strong Talywain team, and in March beat Mountain Ash by 26pts to nil, surpassing the heaviest defeat by Ebbw set thirty five years previously of 21pts to nil. Ebbw

Vale beat Merthyr by a clear 44 pts, Pontypridd by a clear 20pts, and played 'delightful rugby' in convincingly beating Abergavenny by 27pts to 5pts. Ebbw Vale also heavily defeated Briton Ferry by 21pts to 3pts, but the most satisfying result came in one of the best performances by a Welsh against an English side in holding the powerful Wolverhampton pack to a draw. Old Stager remarks that: 'the Ebbw Vale forwards were the better pack, and it was their work in the loose that subdued the lively Wolverhampton forwards' (*Western Mail*, 4th April, 1938).

The Association Football club still lacked the necessary support and failed to find reinvigorated form. By the end of the 1937-8 season there was some doubt about whether it would come out of the corner to fight another round. There was a huge sigh of relief when it decided to 'play for another season' in the First Division of the Welsh League. The Rugby Club's fortunes, however, had seriously improved, both financially and in match winning ability. Success on the field was rewarded with added spectator support.

In the context of a fixture list that included few strong opponents it is remarkable that any Ebbw Vale players reached the final trials for the Welsh team. Surprisingly, then, not only did a number of players participate in the preliminary rounds, but others reached the final trial and progressed as far as the bench. Caps were awarded for the final trial for the 1919-20 season and Harry Thomas of Ebbw Vale played ¾ back for the stripes (possibles). He had a good game and was rewarded with a place on the bench against Scotland, France, and Ireland. In the 1923-4 season Joe Lawrence, who played in the forwards and who captained Ebbw Vale in the 1920-21 season, progressed to the final trial, as did Ellis Jones in 1933-34. Dai 'Reagan' Jones, who captained Ebbw Vale 1929-31 and 1933-6 made the Welsh bench in the 1932-3 season, and so did Ben Southway in 1936-7. Almost a decade later Southway and Percival of Ebbw Vale were selected to play in the famous Monmouthshire side which beat the touring New Zealand Services by 15pts to nil. A. H. Rowlands, Newport's right centre, scored three tries, one of which was converted by Southway. 4pts from a drop goal by J. Hawkins of Newport, the Monmouthshire captain, completed the points tally.

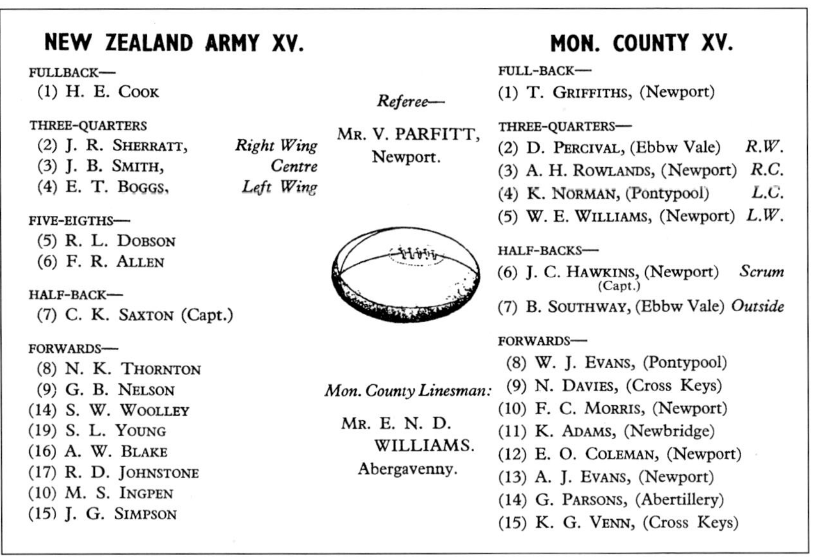

NEW ZEALAND ARMY XV.

FULLBACK—
(1) H. E. Cook

THREE-QUARTERS
(2) J. R. Sherratt, *Right Wing*
(3) J. B. Smith, *Centre*
(4) E. T. Boggs, *Left Wing*

FIVE-EIGTHS—
(5) R. L. Dobson
(6) F. R. Allen

HALF-BACK—
(7) C. K. Saxton (Capt.)

FORWARDS—
(8) N. K. Thornton
(9) G. B. Nelson
(14) S. W. Woolley
(19) S. L. Young
(16) A. W. Blake
(17) R. D. Johnstone
(10) M. S. Ingpen
(15) J. G. Simpson

Referee—
Mr. V. PARFITT,
Newport.

Mon. County Linesman:
Mr. E. N. D.
WILLIAMS.
Abergavenny.

MON. COUNTY XV.

FULL-BACK—
(1) T. Griffiths, (Newport)

THREE-QUARTERS—
(2) D. Percival, (Ebbw Vale) *R.W.*
(3) A. H. Rowlands, (Newport) *R.C.*
(4) K. Norman, (Pontypool) *L.C.*
(5) W. E. Williams, (Newport) *L.W.*

HALF-BACKS—
(6) J. C. Hawkins, (Newport) (Capt.) *Scrum*
(7) B. Southway, (Ebbw Vale) *Outside*

FORWARDS—
(8) W. J. Evans, (Pontypool)
(9) N. Davies, (Cross Keys)
(10) F. C. Morris, (Newport)
(11) K. Adams, (Newbridge)
(12) E. O. Coleman, (Newport)
(13) A. J. Evans, (Newport)
(14) G. Parsons, (Abertillery)
(15) K. G. Venn, (Cross Keys)

New Zealand Services versus Monmouthshire, February 27th 1946. Played at Pontypool.

Rugby and the War

The outbreak of war necessitated the mobilisation of all able bodied men for the armed forces, but in vital industries, such as coal and steel, labour was required to contribute to the war effort by continuing to work. In these areas sporting teams were not as badly affected as those where most of the young male population enlisted or were conscripted into the armed forces. In the Ebbw Vale area rugby remained strong during the war, but elsewhere activities were suspended and games played on an occasional basis.

The Welsh Rugby Union issued a circular to clubs on 6 September informing them of the Government's Emergency Act banning entertainments and the gathering of crowds, and therefore suspended fixtures for the 1939-40 season. On the 25th September, the position was clarified. The WRU reiterated its position, but informed affiliated clubs that the Home Secretary had recommended that recreation, entertainment and sport should continue to a limited extent, on condition that it did not interfere with National Security and Public Safety. This meant that sporting organisations were able to continue their activities if they so wished. The statement went on to inform clubs that: 'The Welsh Rugby Union take this early opportunity of acquainting their affiliated Clubs and subsidiary organisations that if they are desirous of playing games in accordance with the recommendation of the Government, they must themselves make and be responsible for the whole of the arrangements, which must comply with the Government regulation, viz: – that before matches can be arranged the permission of the local police must be obtained.'

Wales played its last international game before the War on 11th March, 1939 against Ireland. Ireland was on target to take the triple crown but was deprived of it for the seventh time in a game that saw no score for the first 75 of the 80 minutes. The Irish managed to smother Wilf Wooller, preventing him from successfully dropping a goal. Wales changed tactics and created space for Willie Davies, the Swansea fly half to score the only dropped goal of his career, and the last for Wales to be worth 4 points. He also scored the only try of the match making Wales the winner by 7pts to nil. Four of the Welsh team who played that day gained further caps after the war, Haydn Tanner, L. Manfield, W. Travers and the full back Howard Davies. When play resumed after the War Wales played eight Victory internationals for which no official caps were awarded. Full internationals were resumed on 18th January, 1947 when England beat Wales 9 pts to 6 pts.

Most clubs cancelled their regular fixture lists, but carried-on with various games including charity events. Because they were not officially under the auspices of the Welsh Rugby Union, detailed reporting and even detailed records are hard to come by. Newport, for example, decided to play teams within a sixty mile radius because of the inability of sporting fixtures to qualify for petrol rationing. Newport whose records are second to none in comprehensiveness, kept no detailed checklist of its war time activities, and the same was the case with Cardiff. Cardiff played its last official match on 2nd September against Bridgend at The Cardiff Arms Park. Cardiff beat Bridgend 20pts to 9pts. It was six years before another official match was played. A War Emergency Committee was formed and unofficial and charity matches were organised, including games against Ebbw Vale. An air raid on 2nd January 1941 deposited an unexploded bomb behind the goal line which further hindered the playing of rugby. All matches were friendly, and unofficial. Publication of the *Football Argus* and *Football Echo* was suspended indefinitely during the War.

Although there was no official rugby the clubs of Gwent looked favourably upon continuing the game. A valleys committee was formed comprising Abertillery, Risca, Talywain, Cross Keys, Abercarn, Brynmawr, Blackwood, Ebbw Vale, Newbridge, Machen, Blaina, and Crumlin. The first of the unofficial first class games was played between Newport and Cardiff on 14th October, 1939. Two days later Ebbw Vale began its campaign against Cross Keys, losing 3pts to nil. In the following weeks the tables were completely turned and Ebbw Vale beat Cross Keys by 20pts. to 4pts. Almost without exception the Ebbw Vale games were played on Mondays throughout the war years.

Ebbw Vale continued to play rugby, mainly because of the large pool of young men employed in the vital industries. Rugby was kept alive in Ebbw Vale through the organisational skills of Dai Regan Jones, the former Newport and South Wales Borders' wing-forward.

In August of 1940 the Committee of Ebbw Vale Rugby Club met to decided what policy to adopt for the coming season. The Committee resolved unanimously to continue playing as long as it was possible to secure fixtures. In fact, 1940-41 saw Ebbw Vale attain something that it had never done previously nor since, that is a 100% victory, winning all thirty of their games, captained by the irrepressible Wally Talbot. The *Football Echo*, May 6, 1950 compared Maesteg's similar achievement in the 1949-50 season with that of Ebbw Vale: 'for the sake of those who are always on the look out for records it can by pointed out that in the season 1940-41 Ebbw Vale, who continued to keep the rugby flag flying during the war years, fulfilled a complete list of fixtures with English and Welsh clubs who also operated during that period – and they had a similar unbeaten record. In fact that record was unique since through the whole of that season they did not draw a match, every one was a clear victory. They scored 629 points with only 103 against'.

This achievement should not be underestimated. Even though it was the war years Ebbw Vale played some formidable opponents. The Valians beat the RAF by 27pts to 3pts; the South Wales Borderers by 20pts to 8pts; an Army XV by 55pts to nil; and the British Empire XV by 16pts to 3pts. Cardiff continued to have a strong side during the War years and played Ebbw Vale twice in the 1940-41 season, losing 10pts to 15pts, and 3pts to 10pts. In the first of these games Wilfred Wooller captained the side which had Jack Jermain, Les Spence, Wendy Davies and Jumbo Thomas in the pack. Ebbw Vale trailed at half time by 6pts to 10pts. In the second half the visitors persisted in attack and a delicate cross kick from Percival to Ken Davies resulted in a try converted by Chaplain to edge Ebbw Vale into the lead by one point. Cardiff's fate was sealed by a dropped goal. Ebbw Vale also beat Llanelli by 16pts. to nil.

What is even more remarkable is that beyond this invincible season Ebbw Vale remained undefeated up until the end of the following season. Again the fixture list was strong, but under war conditions newspapers were disinclined to report sporting activities. Ebbw Vale met Newport at the beginning of April at Rodney Parade to defend its two seasons unbeaten record. Newport immediately exerted pressure and went ahead with a penalty goal by R. Morgan. Not to be out manoeuvred, the Valians replied with a clever try from J. T. Knowles, drawing the scores level. In the second half Newport mounted a counter-offensive which was repelled by some heroic defensive play, creating an opportunity for Knowles to score a second try. Ebbw Vale was now in the driving seat and exerted more pressure, resulting in a try by W. Sheen and converted by Southway, making the score 11pts to 3pts.

The record was lost to Percy Jones' XV. Jones, a veteran Welsh international selected a team to play at Blackwood in aid of the Red Cross. It was well attended with dignitaries, including the local MP Sir Charles Edwards and the Chief Constable of Monmouthshire

Invincible Season 1940-41

Back row, left to right: W. Whitson, J. D. Rees, R. J.Criddle, J. Rudman, H. Mortimer, W. Morris, J. Wilding, A. J. Powell, T. J. Payne.
Second: W. Sheen, D. Percival, J. Gardner, W. Millet, H. Caswell, E. Jones, G. M. Chaplin.
First: A. J. Coward, R. W.Wiltshire (Treas.), A. Bricknell, D. Jones, M. J.Richards, G. Sherbourn, R. John, R. Box, I. J.Baker, J. Flinn.
Seated: G. Cugley (VC), Dai Reagan Jones (Hon. Sec.), W. Talbot (Capt.), F. Bedell (Chair), A. Gardner, J. Rodway (Fin. Sec.), Mog Price (Trainer). On Ground: Ben Southway, Mel Rees, (J. Redmund: Absent).

Major W. R. Lucas D.S.O. Capt Geoffrey Crawshay kicked off in the first half, and Major P. H. Varwell in the second. Ebbw Vale lost by the narrowest of margins. Both teams scored a penalty goal and a try, but Tamplin sealed the victory for Jones' team by converting the try.

Ebbw Vale's fortunes collapsed in the 1943-44 season with a series of defeats by strong and weak sides alike. Losing, for example, to Cardiff (twice), Newbridge, Newport, Joe Davies' Blaenavon XV, and Newbridge Welfare. Of some consolation was the knowledge that the team beat Newport twice. The deciding match in a series of three was played at Rodney Parade on 15th January 1944. The match was kicked off by a Victoria Cross holder who supported Ebbw Vale, ex-company sergeant-major Jack Williams. Both teams fielded extremely strong sides in a game distinguished by 'merciless and keen' tackling. The 'enthusiasm and keen rivalry produced play of a very robust nature' (*Western Mail*, 17th January, 1944). At the start of the following season Newport immediately avenged the defeat. Ebbw Vale was to prove that its lack of form in 1943-44 was not just a temporary aberration because against the stronger sides Ebbw Vale failed to register. Ebbw Vale went on to beat Percy Jones' XV, Abercarn (twice) Cardiff Varsity, Blaina, Brynmawr, Brecon ITC, Abertillery and Bristol Aeroplane Works. The exception was a superb win against Llanelli by 26pts to 9pts, and a couple of credible draws against Llanelli and Wasps. Ebbw Vale was, however, defeated by stronger sides in addition to Newport, such as Cardiff (twice), Newbridge, and Bristol, doing little to sustain its claims to first class status.

Wally Talbot captained Ebbw Vale throughout the war years and continued to play a central role in the affairs of the club, and the Monmouthshire Rugby Union, for many years after. He was a formidable and convivial character who as secretary kept most of the details of meetings, and club records in his head. In 1949 he was praised in the *Western Mail* for the efficiency with which he discharged his secretarial duties. As landlord of the Bridge End Inn he and his wife Bella played host to supporters and team members alike, regaling them with tales of triumphs, near misses and disasters. The walls were adorned with rugby club memorabilia, and echoed to

Wally Talbot, with his wife Bella, holding forth at the bar of the Bridge End Inn.

the sound of celebrations and commiserations as the home and away supporters poured in before and after the final whistle. One of his favourite tales was about a pre-war fixture with Mountain Ash. When the charabanc was late arriving the Treasurer became nervous about having to return the gate receipts, and was crest fallen when he saw the telegram boy hurtling down Comer's Hill on his bicycle with his coat tails flying in the wind, bringing news that 'The Old Firm' had to cancel and a fuller explanation would follow. Wally Talbot decided that the afternoon should not go to waste and the players and committee made a hefty dent in the anticipated compensation from Mountain Ash by passing most of it over the bar.

The Campaign for First Class Status

The table printed below indicates how Ebbw Vale made a sustained and concerted effort to establish its claim to first class recognition. Between 1946 and 1949 Ebbw Vale was consistent in its impressive record against ever increasingly strengthened opposition.

Year	*Played*	*Won*	*Drawn*	*Lost*	*For*	*Against*
1945-46	42	25	2	15	402	300
1946-47	34	23	3	8	404	210
1947-48	25	24	3	8	409	208
1948-49	36	25	2	9	347	220

Post War campaign.

The 1948-49 season was crucial in the campaign for first class status. The fact that the Welfare Committee declared the ground unfit to play did not help matters in the short term because Ebbw Vale was forced to find alternative arrangements while the necessary resurfacing work commenced. It had to rely upon the good will of neighbouring clubs to allow the use of their grounds. During this difficult period deliberate attempts were made to sour relations between the Ebbw Vale Club and her allies in the hills by the spread of rumours concerning the intention of its committee to break faith and drop the likes of Tredegar and Brynmawr from the fixture list for the 1950-51 season. There was no foundation to the rumours and Ebbw Vale affirmed that both clubs must in future figure in the fixture lists. The press was supportive of Ebbw Vale and was sympathetic, not only towards the inability to use its own ground, but also because of the loss of revenue this entailed. Many employers, including Richard Thomas and Baldwins, were helping to increase season ticket sales by collecting subscriptions through the weekly wage packet. The National Coal Board, however, refused to operate the scheme, despite the fact it had something like 200 applications from rugby followers to deduct 6d per week from their wages to be paid to the Club.

Rugby had gone from strength to strength during the war years and after, but Ebbw Vale still found it difficult to lure the successful South Wales clubs to the North Monmouthshire valley town, despite the fact that Ebbw Vale had provided them with formidable opposition during the War. Llanelli, Swansea, Neath, Cardiff and Newport all remained aloof. Nevertheless, the less fashionable clubs of Newbridge, Penarth, Pontypool and Pontypridd were firmly ensconced on the fixture list. The Ebbw Vale Committee also adopted an adventurous policy in attracting English encounters with British Aero, Taunton, Lydney, Devonport Service, London Saracens, and Kenilworth. None of the English clubs were able to conquer the formidable force of Ebbw Vale, but in an exciting game Taunton secured a draw. On the day after Boxing day, 1948, in a display that was almost textbook rugby, the West Country team commenced its onslaught. It was only a brilliant tackle by V. Edwards that saved Ebbw Vale from conceding a try by Lloyd of Taunton, and shortly after, Daniel, on the opposite wing, almost reached the line. Ebbw Vale, looking rattled in the first few minutes, settled down and began to dominate the scrums. The forwards took control from then on with Griffiths having an outstanding game, supported ably by A. Edwards the former Welsh international schoolboy. The *South Wales Echo* (27th Dec.) comments that the 'forwards played rousing football and produced many terrific rushes'. Teddy. Williams gave the Ebbw Vale backs fine service, and he intercepted the ball in the Taunton twenty-five, ran up to the line and passed it to Pugh who touched down almost under the posts. At half time Ebbw Vale led by 5pts to nil, and continued to dominate the game in the second half. It was only desperate tackling by Taunton that held the score. After losing Gunter, Taunton went against the run of play in sending Lloyd over for a spectacular try under the posts. Taunton was lucky to hold a side which dominated throughout to a 5pt draw.

First Class Rugby[2]

Ebbw Vale's overall record for the 1948-9 season was impressive, given the difficulties of playing home games on neighbouring grounds, and the consequent financial loss which put a strain on the club during a crucial period in its history. Of the thirty-six games recorded, Ebbw Vale won twenty-five, drew two, and lost nine. Pontypool and Maesteg were the only teams to beat the Valians twice. Among the other defeats were Pontypridd, Newbridge, and Resolven. The record was enough to secure the status that Ebbw Vale had strove to achieve for almost seventy years. On 3rd September 1949 Ebbw Vale ran out of their refurbished changing rooms, onto their newly laid ground, fenced with iron railings all around. The President of the WRU, David Rocyn Jones met the players and kicked-off the game. As we saw in the last chapter Newbridge gained the upper hand on the day, but Ebbw Vale's first season in the upper echelons of Welsh Rugby was nothing short of amazing given the ground difficulties that bedevilled it throughout.

On Saturday 3rd October, 1949 the *South Wales Football Echo* summed-up the mood of the club and its supporters under the headline 'RUGBY OPTIMISM AT EBBW VALE':

> 'The revival of Welsh Rugby in Ebbw Vale on the scale desired by the present enthusiastic committee is making admirable progress, and generally speaking there is greater interest taken in the affairs of the club just now than there has been for many years. Gates are improving, the standard of football is steadily going up and the barometer of progress is certainly "set fair".'

In the unofficial championship competition there was no fixed number of games, nor did those in competition have to play each other. Clubs were responsible for arranging their own fixtures. It was often complained when some of the less prestigious clubs topped

2. Volume 2 of this history will cover this period in much more detail.

the table that their fixture lists were not as strong as the likes of Cardiff and Newport. The Ebbw Vale fixture list was very impressive, but the big South Wales clubs, Newport, Cardiff, Swansea and Llanelli were once again conspicuous by their absence. To compensate Ebbw Vale went all out to attract strong English opposition, beating Barnstable, Aldershot Services, Devonport Services, Wolverhampton, Western Super Mare, Bridgewater, The Royal Corps of Signals, and Penzance Newlyn, and drawing with Nuneaton. Ebbw Vale twice lost narrowly to the eventual leaders of the championship table Maesteg, first by 3pts to 6pts, and second by 11pts to 12pts.

Ebbw Vale got off to a shaky start with defeats by Newbridge and Pontypool, but soon settled down with wins over Tredegar and Barnstable. The two hundred mile journey to Barnstable did not mar the standard of play. Barnstable was taken by surprise at the very high standard of rugby and by the delightfully open play. After the Barnstable game the *Football Echo* reviewed Ebbw Vale's prospects. The whole atmosphere of the club was buoyant and the gates were steadily improving as Ebbw Vale played fast open rugby. Against Penygraig Ebbw Vale played marvellously with the pack once again dominating as George Gwynne, Gwyn Griffiths and Ron Evans played excellent rugby. The backs were not as quick in handling as they should have been and Jack Lawrence, while showing improvement was not servicing the backs quickly enough to provide maximum opportunities. Lawrence had first started playing for the club in 1944, but was conscripted in 1947. On his return he played consistently for Ebbw Vale until 1957, and then continued with the Athletic. One of Ebbw Vale's star players at outside half, Teddie Williams, was criticised for falling well below his usual standard, a criticism which he took to heart. Two weeks later against Aldershott Services in a 'thrilling and spectacular' display by the whole team, Teddie Williams excelled in a deluge of scoring. The *Football Echo* singled him out for praise: 'special tribute must be paid to Teddy Williams (right centre) who played as one inspired and scored two excellent tries. He tore holes in the Services defence despite the efforts of the Scottish Trialist captain J. Stewart and Corporal D. Williams (right centre) to check the onslaught.

Teddy Williams. Ebbw Vale's outside half 1949.
(Cartoon from *South Wales Argus*).

After twelve games Ebbw Vale had only lost two, but five of them were drawn. Out of eighteen Ebbw only suffered four defeats but was settled in the middle of the table because six of the games had been drawn. At the halfway mark, after twenty-two games eleven had been won, six drawn and five lost. The second half of the season saw Ebbw Vale develop into a formidable force, and of the remaining twenty two games the Valians won seventeen, drew one and lost four. Ebbw Vale had secured fourth place in the merit table with an average percentage of 71.59%. Only Cardiff and Swansea scored more points.

In 1950 Ebbw Vale's talent began to be recognised and two players

Unofficial Champions for the first time 1951-2.

were selected to play in Crawshay's XV. Ebbw Vale had long had a link with Crawshay's touring team through a former Captain, Honorary Secretary and Fixture Secretary of the Club, Dai 'Regan' Jones. He captained Ebbw Vale between 1929-31, played for Newport and returned to resume the captaincy 1933-36. He was dynamic, forceful and an imposing personality who gave a friendly welcome to everyone at the Club. He was a Welsh reserve and also played for the Army XV. He worked closely with Captain Crawshay on the tours and had a good deal of say in the selection of the teams.

Despite the horrendous problems with the new drainage system Ebbw Vale managed to climb one step nearer to the top against some very tough opposition, coming third to Newport and Cardiff, losing only six of the forty-one matches played, and scoring a remarkable 508 points, conceding only 132. The team defeated nine clubs by in excess of twenty points. Ebbw Vale had an almost unblemished home record, going down only to a very strong Swansea side. In this outstanding season Ernie Lewis and John Pugh scored over a hundred points. John Pugh had first played for Ebbw Vale in 1944 while serving in the Royal Navy. His brilliant attacking style and versatility in being able to play almost any position made him one of the leading figures in transforming Ebbw Vale into a first class team. He gained a Monmouthshire cap and went on to captain the team 1955-6. Ernie Lewis played between 1949-53. Lewis had a sharp tactical mind and at outside half orchestrated the Vale game with brilliant displays of elusive running. He was joint captain of the club 1952-3.

After seventy-two years Ebbw Vale overcame all the odds and under the captaincy of George Gwynn achieved the ultimate accolade in becoming the undisputed champions of Welsh rugby in 1951-2. In a tightly fought campaign the Valians fought off a strong challenge by Newport. Lewis once again topped the hundred mark, and the Vale went undefeated for the last twenty-five games. Overall Ebbw Vale scored six hundred and forty-four points in thirty nine games, winning thirty-one and drawing two. There was only one home defeat, giving Ebbw Vale an overall percentage of 82.05. It was not all plain sailing, however, because from 24th November Ebbw Vale suffered four narrow defeats against Newbridge, Maesteg, Bective Rangers and Nuneaton which exposed the lack of depth in the squad. Ebbw Vale bounced-back after the four defeats in November and December 1951 to mark-up a convincing victory over Pontypool by 18pts to 5pts, followed by a 17pts to nil victory over Crosskeys. Brynmawr and Penygraig were the next victims against which the team scored 49pts, conceding only 3pts. There are a number of different accounts of the final tally, but the *Football Echo* suggests that overall Ebbw Vale played 37 games, of which twenty nine were won, and two drawn. The team achieved a points record of 625 (J. B. G. Thomas records it as 644) to 140, making an average of over 16 points per game to its opponents' average of 3pts. The previous points record at Ebbw Vale had been 620.

BIBLIOGRAPHY

Newspapers

Merthyr Express, South Wales Daily Argus, South Wales Weekly Argus, Western Mail, South Wales Daily News, Monmouthshire Merlin, Star of Gwent, South Wales Gazette, South Wales Football Echo.

Books and Articles

Minute Books of the Welsh Rugby Union.

John Billot, *History of Welsh International Rugby* (Ferndale, Glamorgan, Ron Jones Publications, 1970).

Emrys Evans, *South Wales Rugger Souvenir* (London, Findon Publications, 1950).

Duncan Gardiner and Alan Evans, *Cardiff Rugby Football Club 1876-1939* (Stroud, Tempus, 1999).

Steve Lewis, *Newport Rugby Football Club 1874-1950* (Stroud, Tempus, 1999).

Jack Davis, *One Hundred Years of Newport Rugby 1875-1975* (Risca, Starling Press, 1974).

Appendix One

Achievements

RUGBY SCORING

Season	*Try*	*Conversion*	*Penalty*	*Drop G*	*Mark G*
1890-91	1 pt.	2 pts.	2 pts.	3 pts.	3 pts.
1891-92	2 pts.	3 pts.	2 pts.	3 pts.	3 pts.
1892-93	2 pts.	3 pts.	3 pts.	4 pts.	4 pts.
1893-94	3 pts.	2 pts.	3 pts.	4 pts.	4 pts.
1905-06	3 pts.	2 pts.	3 pts.	4 pts.	3 pts.
1948-49	3 pts.	2 pts.	3 pts.	3 pts.	3 pts.
1971-72	4 pts.	2 pts.	3 pts.	3 pts.	3 pts.
1992-93	5 pts.	2 pts.	3 pts.	3 pts.	n/a

ACHIEVEMENTS 1880-1953

Invincible Season

1940-41 30 games played, 30 won. 629 points for, 103 against. 100%

Post War campaign

	Played	*Won*	*Drawn*	*Lost*	*For*	*Against*
1945-46	42	25	2	15	402	300
1946-47	34	23	3	8	404	210
1947-48	35	24	3	8	409	208
1948-49	36	25	2	9	347	220

First Class Rugby

	Games Played		Won	Drawn	Lost	For	Against	Ave. %
1949-50	44	Home	14	3	2	207	71	
		Away	14	4	7	265	120	71.59

CLUB CAPTAINS

1880-83	Len Williams	1883-84	G. Skinner
1884-85	D. J. Richards	1885-86	A. Parry
1886-87	A. Parry/ C. J. Jones	1887-88	E. Prosser/ W. E. Williams
1888-89	E. Jones	1889-90	E. Jones
1890-91	M. Kinsey	1891-92	T. Giles
1892-93	T. Jones	1893-94	Charlie Marchant
1894-95	Windsor James/ Evan Owen	1895-6	E. J. Giles
1896-97	B. Simmonds	1897-99	J. Kerton
1899-00	J. Pugh	1900-02	A. Rodway
1902-06	*Ebbw Vale senior side ceased to play. Crusaders played Junior rugby*		
1906-07	Amos Hudson	1907-08	A. Monks
1908-9	W. Higgins	1909-10	Dai Davies
1910-11	Chick Jenkins	1911-12	Chick Jenkins (?)
1919-20	Mike Hurley	1920-21	Joe Lawrence
1921-22	Bob Amos	1922-23	Bert Price
1924-25	Tom Watkins	1925-29	Tom Kerton
1929-31	Dai 'Regan' Jones	1931-33	Albert Kerton
1933-36	Dai 'Regan' Jones	1936-37	Wally Talbot
1937-38	Eddie Williams/ W. Talbot (joint)	1938-44	Wally Talbot
		1945-46	W. Talbot (?)
1946-49	Ron Evans	1949-51	Eric Finney
1951-52	George Gwyn	1952-53	I. Williams/E. Lewis

WELSH PLAYERS, TRIALISTS AND RESERVES

Great Britain Northern Union

Oliver Burgham (Halifax) (1911)
T. E. (Chick) Jenkins (Tour party to Australia 1910.
No Test appearances)
T. Howley (Wigan) (1924)
Ron Morgan (Swinton) (1963)

Wales Northern Union

Oliver Burgham, Welsh International (1908)
Jack Foley, Welsh International (1908-11)
Llew J. Llewellyn, Welsh International (1910-12)
T. E. (Chick) Jenkins, Welsh International (1908-12)
W. J. Saunders, Welsh International (1908)
H. Smith, Welsh International (1911)
G. Hitchins, Welsh International (1911)
F. Roffey,Welsh International (St. Helens) (1921 and 1926)
T. Howley, Welsh International (Wigan) (1921 and 1925)

Northern Union Welsh League

Syd Jenkins
W. Higgins

Rugby Union

Harry Thomas,	Welsh Reserve	1919-20
Joe Lawrence	Welsh Trialist	1923-24
Dai (Regan) Jones	Welsh Reserve	1932-33
Ellis Jones	Welsh Trialist	1933-34
Ben Southway	Welsh Reserve	1936-37
Eric Finney	Welsh Reserve	1952-55
Ben Edwards	Welsh Cap (Newport)	1951
Albert Jackson	Welsh Trialist	

Captain Geoffrey Crawshay's Welsh XV

Dai 'Regan' Jones	1930
A. Gardner	1939
E. Finney	1950
G. Griffiths	1950

Highest Northern Union Try Scorer

Season	Llew J. Llewelyn	24 (1910-11)
Match	Llew J. Llewelyn	5 (1910-11)

Highest 1st XV Try Scorer

Season	John Pugh	37 (1951-52)
Match	John Pugh	6 (1951-52)

Presidents of the Welfare Association 1918-1960

Founder Sir Frederick Mills, Bart., J.P., Ebbw Vale Steel, Iron and Coal Company

Mr. Evan Davies M.P., 1919-1929

Sir John Beynon, Bart., Ebbw Vale Steel, Iron and Coal Company, 1930-1936

Sir William Firth, Richard Thomas and Co. Ltd., 1937-1941

Rt. Hon. Aneurin Bevan, M.P., P.C. 1941-1960

Appendix 2

(From the *Merthyr Express*, 17th May, 1930)

Ebbw Vale R.F.C.'s Record

CO-OPERATION THE KEYNOTE OF SUCCESS

The season 1929-30 has been one of the best experienced by Ebbw Vale from a football point of view for many years. Not since the days of Tommy Howley, "Darby" Hopkins, Tommy Coles, Jimmy James (Ginger), Billy Wheatly, and Jimmy Williams, has Rugby been of such a high standard. The unfortunate local industrial depression played havoc with the "gates", and the usual "hillside sportsmen" were to be seen in hundreds viewing the games from the many points of vantage that unfortunately overlook the Ebbw Vale Sports Ground. The club has suffered its share of ill-luck by the way of players being injured. Gwyn Evans broke his leg at Pill, and Curford Davies broke his leg at Ebbw Vale. Stan Williams broke his collar bone and Ron Davies injured his ankle in home games. All were kept from playing during the last eight matches. Fortunately for the Valians they had an abundance of good talent, which always fitted in nicely. They unearthed the usual crop of outstanding personalities and players. Jack Rees, the fly half, was among the brilliants, and Dai Jones (Regan), captain, was the inspiration of the side. He possesses a fine personality , commands the respect of every player, and expounds in practice how rugby should be played. The following is a pen picture of the club's players.

H. TURNER (full back). – Age 20; steel worker; born at Tredegar, and played with Tredegar Excelsiors, a clever junior side from that district. Came to Ebbw Vale as a centre, but soon developed into a clever full back. Kicks well with both feet, a fearless tackler, with a deceptive turn of speed.

JACK PRICE ("Iron") (right wing). – Born at Ebbw Vale; very fast; a prolific try getter; takes a ball cleanly and kicks well. Assisted Mon. County on five occasions. Senior player of the club, having played ten consecutive seasons.; also vice captain. Age 30.

WINDSOR KERTON (right Centre or fly half). – Age 23 years; very clever all round player; sound tackler and good at making an opening; nephew of the famous Jimmy Kerton.

G. R. S. FARNIE (centre or wing). – Age 19; bank clerk; good all round footballer; a fearless player who always goes straight for the line, and kicks a splendid length. He is the product of a Scottish public school.

IVOR FROWEN. – Age 21; a product of Tredegar Excelsiors. A brilliant inside half who is at home in any position. Has all the qualities of a first class player; a desperate tracker and good try scorer.

JACKY REES. – Aged 18; born in Ebbw Vale. Learnt his "Rugger" with the Ebbw Vale County School. Played for Mon. County on two occasions. The cleverest outside half seen in Ebbw Vale. Scores the most amazing tries and can win matches by doing the most unorthodox things. Really a brilliant player.

DAI JONES ("REGAN"). – (captain) – Age 26. Born at Ebbw Vale. A brilliant player. The life of the side. Played his first rugby with Ebbw Vale juniors; played five years in Army Football; a regular touring member of Captain Crawshay's XV. Played for his County twice. Played for Leicester, British Army, SWB Fifteen, and also the Final Welsh Trial.

H. CASWELL. – Age 22, 5ft 10in., 13 stone. Born at Ebbw Vale. Learnt his football with the Ebbw Vale Crusaders. A real grafter.

H. TALBOT. – Age 23. Born at Ebbw Vale; 6ft., 12 stone; most improved forward of the side; a brainy player. Learnt his "Rugger" with the Crusaders. A genius for obtaining possession in the lineout.

FRED TALBOT. – Age 20, 5ft 10in., 13 stone; hard working forward, very fast and good tackler. Learnt his "Rugger" with E.V. Crusaders.

TOM HARRIS. – Age 26, 5ft 8in., 12 stone. Front rank forward from Tredegar. Brainy and clever all-round player.

HOWARD WILLIAMS. – Age 20, 5ft 7in., 11 stone. Learnt his football at college. Secondary Schoolboy Welsh International. The outstanding wing forward. Very clever. Can control a ball with perfect ease; a brilliant tackler. Born at Ebbw Vale.

PHIL HUGHES. – Age 23, 5ft 8in., bank clerk; very fast, clever in the open. Quite at home in the three quarter line. Came to Ebbw Vale from Newbridge R.F.C.

EMLYN WAKLEYN. – Aged 20; 5ft 7in., 12 stone. Welsh Schoolboy International. A clever brainy forward, always ready to take a pass in the three quarter line. A demon tackler.

W. BROOKS. – Age 32, 5ft 8in., 12st. 10lbs., a good hooker, hard working forwards, a safe pair of hands. Also plays full back. Born at Ebbw Vale and a product of local Rugby.

CHARLES MACNAB. —6ft. 1in., 13 stone, aged 24; a clever long-line forward; a member of the old Tredegar Club. Possesses a good turn of speed. A class player who always opens up the game.

STAN WILLIAMS. – Age 28. 12st. 6lb., 5ft. 9in., a good fast, open forward. Born at Ebbw Vale and a product of local Rugby.

H. Phillips, Gwyn Evans, T. H. Phillips and T. Sugrue are other very able players who have assisted Ebbw Vale and acquitted themselves with credit.

Alf Davies ("runner") has also given good service.

JOE LAWRENCE assisted the club on several occasions. The game he played against Tredegar on Monday last will be the last time for him to don the "kit" for playing purposes. This brings to a close 20 years' regular play. He commenced his "Rugger" at the early age of 15 and has done credit to the game ever since. Well done Joe!

The club will be holding its annual dinner on Saturday, May 24, at 6.30 pm. At the Victoria Hotel.

The time and place of the annual meeting of the Rugby Club during the first week in June will be announced later. There will be nine vacant seats to be filled on the committee. All persons who intend nominating candidates should send in their nominations to the hon secretary, Mr. J. D. Rees, 117 Pennant Street, Ebbw Vale. They must be Welfare members. It is also hoped that a meeting will be arranged at an early date for the Reserves "Old Crusaders").

VALIAN

Appendix 3

The Crusaders and the formation of the Athletic team

From the early days of its formation there are sporadic reports of an Ebbw Vale 2nd XV, and as we saw the Ebbw Vale Crusaders who became the Reserves took over where Ebbw Vale left off in the early years of the 20th Century by wining the junior league twice. The only Ebbw Vale 2nd XV season that gets much attention is 1893-94. Up to November 1893 the team had not lost a game and included in its ranks players who were to become central figures in the first team, J. Kerton and Tom Marchant. By December the 2nds had played 13 games and lost only one to New Tredegar. On that occasion the services of many of its regular players were called up for first team duty. The Crusaders continued to play when Ebbw Vale became a Northern Union Club, and ceased to play only with the onset of the First World War.

When Eugene Cross reformed the Crusaders after the First World War it was to form the backbone of the resurrected Ebbw Vale Rugby Club. The Crusaders were the Ebbw Vale 2nds and provided invaluable support to the senior team. It is difficult to determine with any accuracy the overall strength of the Reserve teams or a clear picture of the fixtures played. We know, for instance, that the Crusaders opened the 1925-6 season against Ebbw Vale, going down by 20pts to nil, and played Cwm four times in the 1926-7 season, losing the first and wining the second. There is no report of the remaining games. At the same time they were narrowly defeated by Abertillery

Quins by 3pts in a game that the Crusaders deserved to win. In April 1928 they were congratulated for their enterprise in having a fixture with a Public Schools side that included secondary school internationals. This was the season in which P. H. Lloyd was player secretary. It looks as if the Reserves ceased to play during the 1929-30 season, because in April 1930 an application was approved by the Ebbw Vale Welfare Association for the Crusaders to use the Top Field with a view to 'reforming the Rugby Reserves'. Eugene Cross of 34 Eureka Place is cited as the contact person for all interested players.

After the Second World War Ebbw Vale had no reserve team. Injuries severely weakened the Ebbw Vale side in the early part of its first championship season, and with no second XV to call upon doubts were raised about the long-term viability of continuing without a reserve team. The committee was well aware of the problem, but could see no immediate resolution because of the unavailability of grounds in the area. The issue came to the fore again in January, 1952 when the possibility of merging with Cwm became a point of discussion. Negotiations came to nothing, but the determination to solve the problem continued unabated. In the 1953-4 season Beaufort Rugby Club was invited to become the Ebbw Vale second team. Beaufort had a chequered history, with intermittent periods of existence, followed by collapse. There was no club in existence immediately after the Second World War until during the 1947-8 season John Lloyd, a Laboratory Technician at Richard, Thomas and Baldwins Steel Works, put together a side to play in a competition at Tredegar. The players decided to form a club and successfully applied to use the lower Beaufort Welfare Ground. A number of people prominent in the Beaufort team subsequently came to be heavily involved with the Ebbw Vale club both as officials and players. They include Laurie Rudman, John Dentus, Ivor George, Dickie King, John Hughes, Marsden Evans, Arnold Byles, Ivor Rogers, Glyn Davies, Harry Sturdy, Benarr Thomas and Tom Bourton.

Street by Street

LOUGHBOROUGH

COALVILLE, MELTON MOWBRAY, SHEPSHED, SYSTON

Barrow upon Soar, Burton on the Wolds, Castle Donington, Diseworth, East Goscote, East Leake, Kegworth, Mountsorrel, Quorn, Sileby, Thrussington, Whitwick, Woodhouse Eaves

2nd edition July 2008

Original edition printed November 2002

Published by AA Publishing (a trading name of Automobile Association Developments Limited, whose registered office is Fanum House, Basing View, Basingstoke, Hampshire RG21 4EA. Registered number 1878835).

Produced by the Mapping Services Department of The Automobile Association. (A03713)

A CIP Catalogue record for this book is available from the British Library.

Printed by Oriental Press in Dubai

Ref: ML218z

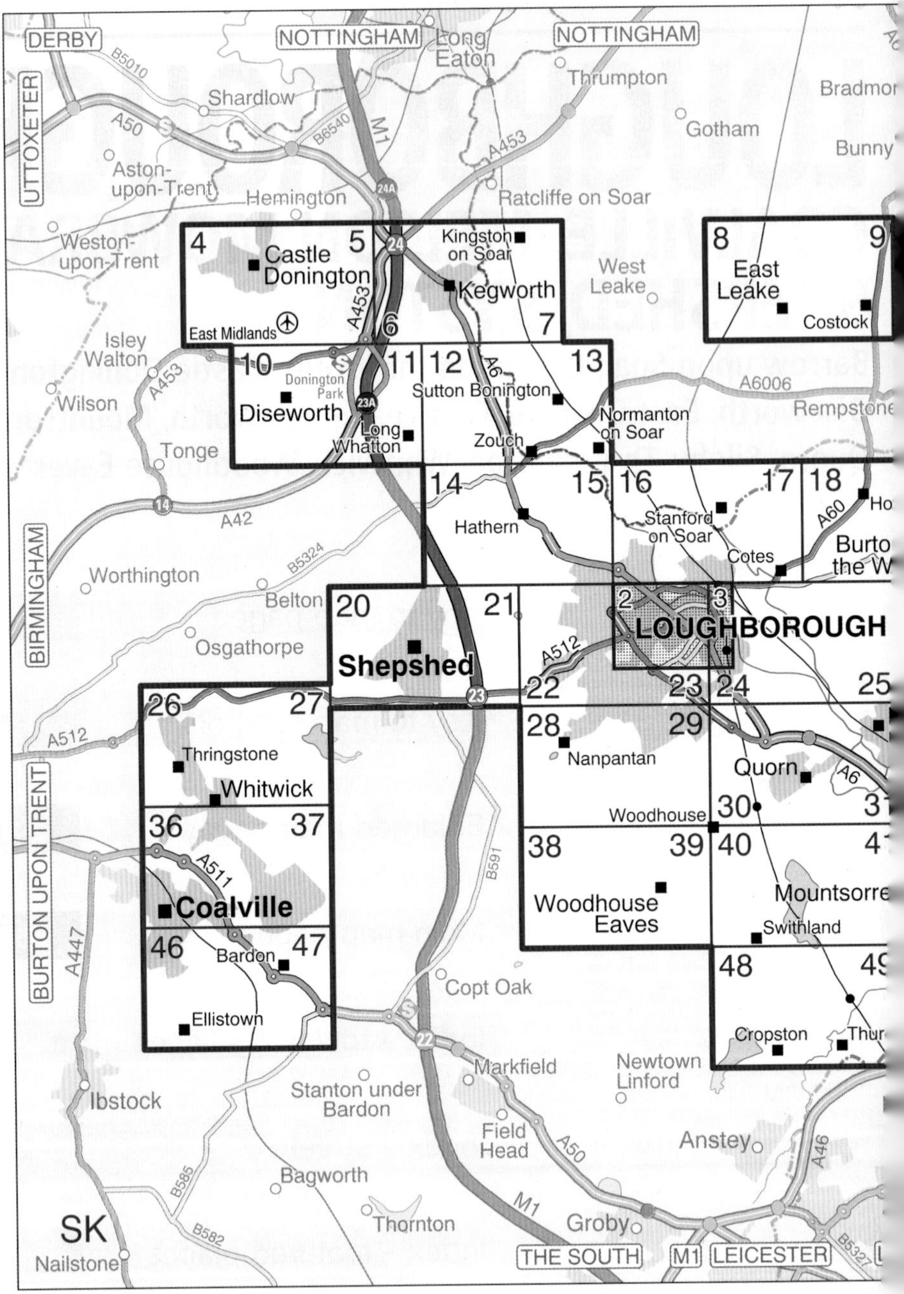

DERBY
NOTTINGHAM
Long Eaton
NOTTINGHAM
UTTOXETER
B5010
Shardlow
Thrumpton
Bradmore
A50
B6540
M1
Gotham
Bunny
Aston-upon-Trent
A453
Hemington
24A
Ratcliffe on Soar
Weston-upon-Trent
4
5
24
Castle Donington
Kingston on Soar
West Leake
8
9
East Leake
A453
Kegworth
Costock
East Midlands
6
7
Isley Walton
10
11
12
13
Donington Park
A6
A6006
Wilson
A453
Diseworth
23A
Sutton Bonington
Rempstone
Normanton on Soar
Long Whatton
Zouch
Tonge
14
15
16
17
18
14
A42
Stanford on Soar
A60
Hathern
BIRMINGHAM
B5324
Cotes
Burton on the Wolds
Worthington
Belton
20
21
2
3
Osgathorpe
LOUGHBOROUGH
A512
Shepshed
22
23
24
25
23
26
27
A512
28
29
Thringstone
Nanpantan
Quorn
Whitwick
A6
Woodhouse
30
31
36
37
A511
38
39
40
41
B591
BURTON UPON TRENT
Woodhouse Eaves
Mountsorrel
Coalville
A447
Swithland
46
47
Bardon
48
49
Copt Oak
Ellistown
22
Cropston
Thurcaston
Markfield
Newtown Linford
Stanton under Bardon
Ibstock
Field Head
Anstey
A50
A46
B585
Bagworth
M1
Thornton
Groby
SK
B582
B5327
THE SOUTH
M1
LEICESTER
Nailstone

Scale of enlarged map pages 1:10,000

6.3 inches to 1 mile

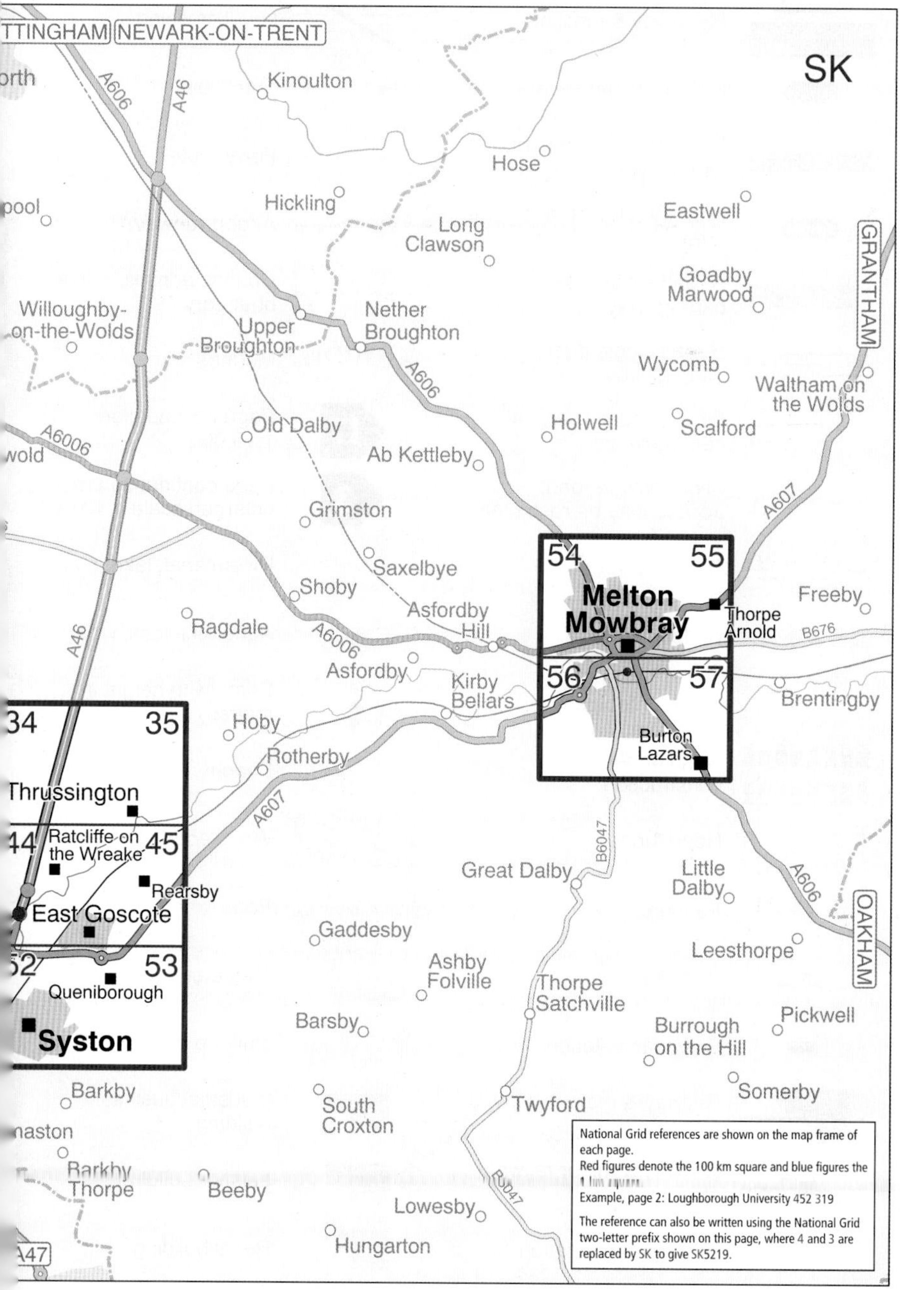

TTINGHAM
NEWARK-ON-TRENT
SK
orth
A606
A46
Kinoulton
Hose
Hickling
pool
Long Clawson
Eastwell
GRANTHAM
Goadby Marwood
Willoughby-on-the-Wolds
Upper Broughton
Nether Broughton
Wycomb
Waltham on the Wolds
A606
Old Dalby
Holwell
Scalford
A6006
wold
Ab Kettleby
A607
Grimston
Saxelbye
54
55
Melton Mowbray
Shoby
Freeby
Thorpe Arnold
Ragdale
Asfordby Hill
B676
A6006
Asfordby
Kirby Bellars
56
57
Brentingby
A46
34
35
Hoby
Burton Lazars
Rotherby
Thrussington
A607
44
Ratcliffe on the Wreake
45
B6047
Great Dalby
Little Dalby
A606
Rearsby
East Goscote
OAKHAM
Gaddesby
Leesthorpe
52
53
Ashby Folville
Thorpe Satchville
Queniborough
Pickwell
Barsby
Burrough on the Hill
Syston
Barkby
Somerby
South Croxton
Twyford
naston
Barkby Thorpe
Beeby
B6047
Lowesby
Hungarton
A47
National Grid references are shown on the map frame of each page.
Red figures denote the 100 km square and blue figures the 1 km square.
Example, page 2: Loughborough University 452 319
The reference can also be written using the National Grid two-letter prefix shown on this page, where 4 and 3 are replaced by SK to give SK5219.

4.2 inches to 1 mile

Scale of main map pages 1:15,000

0
1/4
miles
1/2
3/4
1
0
1/4
1/2
kilometres
3/4
1
1 1/4
1 1/2

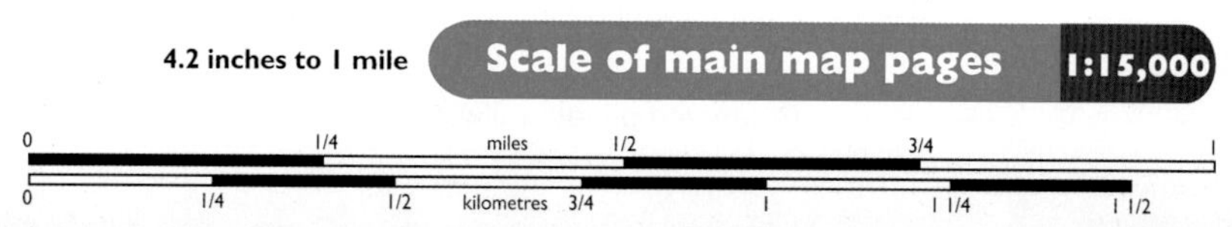

Symbol	Meaning
Junction 9	Motorway & junction
Services	Motorway service area
	Primary road single/dual carriageway
Services	Primary road service area
	A road single/dual carriageway
	B road single/dual carriageway
	Other road single/dual carriageway
	Minor/private road, access may be restricted
	One-way street
	Pedestrian area
	Track or footpath
	Road under construction
	Road tunnel
P	Parking
P+	Park & Ride
	Bus/coach station
	Railway & main railway station
	Railway & minor railway station
	Underground station
	Light railway & station
	Preserved private railway
LC	Level crossing
	Tramway
	Ferry route
	Airport runway
	County, administrative boundary
	Mounds
17	Page continuation 1:15,000
3	Page continuation to enlarged scale 1:10,000
	River/canal, lake, pier
	Aqueduct, lock, weir
465 Winter Hill	Peak (with height in metres)
	Beach
	Woodland
	Park
	Cemetery
	Built-up area
	Industrial/business building
	Leisure building
	Retail building
	Other building

Symbol	Meaning
	City wall
A&E	Hospital with 24-hour A&E department
PO	Post Office
	Public library
	Tourist Information Centre
	Seasonal Tourist Information Centre
	Petrol station, 24 hour Major suppliers only
	Church/chapel
	Public toilets
	Toilet with disabled facilities
PH	Public house AA recommended
	Restaurant AA inspected
Madeira Hotel	Hotel AA inspected
	Theatre or performing arts centre
	Cinema
	Golf course
	Camping AA inspected
	Caravan site AA inspected
	Camping & caravan site AA inspected
	Theme park
	Abbey, cathedral or priory
	Castle
	Historic house or building
Wakehurst Place (NT)	National Trust property
	Museum or art gallery
	Roman antiquity
	Ancient site, battlefield or monument
	Industrial interest
	Garden
	Garden Centre Garden Centre Association Member
	Garden Centre Wyevale Garden Centre
	Arboretum
	Farm or animal centre
	Zoological or wildlife collection
	Bird collection
	Nature reserve
	Aquarium
V	Visitor or heritage centre
	Country park
	Cave
	Windmill
	Distillery, brewery or vineyard

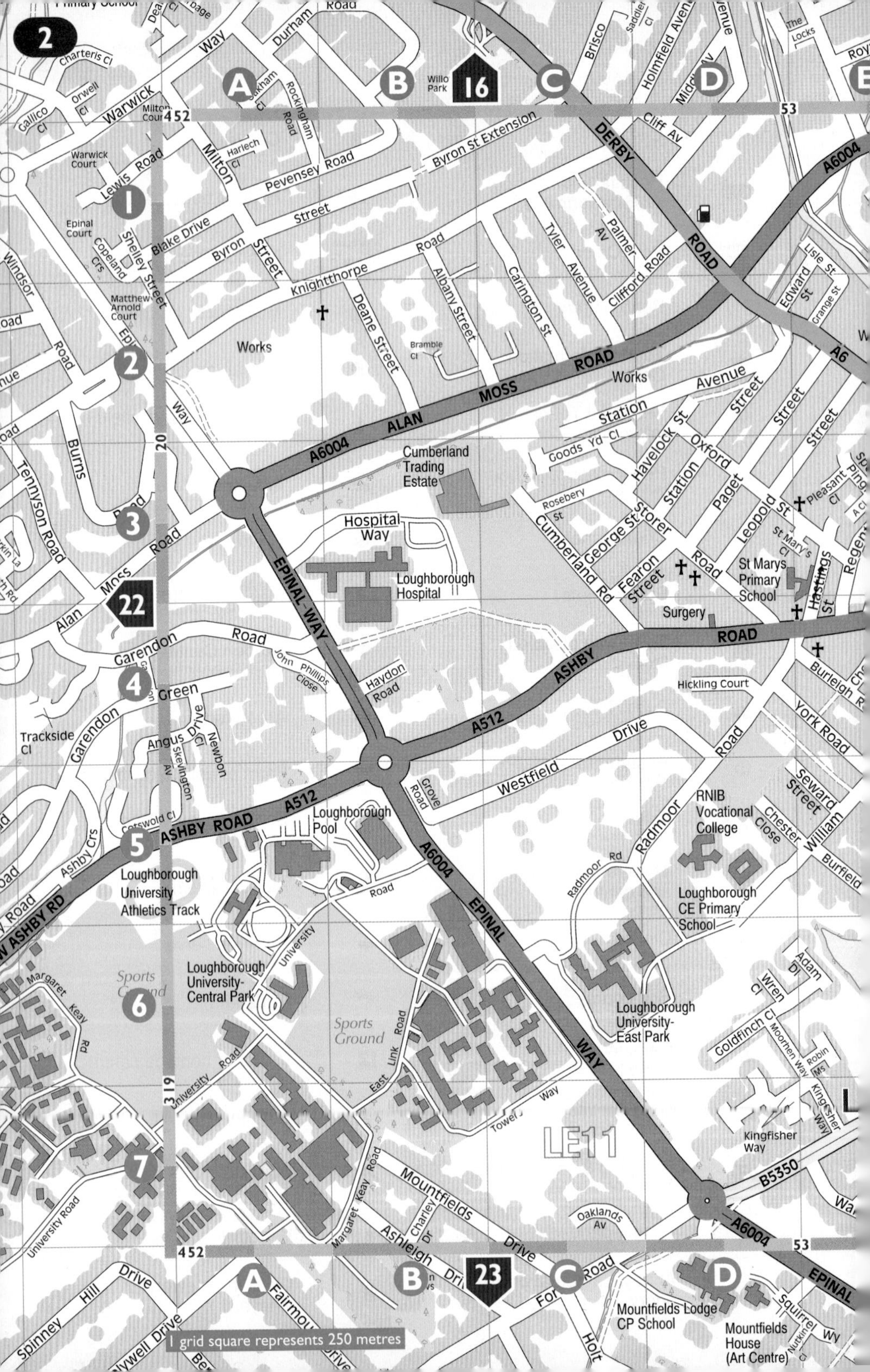
2
A
B
C
D
E
16
22
23
452
53
20
319
1
2
3
4
5
6
7
Primary School
Charteris Cl
Orwell Cl
Gallico Cl
Warwick Way
Milton Court
Durham Road
Oakham Cl
Rockingham Road
Willow Park
Brisco
Saddler Cl
Holmfield Avenue
Avenue
Middle Av
The Locks
Warwick Court
Lewis Road
Milton Street
Harlech Cl
Pevensey Road
Byron St Extension
Cliff Av
DERBY ROAD
A6004
Epinal Court
Copeland Crs
Shelley Street
Blake Drive
Byron Street
Knightthorpe Road
Palmer Av
Tyler Avenue
Clifford Road
Lisle St
Edward St
Grange St
Windsor Road
Matthew Arnold Court
Deane Street
Albany Street
Carington St
Bramble Cl
Works
A6
ALAN MOSS ROAD
Station Avenue
Goods Yd Cl
Havelock St
Street
Oxford Street
Burns Road
Tennyson Road
Way
Cumberland Trading Estate
Rosebery St
Station Street
Paget Street
Leopold St
Pleasant Cl
Hospital Way
Cumberland Rd
George St
Storer Road
St Mary's Cl
Loughborough Hospital
EPINAL WAY
Fearon Street
St Marys Primary School
Hastings St
Regent
Alan Moss Road
Surgery
ASHBY ROAD
Garendon Road
John Phillips Close
Haydon Road
Hickling Court
Burleigh Rd
Trackside Cl
Garendon Green
A512
Westfield Drive
Road
York Road
Angus Drive
Skevington Av
Newbon Cl
Grove Road
Seward Street
RNIB Vocational College
Chester Close
William
Cotswold Cl
ASHBY ROAD
A512
Loughborough Pool
A6004 EPINAL
Radmoor Road
Radmoor Rd
Burfield
Ashby Crs
Loughborough University Athletics Track
Road
Loughborough CE Primary School
ASHBY RD
University Road
Adam Dl
Wren Cl
Sports Ground
Loughborough University-Central Park
Margaret Keay Rd
Sports Ground
East Link Road
Loughborough University-East Park
Goldfinch Cl
Moorhen Way
Robin Ms
WAY
Kingfisher Way
University Road
Towers Way
LE11
Kingfisher Way
Margaret Keay Road
Mountfields Drive
B5350
Charley Dr
Oaklands Av
Ashleigh Drive
A6004
EPINAL
Drive
Hill
Spinney
Fairmount Drive
Forest Road
Holt
Mountfields Lodge CP School
Mountfields House (Art Centre)
Squirrel Wy
Nutkin Cl
1 grid square represents 250 metres

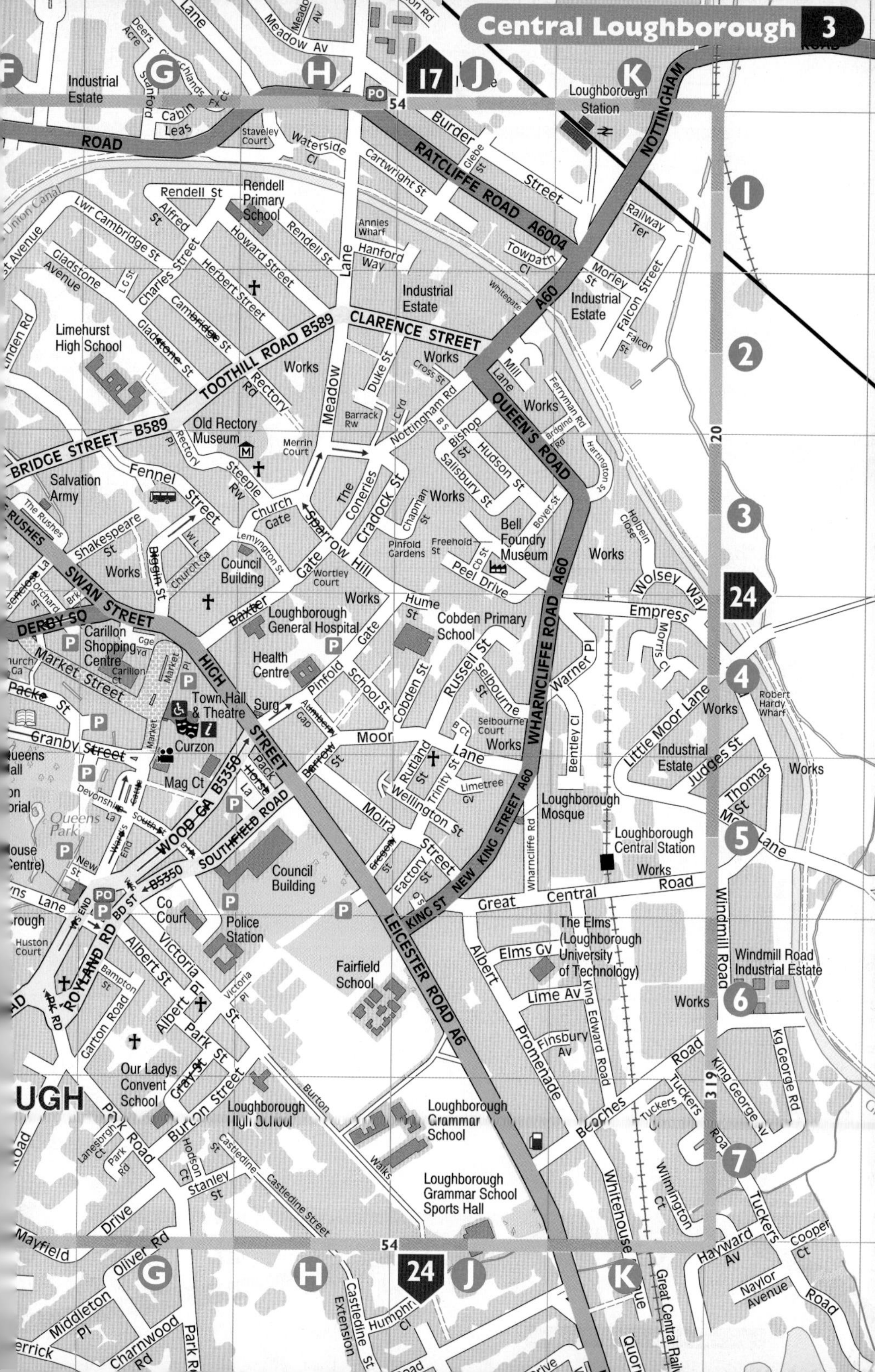
Industrial Estate
Loughborough Station
Ratcliffe Road A6004
Nottingham Road
Rendell Primary School
Limehurst High School
Toothill Road B589
Clarence Street
Bridge Street B589
Old Rectory Museum
Salvation Army
Queen's Road
Bell Foundry Museum
Swan Street
Derby Sq
Carillon Shopping Centre
Loughborough General Hospital
Health Centre
Cobden Primary School
Town Hall & Theatre
Curzon
High Street
Wharncliffe Road A60
Empress Road
Little Moor Lane
Loughborough Mosque
Loughborough Central Station
Great Central Road
Southfield Road
Council Building
Police Station
Fairfield School
Leicester Road A6
The Elms (Loughborough University of Technology)
Windmill Road Industrial Estate
Windmill Road
Loughborough High School
Our Ladys Convent School
Loughborough Grammar School
Loughborough Grammar School Sports Hall
Park Road
Beeches Road
Tuckers Road
Hayward Av
Naylor Avenue
Cooper Ct
17
24
54
20
319

4
A
B
C
D
1
2
3
4
5
443
44
28
27
326
Trent
Lane
Willow
Works
Oakridge Pk
Hawthorn Road
Short Lane
West Meadow Ri
Walton Hl
Hazelrigg Cl
Spittal
Campion
Hill
Tanyard Close
Bentley Road
Shirley Cl
Darsway
Salter Cl
Fosbrook Dr
Fox Road
Queensway
Staunton Cl
School La
Huntingdon
Haulton Dr
Drive
Harcourt Place
Bondgate
Hillside
Orchard Primary Sch
Roby Lea
Minton Rd
The Green
Grange Drive
Surg
PO
Stdbrk Cl
Cordwell Cl
Kirkland Close
Ferrers Close
Orchard Avenue
Tipnall Road
Cr Cl
Peartree Cl
Surg
Borough St
Market St
St An La
Apiary Gate
Park Lane
Park Lane
Donington Manor Hotel
St Edwa
CE Prin
School
Bosworth
Starkie Av
Park Av
Paddock Cl
Road
Shields Crescent
Towles Pastures
Devon La
Delven Lane
Mnt Pl
Barn Close
D La
Cheribough Rd
Hall Farm Close
Eaton Road
Hastings St
Cooks Av
High Street
Orly Av
Fields
Cvh Cl
Harvey Rd
Wndml Cl
Crabtree Close
Bakewell Drive
Hallam St
Edward's Rd
Meadow Crs
Stonehill
Cedar
Hill Top Farm
Hill Top
Diseworth Road
Anson Road
Vanguard Road
Dakota Road
P
A453
A453
A453
HILL
10
1 grid square represents 500 metres

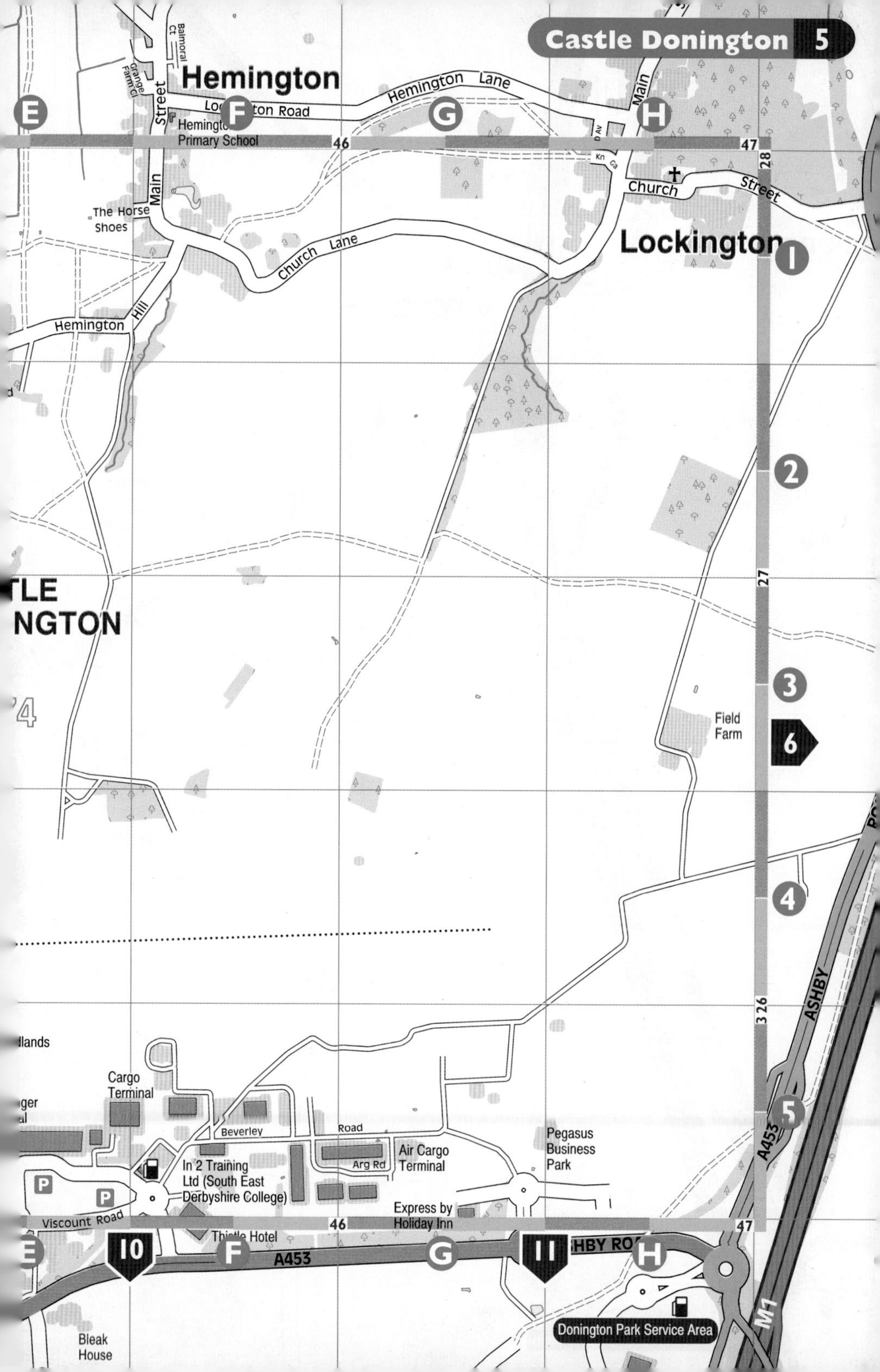
Hemington
Balmoral Ct
Grange Farm Cl
Street
Lockington Road
Hemington Lane
Hemington Primary School
Main
The Horse Shoes
Church Lane
Hemington Hill
Hemington
Church Street
Lockington
Field Farm
6
ASHBY
A453
M1
Cargo Terminal
Beverley Road
Arg Rd
Air Cargo Terminal
Pegasus Business Park
In 2 Training Ltd (South East Derbyshire College)
Viscount Road
Express by Holiday Inn
Thistle Hotel
A453
10
11
Donington Park Service Area
Bleak House
46
47
28
27
26
E F G H
1 2 3 4 5

6
A
B
C
D
447
48
28
27
326
1
2
3
4
5
Church Street
ockington
A453
Junction 24
A6
ASHBY ROAD A453
M1
Long Lane
Citrus Grove
Works
Side Ley
Nottingham Road
DERBY ROAD
Kegworth Squash Club
Nine Acres
Best Western Premier Yew-Lodge Hotel
Packington Hill
Works
Kegworth Museum
Sibson Drive
Peppers Drive
Windmill Way
Suthers Road
Road
High Street
Ashby
Langley Drive
W Bank
Springfield
Oldershaw Av
Broadhill Road
Staffords Acre
Kegworth Primary School
Pleasant Pl
Heafield Dr
The Croft
Mulberry Gdns
Whatton Road
Cem
ROAD
Foxhills
Sutton Rd
St Andrew's Rd
Hillside
Burley Rise
Bedford Cl
Gerrard Crescent
Thomas Road
Roberts Close
Shepherd Wk
Kirby Drive
The Lodge
New Brickyard Lane
ASHBY
Whatton Road
A453
Spring House Farm
11
12
M1
1 grid square represents 500 metres
Slade Farm
PO

Kingston on Soar
GWORTH
Gotham Road
Kegworth Rd
St Winifreds Ct
Kingston Lane
Road
Station Road
River Soar
Station Ter
Old Bull Farm Cl
Chestnuts Cl
Station Road
Melton Lane
Sutton Fields House
University of Nottingham - Sutton Bonington Campus
College Road
Soar Lane
Landcroft La
Cemetery
Marle Pit Hill
Bollard's La
Buc
Main
St Ann's Manor
Kingston Brook
E
F
G
H
I
2
3
4
5
50
51
28
27
3 26
12
13

8
A
B
C
D
1
2
3
4
5
454
55
28
27
326
Midshi
Bunny Lane
Golf Course
The Rushcliffe Golf Club
Gotham Rd
East
Leake
Works
Rushcliffe Halt
Stocking Lane
Stocking Lane
Rshclf Gv
Roulstone Crs
Angrave Rd
Hollis
Meadow
Sharpley Dr
St Mary's Crescent
Weavers Cl
Manor Rd
Ryeholme Cl
Thistle Bank
Cottage Cl
Northfields Wy
St Ls Dr
Holme Av
Elm Av
Harefield
Towson Fld
The Crs
The Arches
Brookfields Wy
Wtn Cl
Lantern
Brookend
Halls Brook
Nixon Wk
Osier Fields
Lantern Lane Prim Sch
The Burrows
Pkyns Pce
Tn Cl
Kingston Brook
East
Leake
Gotham Rd
Carlton Crs
Monks Mdw
Stonebridge Drive
Moore Cl
Bateman Rd
York Cl
Southwell
Exeter Cl
Truro Cl
S Cl
Mr Fm Mw
De Ferrers Cl
Surg
Health Centre
Birch Lea
Rope Wk
Wr Cl
Arley House
PNEU School
Main Street
PO
Station Road
Church Cl
The Green
Brookside
Prim Sch
Salisbury Av
West Leake Road
Field End Cl
Twentylands Dr
Sch Gn
Old Rectory Cl
The Nook
Bmy Cl
Cromwell Dr
Hawley Cl
Oldershaw Rd
Leivers Cl
Burton Wk
Brookside Av
Oak Crs
Burton Wk
Burton Wk
Potters Lane
Maple Cl
Willow Cl
Pine Cl
Yew Cl
Hall Gdns
Castle Hill
Ash Wk
Poplar Av
Beech Av
Brookside
Cedar Av
Orchard Cl
Bley Av
Kirk Ley Rd
Woodgate Rd
Rempstone Road
Loughborough Road
Woodgate Far
1 grid square represents 500 metres

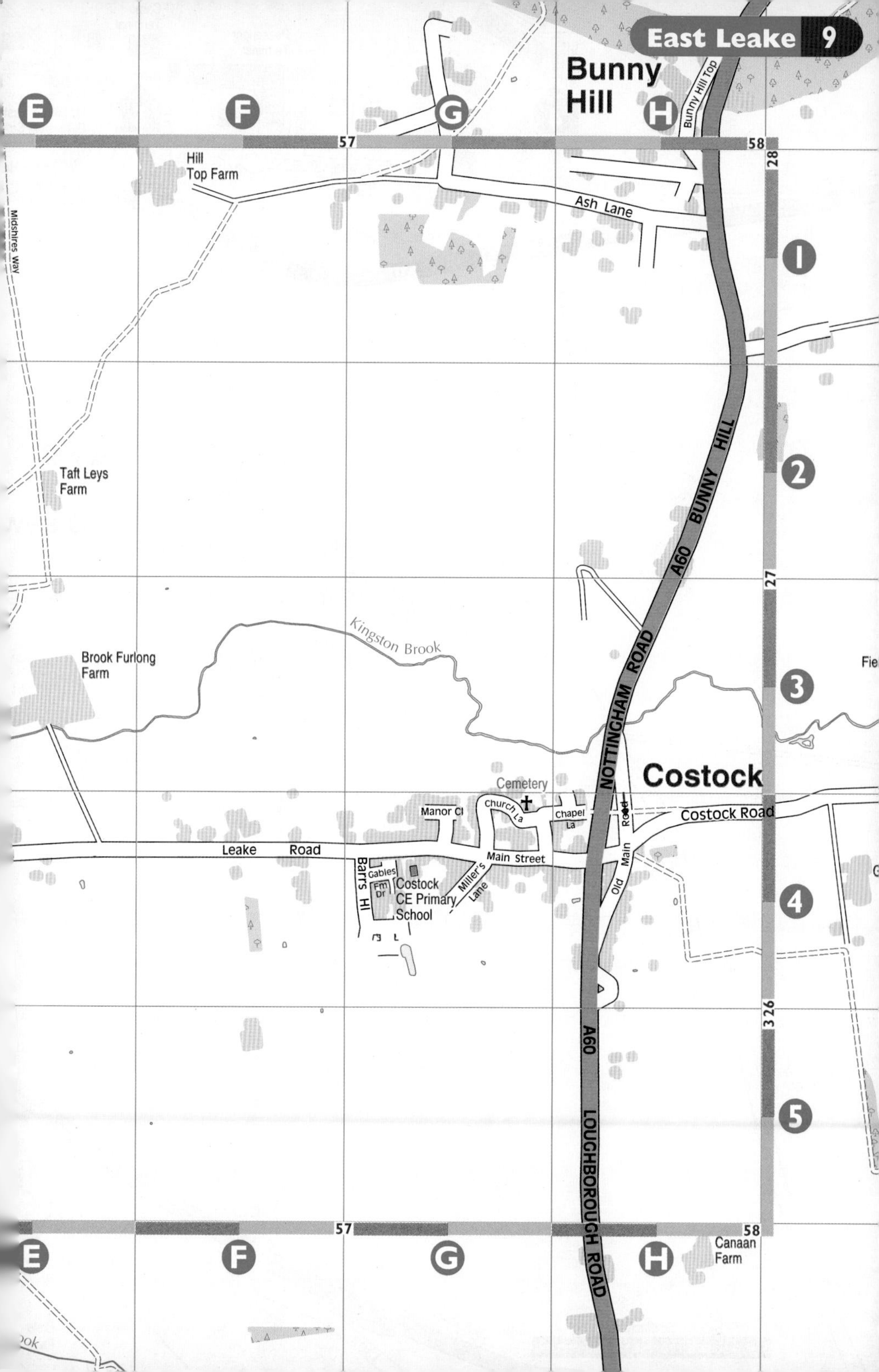
Bunny Hill
Bunny Hill Top
E
F
G
H
57
58
28
Hill Top Farm
Ash Lane
Midshires Way
1
2
Taft Leys Farm
A60 BUNNY HILL
27
Kingston Brook
Brook Furlong Farm
NOTTINGHAM ROAD
3
Fie
Costock
Cemetery
Manor Cl
Church La
Chapel La
Road
Costock Road
Leake Road
Main Street
Main
Old
Barrs Hl
Gables
Fm Dr
Costock CE Primary School
Miller's Lane
4
326
A60
LOUGHBOROUGH ROAD
5
57
58
E
F
G
H
Canaan Farm

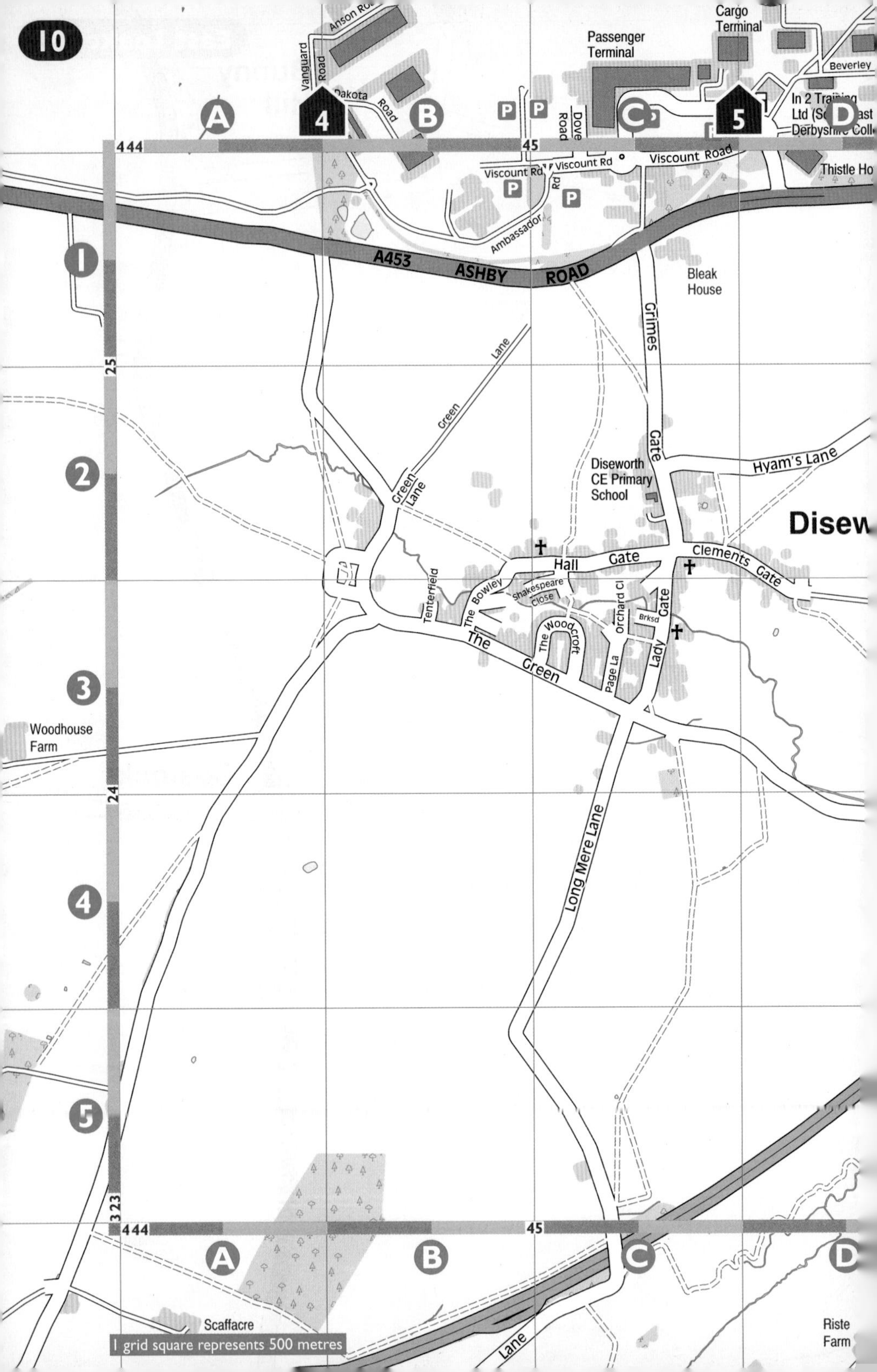

10
Cargo Terminal
Passenger Terminal
Anson Road
Vanguard Road
Dakota Road
Dove Road
Beverley
In 2 Training Ltd
Derbyshire Coll
Viscount Rd
Viscount Road
Thistle Ho
Ambassador Rd
A453 ASHBY ROAD
Bleak House
Grimes Gate
Green Lane
Hyam's Lane
Diseworth CE Primary School
Disew
Hall Gate
Clements Gate
Tenterfield
The Bowley
Shakespeare Close
Orchard Cl
Brksd
The Woodcroft
Lady Gate
The Green
Page La
Woodhouse Farm
Long Mere Lane
Scaffacre
Lane
Riste Farm
1 grid square represents 500 metres

Pegasus
Business
Cargo
E
5
F
G
6
H
Spring House
Farm
47
48
ASHBY ROAD
A453
M1
Donington Park Service Area
Travelodge
I
Whatton
Road
25
2
Windmill
Farm
Junction 23a
Kegworth Lane
3
12
24
Kegworth Lane
A42
West
End
Lester Ct
Lane
4
Main
Street
Brnfld
Cl
Manor
Cl
PO
Crawshaw
Close
Westmeadow
Smithy Lane
Long
Whatton
5
Whatton
Primary School &
Community Centre
M1
323
47
48
E
F
G
H

12
Spring House Farm
A
6
B
C
7
D
448
49
A6
ROAD
1
Slade Farm
River
25
Whatton Road
Windmill Farm
2
Kegworth Lane
Home Farm
LONDON
Whatton House
3
Leicestershire
11
ROAD
24
Kegworth Lane
Marylea Farm
4
Mill Lane
Street
Manor Cl
PO
Brmfld Cl
Mill Lane
Crawshaw Close
Long Whatton Brook
Mill Lane
5
Long Whatton Primary School & Community Centre
The Green
Hathern Road
323
448
49
Piper Cl
Piper Drive
Turvey Lane
Spring Lane
A
B
14
C
B5324 WHATTON ROAD
D
ASHBY ROAD
1 grid square represents 500 metres

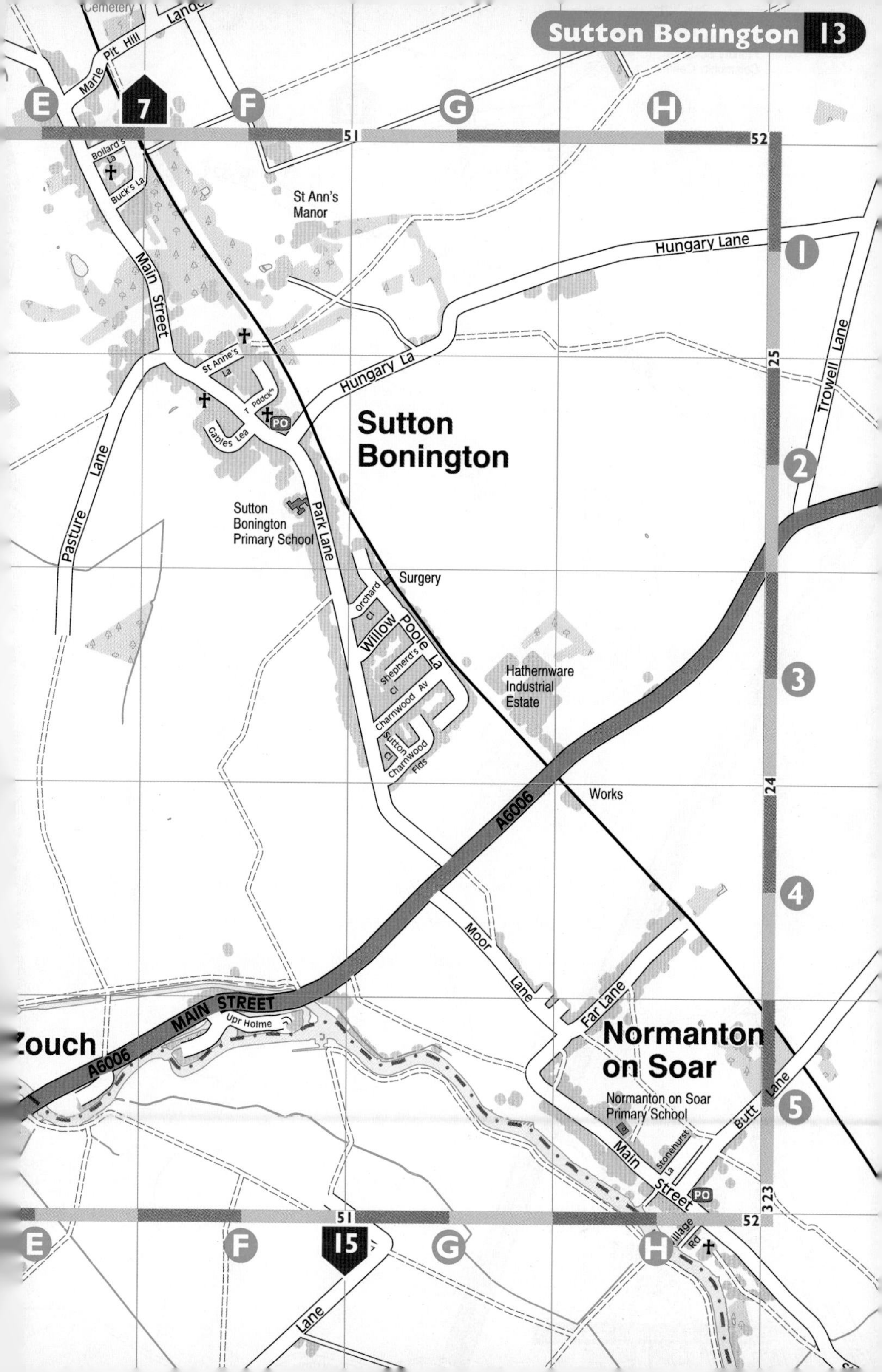
Cemetery
Marle Pit Hill
7
E
F
G
H
51
52
Bollard's La
Buck's La
St Ann's Manor
Hungary Lane
Main Street
St Anne's La
T Pddck
Gables Lea
PO
Hungary La
Sutton Bonington
Pasture Lane
Sutton Bonington Primary School
Park Lane
Surgery
Orchard Cl
Willow
Poole La
Shepherd's Cl
Charnwood Av
Sutton Cl
Charnwood Flds
Hathernware Industrial Estate
Works
A6006
Trowell Lane
1
2
3
4
5
25
24
323
Moor Lane
Far Lane
MAIN STREET
Upr Holme
Zouch
Normanton on Soar
Normanton on Soar Primary School
Butt Lane
Main Street
Stonehurst La
Village Rd
15
Lane

Long Whatton Primary School & Community Centre
The Green
Hathern Road
Piper Cl
Piper Drive
Spring Lane
Turvey Lane
Oakley Drive
Cawdell Dr
B5324 WHATTON ROAD
ASHBY ROAD
B5324
DERBY RO
Oakley Grange Farm
Oakley Wood
Shepshed Road
Lounds Farm
Hathern Road
M1
Oakley
Road
Black
Field Avenue
North Nursery Cl
Tyler Ct
Wood Drive
Highfield Cl
Ringwood Road
Road
Lansdowne Road
Radnor Drive
Oakley
Mill Close
Boundary Way
1 grid square represents 500 metres
A
B
C
D
12
21
1
2
3
4
5
4 48
49
23
22
3 21

Normanton Primary Sch
Main Street
Village Rd
PO
13
E
F
G
H
I
2
3
4
5
16
22
51
52
23
22
21
Pasture Lane
Stan
River Soar
Hathern
Green Hl
Green Hl
The Green
Ash Gv
Church St
Cross St
Surgery
Surg
Pasture La
Gladstone St
St Peters Av
Wesley Cl
Dovecote St
Meadow
Nightingale Av
Old Forge Cl
Swallow Wk
Tanner's La
Wide St
Anchor La
Anchor Cl
PH
LOUGHBOROUGH ROAD
Garendon Av
Loughborough Rd
DERBY ROAD
A6
Black Brook
Messenger Cl
Weldon Road
Cotton Wy
Darwin Crs
Lawrence Wy
Wain Dr
DERBY ROAD A6
Leslie Cl
Lyall Cl
Newton Cl
Alston Dr
Barsby Dr
Roydale Cl
Pear Tree La
Dishley
Irwin Av
Canning Wy
Deighton Wy
Graham Rise
Braddon Rd
Durrell Cl
Francis Dr
Maclean Av
Bagley Cl
Barrett Av
Murdoch Ri
Robert Bakewell Primary School
Deanside Dr
Booth End
B Cl
Colling Cl
Waistrell Dr
Mitchell Drive
Golding Cl
Stonebow
Stonebow Primary School
Wesley Cl
Mortimer Wy
Wyndham Rd
Archer Cl
Christie Dr
Osborne Rd
Gavin Dr
Charteris Cl
Orwell Cl
Stewart Dr
James Av
Cookson Pl
Eden Cl
Monsarrat Wy
Rockingham Rd
Oakham Close
Milton St
Way
Elliot Cl
Me Cl
Maxwell Drive
Duncan Wy
Maxwell Drive
Herriot Wy
Gallico Cl
Warwick
Warwick Court
Lewis Rd
Pevensey Rd
Kingswood Av
Whitby Cl
Mount Grace Rd
Lindisfarne Drive
Byland Wy
Gisborough Wy
Easby Cl
Rufford Cl
Lilleshall Wy
St Olaves Cl
Halley Av
De Montfort Cl
PO
Superstore
Thorpe Acre
Switherland Cl
Kensington Av
Sandringham Dr
Kinross Crs
Windsor Rd
Epinal Way
Epinal Court
Matthew Arnold Court
Shelley St
Blake Dr
Byron Street
Knightthorpe
Conway Cl
Howard
Raynham Dr
Acre Road

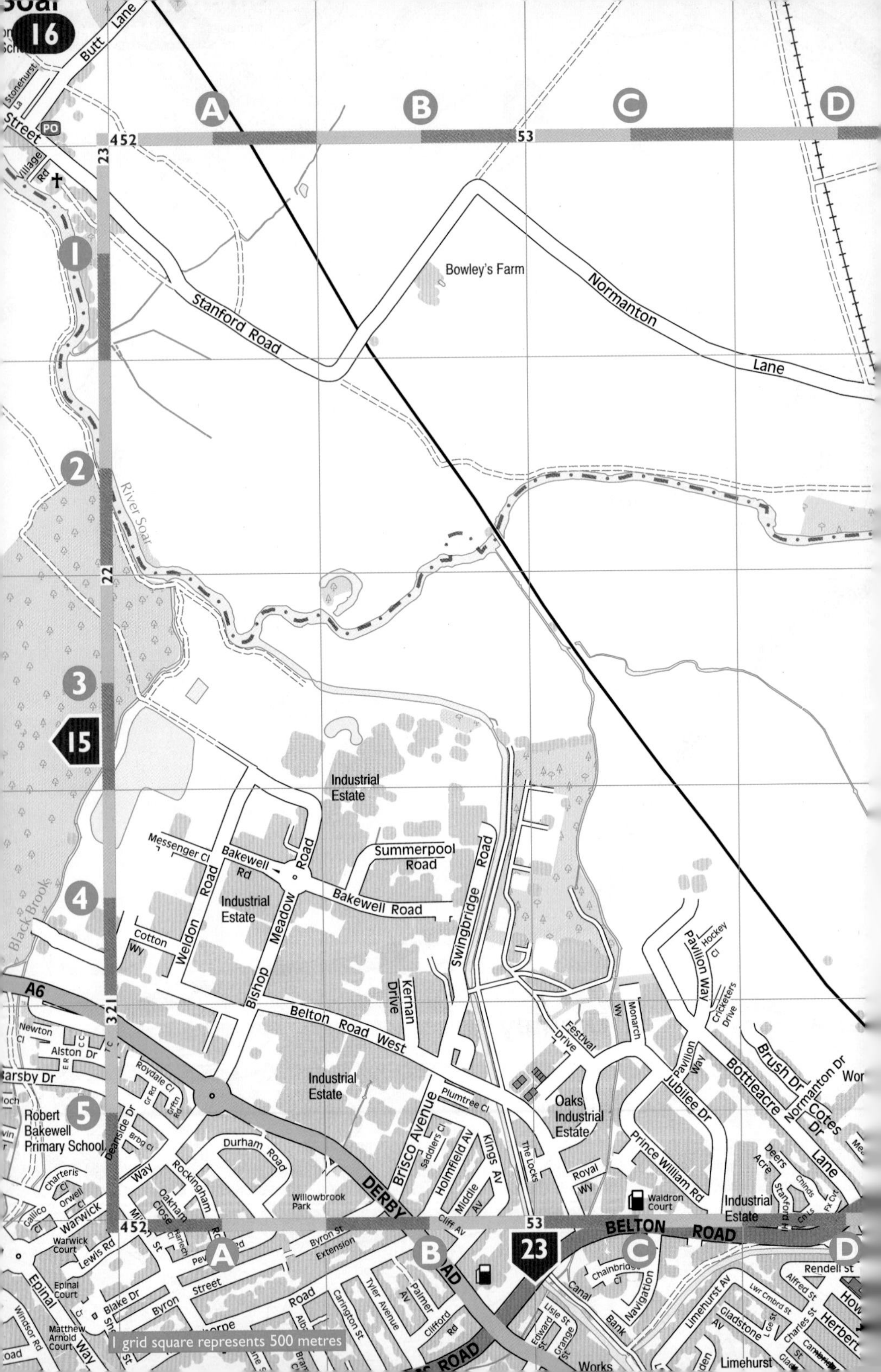
16
15
23
A
B
C
D
1
2
3
4
5
452
53
23
22
321
Butt Lane
Stonehurst La
Street
Village Rd
River Soar
Stanford Road
Bowley's Farm
Normanton Lane
Black Brook
Industrial Estate
Messenger Cl
Bakewell Rd
Meadow Road
Summerpool Road
Weldon Road
Bakewell Road
Swingbridge Road
Cotton Wy
Bishop Meadow Road
Kernan Drive
Belton Road West
A6
Newton Cl
Alston Dr
Barsby Dr
Robert Bakewell Primary School
Roydale Cl
Deanside Dr
Durham Road
Brisco Avenue
Plumtree Cl
Saddlers Cl
Holmfield Av
Kings Av
Middle Av
The Locks
Oaks Industrial Estate
Festival Drive
Monarch Wy
Pavilion Way
Hockey Cl
Cricketers Drive
Brush Dr
Bottleacre Lane
Normanton Dr
Cotes Dr
Jubilee Dr
Prince William Rd
Royal Wy
Waldron Court
Deers Acre
Rockingham Way
Oakham Close
Charteris Cl
Orwell Cl
Warwick
Warwick Court
Gallico Cl
Lewis Rd
Willowbrook Park
DERBY ROAD
Cliff Av
Byron St Extension
BELTON ROAD
Chainbridge Cl
Navigation
Canal Bank
Rendell St
Alfred St
Herbert
Limehurst Av
Gladstone Av
Charles St
Limehurst
Epinal Way
Epinal Court
Matthew Arnold Court
Windsor Rd
Blake Dr
Byron Street
Road
Tyler Avenue
Palmer Av
Carington St
Clifford Rd
Lisle St
Edward St
Grange St
Works
1 grid square represents 500 metres

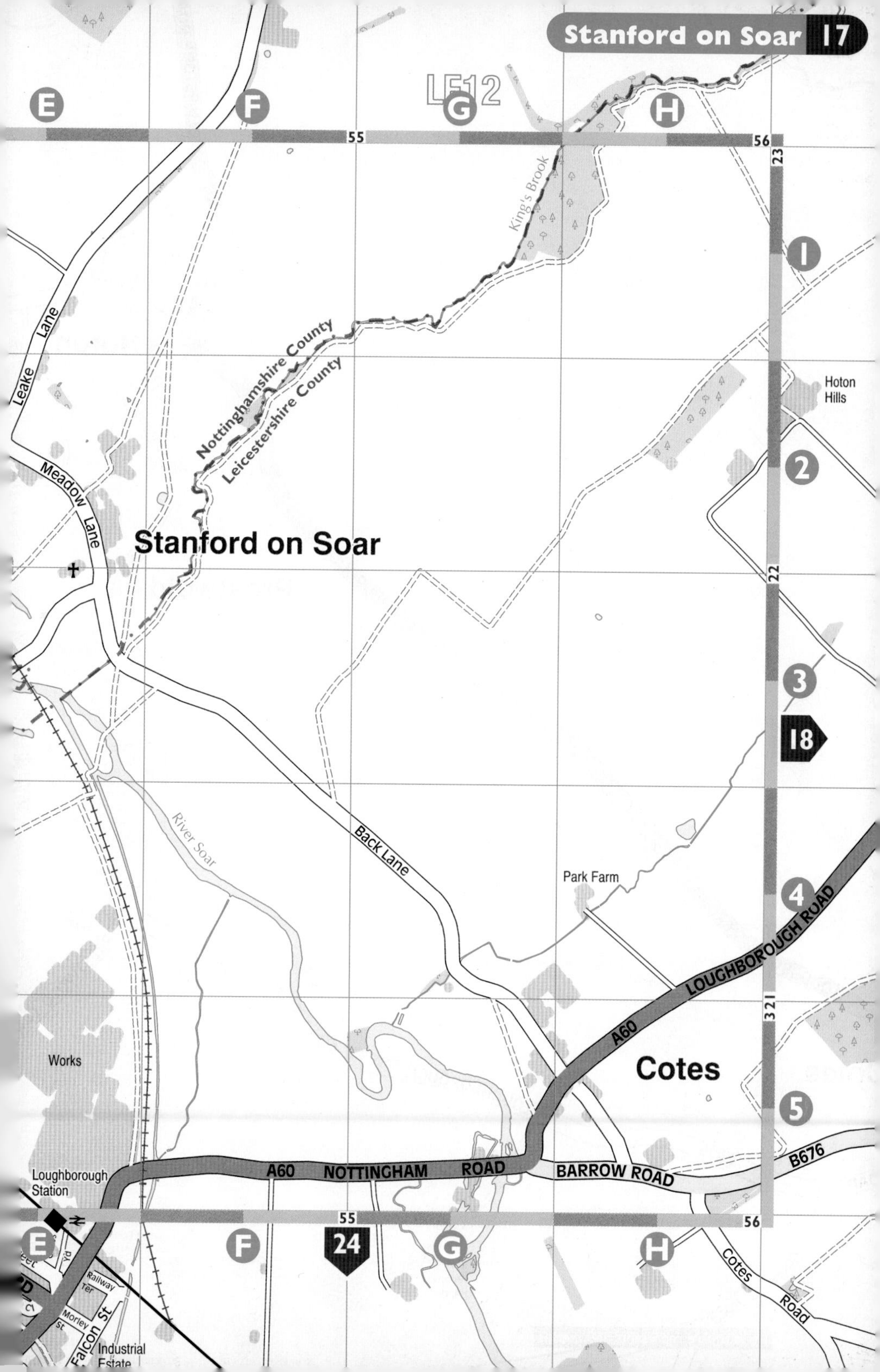
LE12
E
F
G
H
55
56
23
22
21
1
2
3
4
5
King's Brook
Nottinghamshire County
Leicestershire County
Leake Lane
Meadow Lane
Stanford on Soar
Hoton Hills
18
Back Lane
River Soar
Park Farm
LOUGHBOROUGH ROAD
A60
Cotes
Works
A60 NOTTINGHAM ROAD
BARROW ROAD
B676
Loughborough Station
24
Cotes Road
Railway Ter
Morley St
Falcon St.
Industrial Estate

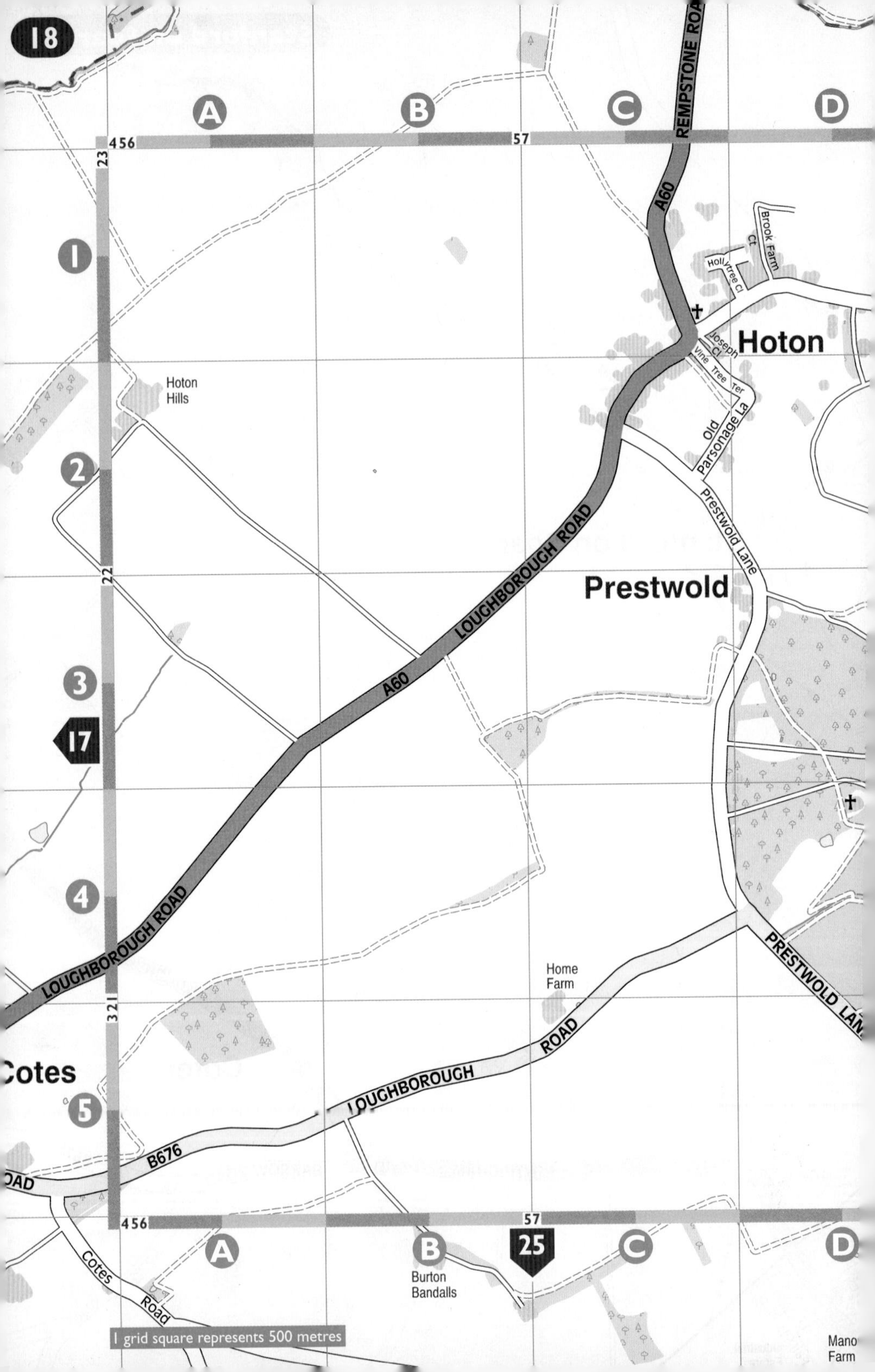
A
B
C
D
456
57
23
22
321
1
2
3
4
5
17
REMPSTONE ROAD
A60
Brook Farm
Ct
Hollytree Cl
Joseph Cl
Vine Tree Ter
Old Parsonage La
Hoton
Hoton Hills
Prestwold Lane
Prestwold
LOUGHBOROUGH ROAD
A60
LOUGHBOROUGH ROAD
PRESTWOLD LANE
Home Farm
LOUGHBOROUGH ROAD
Cotes
B676
ROAD
25
Burton Bandalls
Cotes Road
Mano Farm
1 grid square represents 500 metres

Gorse Farm
Wymeswold Road
Burton Lane
Airfield
(disused)
Wymeswold
Industrial
Park
Burton Lane
The Cliff
Cliff House
Farm
Works
Old
Wood
Wymeswold La
Cemetery
MELTON
ROAD
B676
Hubbard
Rd
Somerset Cl
Brickwood
Place
Mundy
Cl
Brook
St
Hd Cl
St Andrews
Cl
St
Rd
Philips
St Marys
Cl
St Ls Cl
rton on
e Wolds
LOUGHBOROUGH ROAD
Springfield Cl
Hall
Drive
Seals Cl
Sowters
Lane
The Willows
Towles
Fields
Burton on the Wolds
Primary School
Seymour Road
Barrow Road
Burton La
E
F
G
H
59
60
1
2
3
4
5
21
22
23

SHEPSHED
Harboro Farm
Hallamford Road
Tickow Lane
Oxley Primary School
St Winefrides RC Primary School
Loughborough Motorway Trading Estate
Gelders Hall Industrial Estate
Gelders Hall Rd
Cemetery
Industrial Estate
A512 ASHBY ROAD WEST
Charley Road
Brick Kiln Lane
Moscow La
Iveshead Road
Morley Lane
Jolly Farmers La
Pudding Bag Lane
Sandhole Lane
Charnwood Road
Oxford St
King's Rd
Old Station
Ring Fence
Belton St
Factory St
Park Rise
Glenmore Av
Little Haw Lane
Thorpe Road
Grange Road
Anson Road
Conway Drive
Windsor Dr
Belvoir Wy
Springfield Rd
Meadows
The Meadows
Rockingham Cl
Tamworth Cl
Black
27
446
47
20
19
318
1 grid square represents 500 metres

14
22
E
F
G
H
1
2
3
4
5
49
50
20
19
318
Black Brook
Hathern Drive
Mill Close
Boundary Way
Countrymans Way
Butthole Lane
Hind Leys Community College
St Botolphs CE Primary School
Shepshed High School
Forest Street
Forest St
Smithy Wy
Nelson Cl
Westoby Cl
Well Yd Cl
Cumbrian Way
Harrington Rd
Chestnut Cl
The Inleys
Wood Cl
Chiltern Av
Fairway Road
Romway Cl
Homeway Cl
Mendip Cl
Cheviot Dr
Purbeck Av
Pentland Av
New Croft Primary School
Road
Drive
Porlock Cl
Wicklow Cl
Malvern Av
Arbury Dl
Quantock Ri
Fairway Rd
Linley Av
Trueway
Purley Ri
Coombe Cl
S Cl
Pennine Cl
Newlands Av
Polden Cl
Trueway Dr
Park Av
Temple Cl
Road S
Fairway
Brendon Cl
M1
Temple of Venus
Abberton Way
Foxcote
Belmont Wy
Junction 23
ASHBY ROAD EAST
Works
Hurst Farm
Snell's Nook
Longcliffe

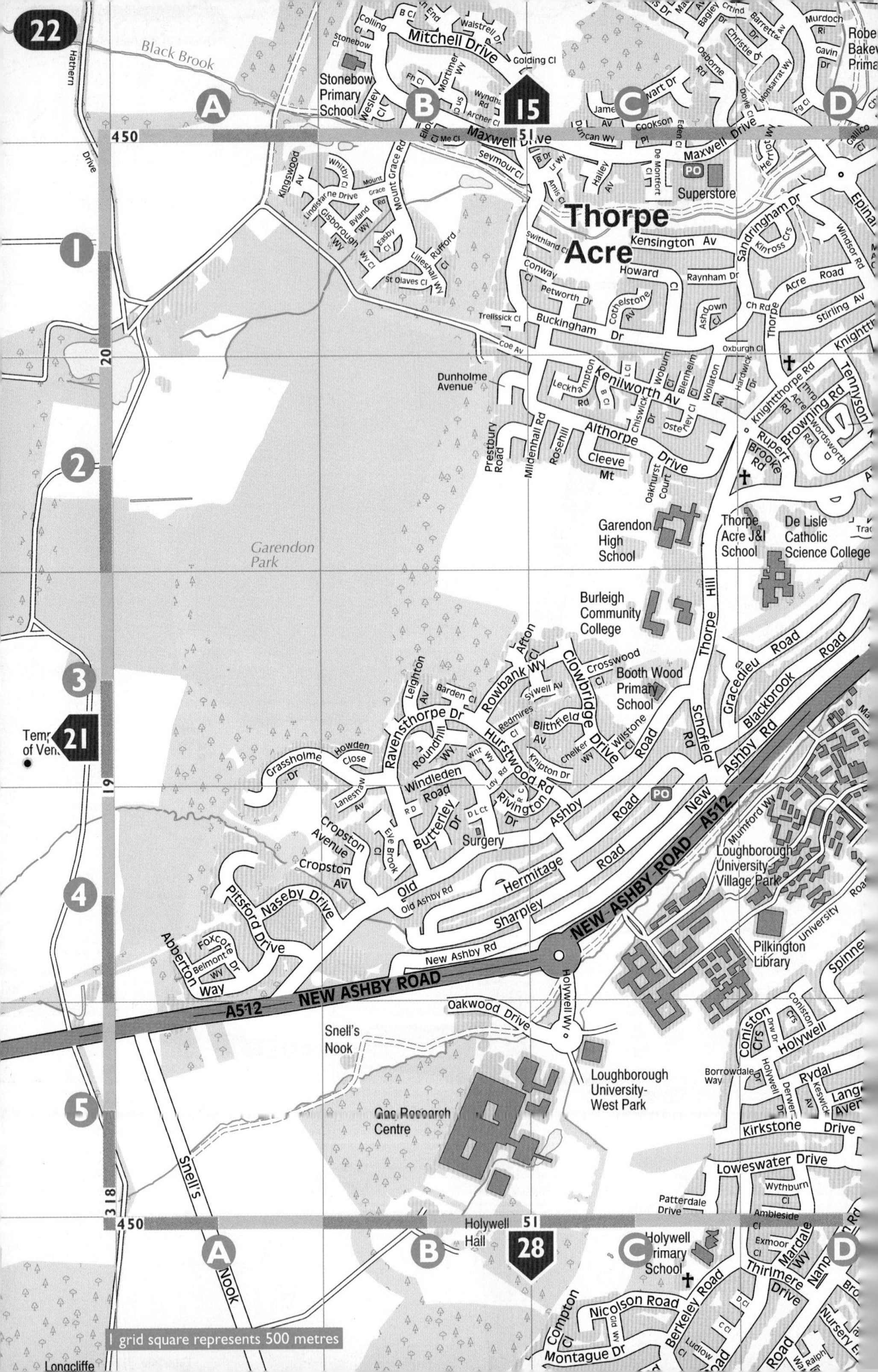
Black Brook
Hathern
Drive
Mitchell Drive
Colling
Stonebow
Walstrell Dr
Golding Cl
Stonebow Primary School
Wesley Cl
Mortimer Wy
Archer Cl
15
Maxwell Drive
Seymour Cl
Kingswood Av
Whitby Cl
Mount Grace Rd
Lindisfarne Drive
Gisborough Wy
Byland Wy
Easby Cl
Rufford Cl
Lilleshall Wy
St Olaves Cl
Duncan Wy
Cookson Pl
Eden Cl
De Montfort Cl
Hailey Av
PO
Superstore
Thorpe Acre
Osborne Rd
Bagley Dr
Christie Dr
Barrett Av
Murdoch Rl
Gavin Dr
Monsarrat Wy
Doyle Cl
Herriot Wy
Sandringham Dr
Kinross Crs
Windsor Rd
Kensington Av
Swithland Cl
Conway Cl
Howard Cl
Raynham Dr
Petworth Dr
Cothelstone Av
Ashdown Cl
Ch Rd
Thorpe Acre Road
Stirling Av
Trelissick Cl
Buckingham Dr
Oxburgh Cl
Coe Av
Dunholme Avenue
Leckhampton Rd
Kenilworth Av
Woburn Cl
Blenheim Cl
Wollaton Av
Hardwick Dr
Chiswick Dr
Osterley Cl
Knightthorpe Rd
Tennyson
Browning Rd
Rupert Brooke Rd
Wordsworth Rd
Prestbury Road
Mildenhall Rd
Rosehill
Althorpe Drive
Cleeve Mt
Oakhurst Court
Garendon High School
Thorpe Acre J&I School
De Lisle Catholic Science College
Garendon Park
Burleigh Community College
Thorpe Hill
Gracedieu Road
Blackbrook Road
Afton Cl
Clowbridge Drive
Crosswood Cl
Booth Wood Primary School
Rowbank Wy
Sywell Av
Leighton Av
Barden Cl
Redmires Cl
Blithfield Av
Ravensthorpe Dr
Roundhill Wy
Hurstwood Rd
Wilstone Cl
Chelker Wy
Knipton Dr
Schofield Rd
Ashby Road
New Ashby Rd
Howden Close
Grassholme Dr
Lanesnaw Av
Windleden Road
Rivington Dr
Butterley Dr
D L Ct
Surgery
Eye Brook Cl
Cropston Avenue
Cropston Av
Old Ashby Rd
Hermitage Road
Sharpley Road
A512
NEW ASHBY ROAD
Mumford Wy
Loughborough University Village Park
University Road
Pilkington Library
Spinney
Naseby Drive
Pitsford Drive
Foxcote Dr
Belmont Wy
Abberton Way
New Ashby Rd
Holywell Wy
Oakwood Drive
Snell's Nook
Loughborough University-West Park
Coniston Crs
Holywell
Borrowdale Way
Rydal
Keswick Av
Derwent Dr
Kirkstone Drive
Loweswater Drive
Wythburn Cl
Patterdale Drive
Ambleside Cl
Exmoor Cl
Mardale Wy
Thirlmere Drive
Napier Rd
Gec Research Centre
Snell's Nook
Temple of Venus
21
1
2
3
4
5
20
19
318
450
51
A
B
C
D
Holywell Hall
28
Holywell Primary School
Compton Cl
Nicolson Road
Berkeley Road
Montague Dr
Ludlow
Nursery
1 grid square represents 500 metres
Longcliffe

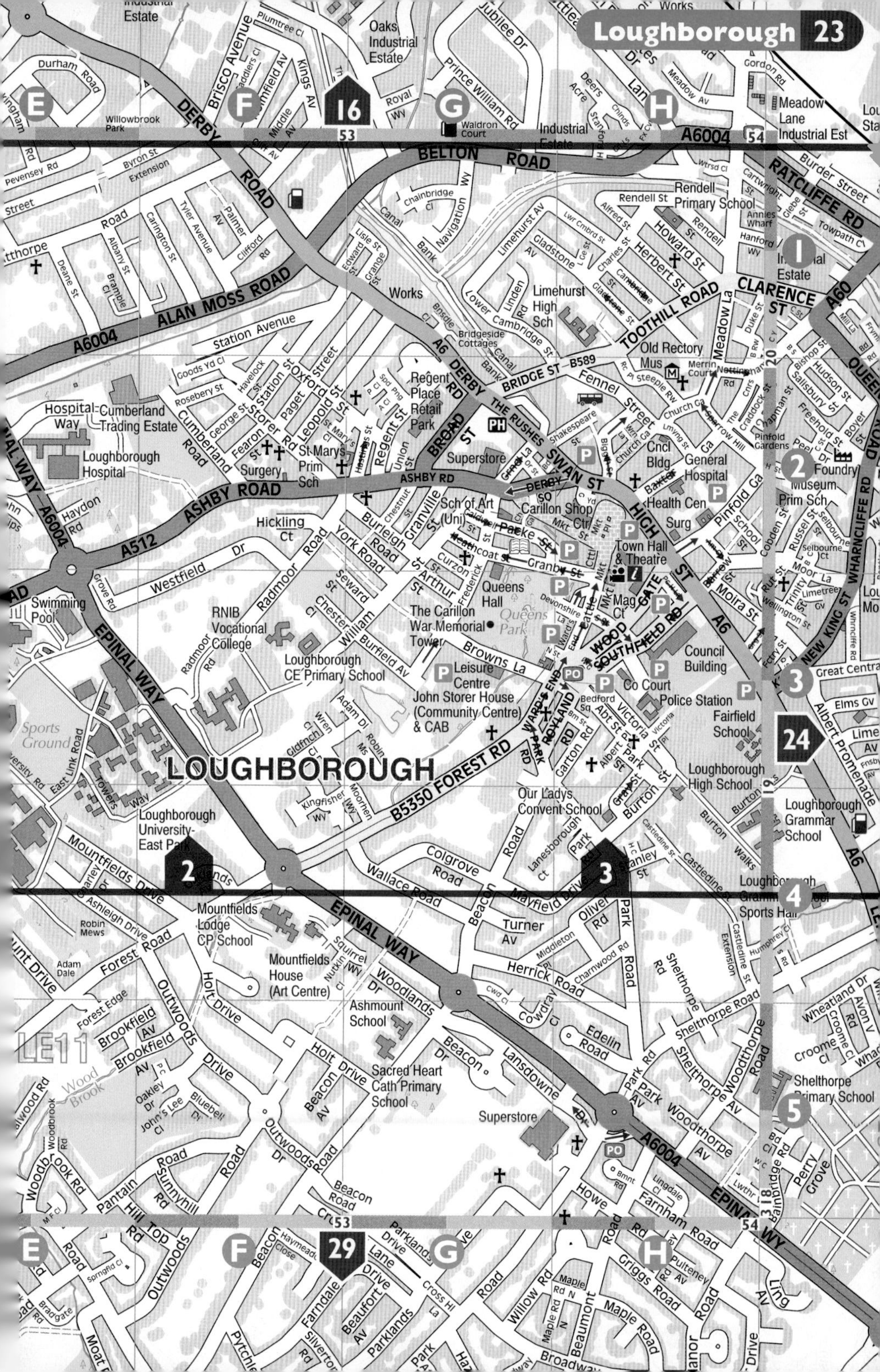
Loughborough 23
16
24
29
2
3
53
54
E
F
G
H
I
1
2
3
4
5
18
19
20
LE11
LOUGHBOROUGH
A6004
BELTON ROAD
ALAN MOSS ROAD
DERBY ROAD
RATCLIFFE RD
ASHBY ROAD
A512
A6 DERBY RD
BROAD ST
THE RUSHES
SWAN ST
HIGH ST
BRIDGE ST B589
TOOTHILL ROAD
CLARENCE ST
WOOD GATE
SOUTHFIELD RD
B5350 FOREST RD
EPINAL WAY
NEW KING ST
WHARNCLIFFE RD
Oaks Industrial Estate
Industrial Estate
Meadow Lane Industrial Est
Willowbrook Park
Waldron Court
Rendell Primary School
Limehurst High Sch
Old Rectory Mus
Regent Place Retail Park
Cumberland Trading Estate
Loughborough Hospital
Hospital Way
Surgery
St Marys Prim Sch
Superstore
Sch of Art (Uni)
Carillon Shop Ctr
Town Hall & Theatre
General Hospital
Health Cen
Surg
Museum
Foundry
Prim Sch
Queens Hall
Queens Park
The Carillon War Memorial Tower
RNIB Vocational College
Loughborough CE Primary School
Leisure Centre
John Storer House (Community Centre) & CAB
Council Building
Co Court
Police Station
Fairfield School
Loughborough High School
Loughborough Grammar School
Our Ladys Convent School
Swimming Pool
Sports Ground
Loughborough University-East Park
Loughborough Grammar School Sports Hall
Mountfields Lodge CP School
Mountfields House (Art Centre)
Ashmount School
Sacred Heart Cath Primary School
Shelthorpe Primary School
Superstore
Works
Station Avenue
Westfield Dr
Radmoor Road
Hickling Ct
Browns La
Colgrove Road
Wallace Road
Mountfields Drive
Forest Road
Holt Drive
Outwoods Drive
Beacon Road
Herrick Road
Park Road
Shelthorpe Road
Woodthorpe Road
Albert Promenade
Lansdowne Dr
Farnham Road
Griggs Road
Maple Road
Beaumont Rd
Pantain Road
Hill Top

24
17
23
3
30
A60
NGHAM ROAD
BARROW RD
A6004
Loughborough Station
Meadow Lane
Industrial Est
RATCLIFFE RD
Burder Street
Rendell Primary School
Industrial Estate
CLARENCE ST
Falcon St
QUEEN'S ROAD
LC
Little Moor Lane
River Soar
Bell Foundry Museum
Prim Sch
WHARNCLIFFE RD
Empress Road
Works
Robert Hardy Wharf
Little Moor Lane
Ind Est
Loughborough Mosque
Moor Lane
Loughborough Central Stn
Windmill Road Industrial Est
NEW KING ST
Great Central Rd
Council Building
Police Station
The Elms (Loughborough Uni of Tech)
Loughborough Moors
Loughborough High School
Loughborough Grammar School
Albert Promenade
King Edward Road
Grand Union Canal
Loughborough Grammar School Sports Hall
LEICESTER ROAD
Great Central Railway
Shelthorpe Road
Woodthorpe Road
Shelthorpe Primary School
Charnwood Water
Loughborough Cemetery
Loughborough Crematorium
Bull in the Hollow Farm
EPINAL WY
A6
LOUGHBOROUGH ROAD
Main Street
Quorn Lodge Farm
Lodge Farm
Farnham Road
1 grid square represents 500 metres

Burton
Bandalls
Manor Lodge
Farm
Walton
Grange
Bandalls La
Walton Lane
Cotes Road
Ryecroft
Farm
Foxhill
Farm
Nottingham Road
Strancliffe
Lane
Willow Road
John Earl Rd
Prkns Cl
Strancliffe Lane
Mrmn Cl
Cotes Road
Cemetery
Pilling's
Lock
Cobbie Cl
Store Dr
Furrows Cl
Willow Rd
Elms Gv
Buttermere Wy
Ullswater Av
Coniston Rd
Birch Av
Ash Cl
Thirlmere Road
Humphrey Perkins
High School
Nottingham Rd
Fishpool
Brook La
Babington
Ellis Cl
Heron Rd
Grasmere Cl
Morgans Orch
Beaumont Rd
Wycliffe Av
Newton Cl
Swan Cl
Barrowcliffe
River Soar
Hovel Lane
A6
A6
B5324
Loughborough
Road
Nottingham
E
F
G
H
18
31
57
58
20
19
18
1
2
3
4
5

Thringstone
New Swannington
Abbey Ford Farm
Grace Dieu Priory
Grace Manor
Grace Dieu Wood
Thringstone Primary School
Whitwick St John the Baptist Sch
Holy Cross Catholic Primary School
Whitwick Health Centre
New Swannington Primary School
Redhill Farm
Swannington Common
A512
ASHBY ROAD
Stordon Lane
Meadow
Lily Bank
Ivanhoe Way
Henson's Lane
Main Street
Loughborough Road
Springfield
Heathfield
Tithe Cl
Rumsey Cl
Glebe Road
Priory Cl
Clover Pl
Homestead Rd
St An Cl
Booth Road
Badgers Cft
Kelso Ct
Melrose Rd
Field Close
John St
Ash Dale
Bishop Dr
Swallow Dale
The Green
Brook La
PO
Talbot Lane
Hill Lane
Whitwick Moor
Talbot St
Talbot
Grace Dieu Road
Turolough Road
Warren
Car Hill Rd
Carter Dale
Cragdale
Farndale
Rosedale
Mossdale
Holcombe Cl
Coverdale
Langton Cl
City of Three Waters
Dumps Rd
North Street
Martin Cl
School Lane
The Elms
Howe Road
Valley Way
Cooper Cl
Howe Ct
Lane
Jarvis Wy
Hervey Woods
Stinson Wy
Briers Way
Pares Cl
Bryan's Cl
Rockland Ri
Temple Hill
Parsonwood Hill
Cademan
The Hockley
Bonchurch Road
Skinner's La
Market Pl
Silver St
Vicarage St
City of Dan
Robinson Rd
Brooks
Thomas Rd
Thomas Road
Victoria Cl
Ashford Rd
Cello Cl
Elsdon Cl
Church Lane
Redhill Lane
Whitwick
Spring
Silver Street
Clarke Close
Barr Crs
Ferrers Road
Thornborough
A B C D
1 2 3 4 5
442 43
18 17 316
36
1 grid square represents 500 metres

E
F
G
H
Woods Lane
Blackbrook Farm
45
46
A512
ASHBY ROAD WEST
Ringing Hill
Swannymote Road
Sandhole
Lane
1
20
18
Spring Burrow Lodge
Finney Farm
2
Warren Lane
Blackbrook Reservoir
3
High Sharpley
Swannymote Road
Way
17
Drybrook Lodge Farm
4
Road
Oaks Road
Oa
5
WICK
Mount St Bernard Abbey
316
45
46
37
E
F
G
H
Hastings Av
Barnard's Road
Abbey Road

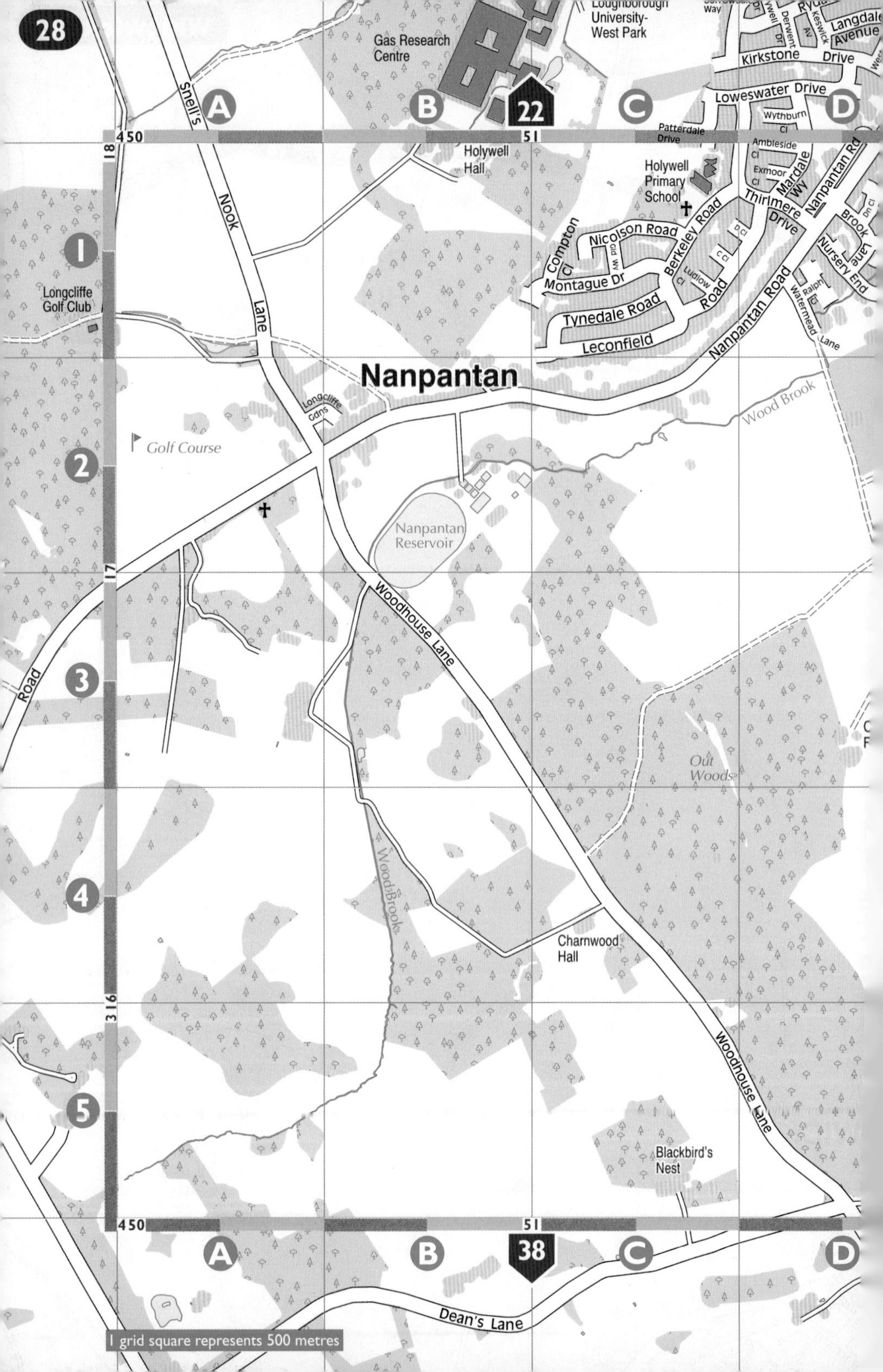

Loughborough University-West Park
Gas Research Centre
Snell's Nook Lane
Kirkstone Drive
Loweswater Drive
Langdale Avenue
Keswick Av
Derwent Dr
Wythburn Cl
Patterdale Drive
Ambleside Cl
Exmoor Cl
Mardale Wy
Thirlmere Drive
Nanpantan Rd
Holywell Hall
Holywell Primary School
Compton Cl
Nicolson Road
Gld Wy
Berkeley Road
Montague Dr
Ludlow Cl
Tynedale Road
Leconfield Road
Nanpantan Road
Brook Lane
Nursery End
Ralph Cl
Watermead Lane
Longcliffe Golf Club
Nanpantan
Longcliffe Gdns
Golf Course
Wood Brook
Nanpantan Reservoir
Woodhouse Lane
Road
Out Woods
Charnwood Hall
Blackbird's Nest
Dean's Lane
450
51
18
17
316
A
B
C
D
1
2
3
4
5
22
38
1 grid square represents 500 metres

Cath Primary School
Superstore
PO
A6004
EPINAL WAY
Oakley Dr
John's Lee Cl
Bluebell Dr
Sandalwood Rd
Woodbrook Rd
Outwoods Dr
Outwoods Road
Beacon Av
Pantain Road
Sunnyhill Rd
Hill Top Rd
Outwoods
Moat Road
Road
Bradgate
Melbreak
Sprngfld Cl
Cross Hill Lane
Parklands Drive
Drive
Beacon Road
Haymeadow Close
Farndale Drive
Beaufort Av
Parklands
Silverton Rd
Hambledon Crs
Pytchley Drive
Cottesmore Dr
Belvoir Dr
Craven Close
Mayo Cl
Ledbury Rd
Tiverton Road
Bramcote Road
Grasmere Rd
Cleveland Rd
Atherstone Road
Jetcott Av
Southdown Rd
Park Atherstone Rd
Cross Hl La
Hazel Road
Walnut Rd
Broadway
Willow Rd
Maple Rd N
Beaumont Road
Maple Road
Griggs Road
Pulteney Rd
Pulteney Av
Farnham Road
Howe Rd
Manor Road
Manor Drive
Maple Rd South
Poplar Road
Ling Av
Perry Grove
Bainbridge Rd
Sheltho
Lilac Cl
Sycamore Wy
Acer Cl
Aspen Av
Redwood Rd
The Osiers
Spruce Av
Cypress Cl
Hollytree Cl
Cherry Cl
Lemontree La
Fairmeadows Way
Juniper Wy
Magnolia Av
Pine Cl
Laurel Road
Outwoods Edge Primary School
Woodbrook Vale High School
Almond Cl
Spindle Rd
Rosewood Wy
Lark Ri
Haddon Way
Freesia Cl
Poppy Cl
Birch
Oak Cl
Laburnam Way
Clumbers Cl
Newstead Way
Calke Cl
Kelham Cl
Newstead Wy
Park Grange
Corydalis Cl
Vale Cl
Allendale Rd
Highland Dr
Hillcrest Dr
Beaumanor Hall
Council Building
May Tree La
Waterloo Spinney Lane
Briscoe Lane
Beaumanor Drive
Forest Rd
Beaumanor Gardens
Home Farm Cl
Vicary Lane
Woodh
Gate
Course
Forest Rd
E F G H
23 30 39
53 54
I 2 3 4 5
18 17 16

30
Shelthorpe Primary School
Loughborough Cemetery
Loughborough Crematorium
Bull in the Hollow
24
A
B
C
D
A6004
EPINAL WY
Lingdale Cl
Farnham Road
Pulteney Rd
Pulteney Av
Road
Manor Road
Manor Drive
Maple Rd
South
Ling Av
Perry Grove
Main Street
Quorn Lodge Farm
A6
LOUGHBOROUGH ROAD
Lodge Farm
Main St
Shelthorpe
Main Street
Woodthorpe
Vale Cl
Allendale Rd
Highland Dr
Hill
Loughborough Road
Farley Way
Pepper Dr
Allen Av
Kelcey Rd
Beardsley Rd
Farnham St
White Street
Loughborough Road
Silver Birches
Warwick Rd
Rumsey Cl
Woodward Av
Woodhouse Road
The Rigsty
The Avenue
The Sandhills
Poulteney Dr
The Deepway
Sutton Cl
The Pingle
Badgers Wk
Whatoff Lodge
Chaveney Road
Chaveney Wk
Beacon Av
Cradock Drive
Elms Dr
Spinney Dr
Forest Rd
Wyvernhoe Dr
Toller Road
Buddon Lane
Chestnut Cl
Quorn & Woodhouse Station
29
Forest Rd
Beaumanor Drive
Beaumanor Gardens
Council Building
May Tree La
Waterloo
Spinney Lane
Briscoe Lane
40
Woodhouse
Home Farm Cl
Great Central Rail
1 grid square represents 500 metres

Pilling's Lock
Cemetery
Cotes Road
Humphrey Perkins High School
River Soar
Barrowcliffe Close
Cotes Road
Beaumont Rd
Wycliffe Av
Woodside Rd
North St
Church La
Church Street
Highfields
Breadcroft La
Thirlmere Road
Coniston Rd
Ennerdale Road
Grasmere Cl
Nottingham Rd
Willow Rd
Birch Av
Ash Cl
Ullswater Av
Buttermere Wy
Furrows
Cobble Cl
Fishpool
Brook La
Babington Rd
Ellis Cl
Heron Cl
Heron Rd
Swan Cl
Pell Cl
Cave Rd
The Banks
The Rookery
Barrow Health Centre
High St
Crossley Cl
Hall Orchard CE Primary School
Beveridge St
New St
Melton Road
Warner St
Grove Lane
Breachfield Road
Illston Gardens
Barrow Road
Bridge St
South Street
Barrow upon Soar Station
Cramps Cl
Holbourne Cl
Lodge Cl
Martin Av
Ribble Drive
Cherwell Rd
Avon Rd
Welland Road
Sileby Road
The Pastures
Mill Lane
Proctor's Park Road
A6
Hovel Lane
Meynell Road
Huntsman's Cl
Swinfield Rd
Brown Av
Victoria St
Catherines Cl
Freehold St
Soar Road
Mansfield St
Disraeli St
Nursery La
Station Road
Steon La
School Lane
Weavers Cl
Cncl Bldg
Quorn Country Hotel
Leicester Rd
The Mills
Armston Rd
Whall Cl
The Brinks
Paddock Close
Selvester Dr
Giles Cl
Northage Close
Northage Close
Wood Lane
Unitt Rd
Leicester Road
Granite Way
North End
Hawcliffe Road
Pepper's Close
Loughborough Road
The Quay
Wood Lane
Works
PH
32
25
41
57
58
E
F
G
H
I
1
2
3
4
5

Barrow upon Soar
Fishpool Brook
Melton Road
Pawdy Farm
Brook La
Fishpool Way
Nottingham Rd
Willow Rd
Birch Av
Babington Rd
Breadcroft La
Highfields
Cave Rd
Ellis Cl
Heron Rd
Swan Cl
Grebe
Branston Av
The Banks
New St
Melton
Warner St
Grove
Breachfield Road
Condon Rd
Illston Gardens
Hall Orchard CE Primary School
Sileby Road
The Pastures
Cherwell Rd
Avon Rd
Welland Road
River View
Huston Cl
Hayhill Lane
Hayhill
Works
Slash Lane
A6
River Soar
The Quay
Sileby Road
Mountsorrel La
Barons
PH
A B C D
1 2 3 4 5
458
59
18
17
316
31
42
1 grid square represents 500 metres

E
F
G
H
I
61
62
18
17
316
2
3
4
5
34
43
Seagrave
Muckle Gate Lane
Green Lane
The Banks
Green Lane Close
Water Lane
The Orchard
Berrycott Lane
King Street
Church St
Swan Street
Butchers Lane
Pond St
Hall Farm
Cemetery
Big Lane
Quebec Farm
Seagrave Road
Belle Isle
Hanover Lodge
Jubilee Avenue
Greedon Rise
Pryor Road
Highgate Primary School
Heathcote
Homefield Road
Greedon Ri
Forest Dr
Bramley Cl
Barradale Av
Weldon Av
Collingwood
Brushfield Av
Albert Av
Seagrave Road
Springfield Rd
Newbold Close
Gibson Road
Drive
Hickling Dr
Moreton Dl
Pochin Way
Marshall Av
Haybrooke Road
Parsons Drive
Barnards Drive
Stanage Road
Ainsworth Dr
Hanover
Park Road
Works
School
Highgate Farm
Swan Street
Highgate
Wellbrook Avenue
Storer Cl
Drive
Cauby Cl
Finsbury Av
Hg Rd
Surgery
PO
PH
Ratcliffe Road
Sileby Stn
Surgery
Moir Cl
Brook
Street
Cemetery
SILEBY

North Hill
Farm
A
B
C
D
462
63
18
Green Lane
Berrycott Lane
The
Banks
Water La
1
King Street
Ivyhouse
Cl.
Church St
wan Street
Pond
St
Butchers
Lane
Hall Farm
2
A46
Park Hill Lane
Travelodge
17
3
Park Hill
Golf Club
33
Hanov
Lodge
Golf Course
Works
4
316
Highgate Farm
5
462
63
A
B
44
C
Spinney Farm
D
Leicestershire Way
A46
Leicestershire Way
1 grid square represents 500 metres

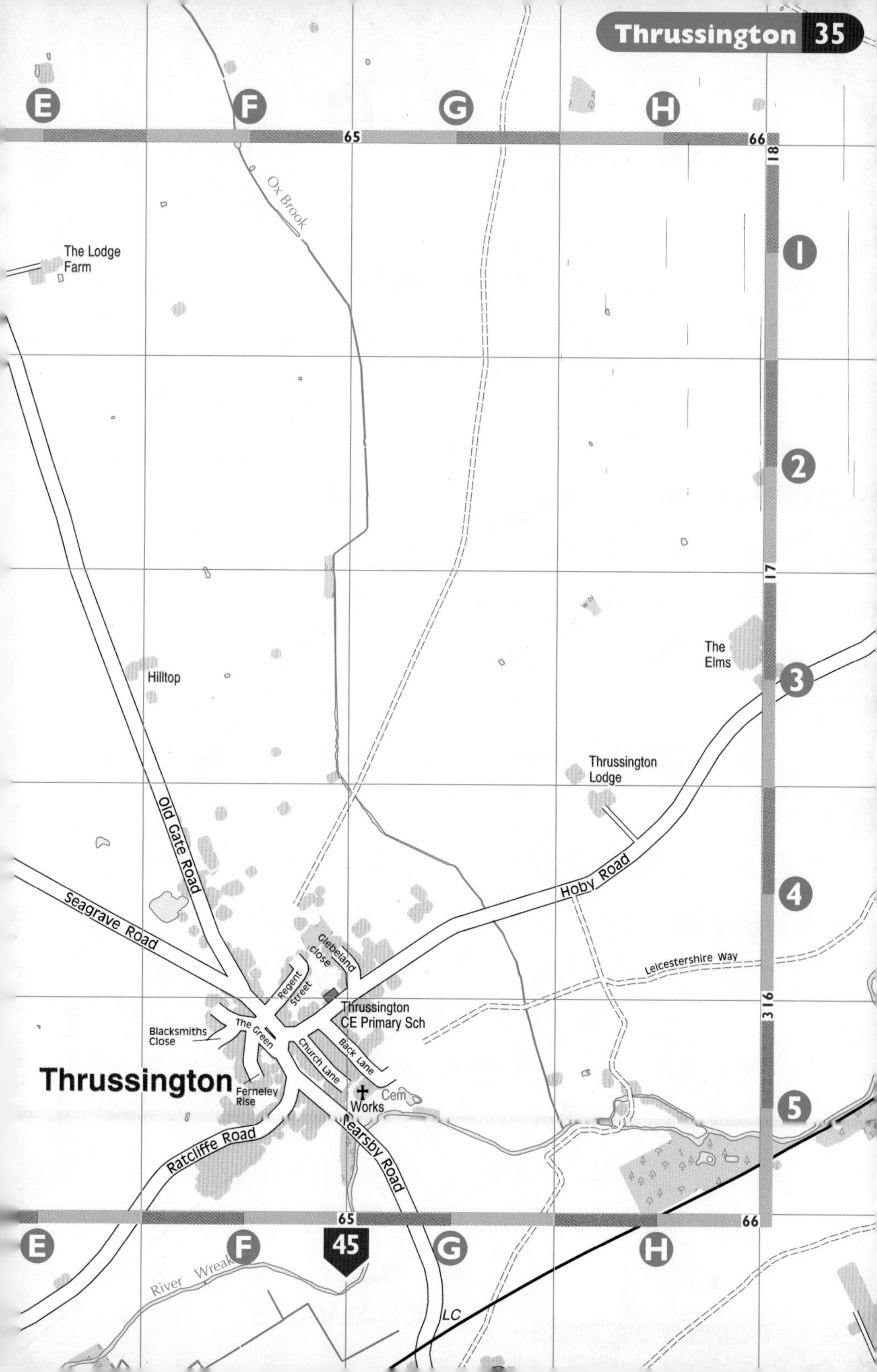
E
F
G
H
65
66
18
17
316
1
2
3
4
5
Ox Brook
The Lodge Farm
Hilltop
The Elms
Thrussington Lodge
Old Gate Road
Seagrave Road
Hoby Road
Glebeland close
Regent Street
Thrussington CE Primary Sch
Leicestershire Way
Blacksmiths Close
The Green
Back Lane
Church Lane
Thrussington
Ferneley Rise
Works
Cem
Ratcliffe Road
Rearsby Road
45
River Wreak
LC

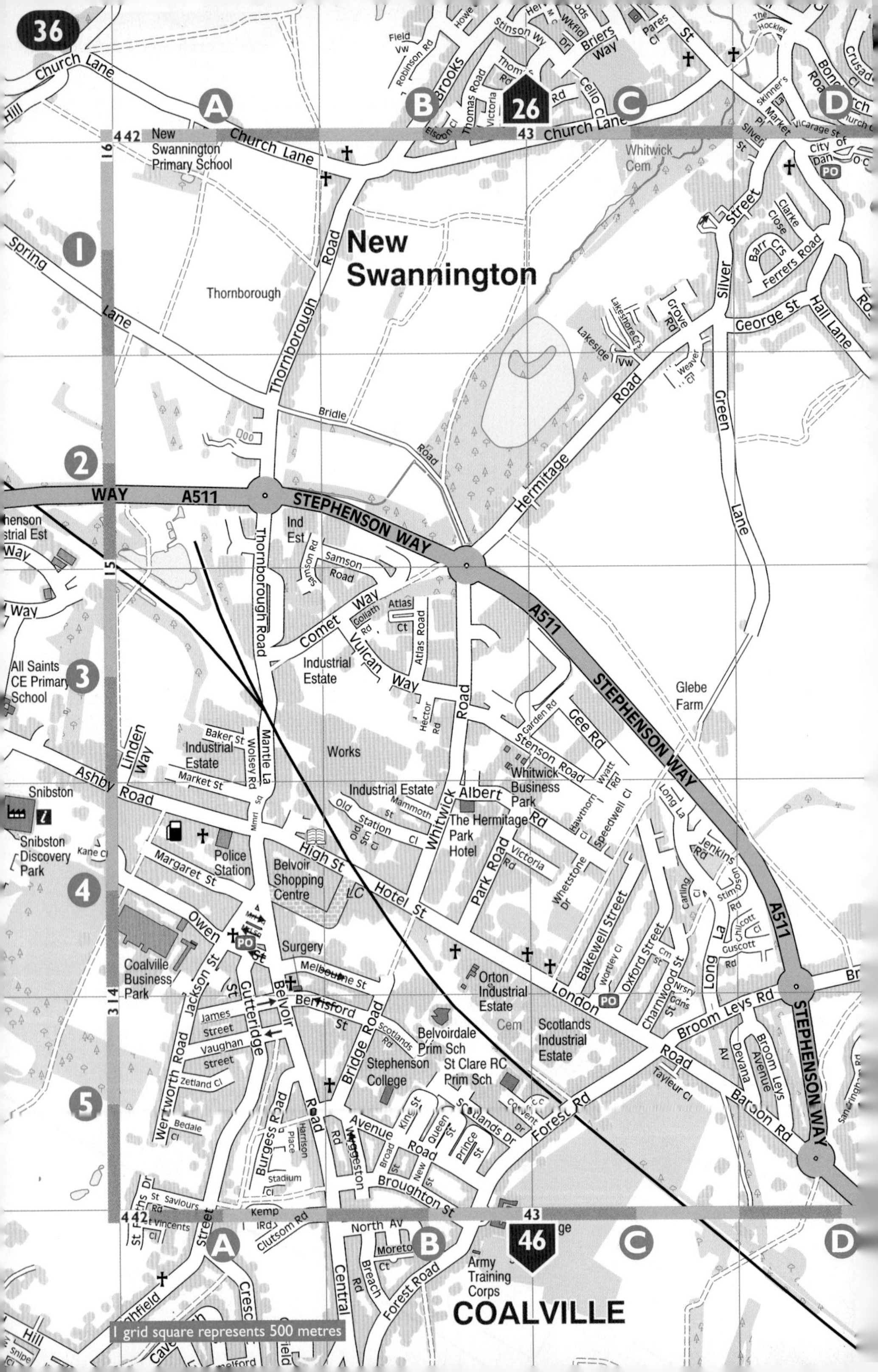
New Swannington
Thornborough
New Swannington Primary School
Church Lane
Spring Lane
Thornborough Road
Bridle Road
Hermitage Road
Whitwick Cem
Silver Street
Green Lane
George St
Hall Lane
Ferrers Road
Barr Crs
Clarke Close
Grove Rd
Lakeside Vw
Lakeshore Crs
Weaver Cl
Brooks
Thomas Road
Victoria Rd
Elsdon Cl
Cello Cl
Briers Way
Stinson Wy
Pares Cl
Field Vw
Robinson Rd
The Hockley
Skinners La
Market Pl
Silver St
Vicarage St
City of Dan
Bond Road
Crusaders Cl
A511
STEPHENSON WAY
WAY
Stephenson Industrial Est
Ind Est
Samson Rd
Samson Road
Comet Way
Goliath Rd
Atlas Ct
Atlas Road
Vulcan Way
Industrial Estate
Hector Rd
Whitwick Road
Garden Rd
Gee Rd
Stenson Road
Wyatt Rd
Whitwick Business Park
Glebe Farm
All Saints CE Primary School
Linden Way
Baker St
Industrial Estate
Wolsey Rd
Mantle La
Market St
Works
Ashby Road
Snibston
Snibston Discovery Park
Kane Cl
Margaret St
Police Station
High St
Belvoir Shopping Centre
Old Station Cl
Mammoth St
Albert Rd
The Hermitage Park Hotel
Park Road
Victoria Rd
Hawthorn Cl
Speedwell Cl
Whetstone Dr
Long La
Jenkins Rd
Stimpson Rd
Chilcott Cl
Guscott Rd
Carling Cl
Hotel St
Owen St
Surgery
Melbourne St
Coalville Business Park
Jackson St
Gutteridge St
Belvoir Road
Bertrisford St
James Street
Vaughan Street
Zetland Cl
Wentworth Road
Bedale Cl
Orton Industrial Estate
Cem
Scotlands Industrial Estate
London Road
Bakewell Street
Wortley Cl
Oxford Street
Charnwood St
Nrsry Gdns
Broom Leys Rd
Broom Leys Avenue
Devana Av
Bardon Rd
Tayleur Cl
Forest Rd
Scotlands Rd
Bridge Road
Belvoirdale Prim Sch
Stephenson College
St Clare RC Prim Sch
Convent Dr
Scotlands Dr
Burgess Road
Harrison Place
Stadium Cl
Avenue Road
King St
Queen St
Prince St
Broad St
New St
Wyggeston Rd
Broughton St
St Saviours Rd
St Faiths Dr
St Vincents Cl
Kemp Rd
Clutsom Rd
North Av
Moreton Ct
Breach Rd
Central Rd
Forest Road
Army Training Corps
COALVILLE
Crescent
Hill
26
46
43
442
1 grid square represents 500 metres

TWICK
Mount St Bernard Abbey
High Tor Farm
Abbey Road
Leicester Road
Ivanhoe Way
Meadow Lane
Warren Hills Road
King Edward VII College
Castle Rock High School
Warren Hills Primary School
Agar Nook
Greenhill Road
Cemetery
Broom Leys Prim Sch
Greenhill
RAF Building
Forest Way School
Barnard's Road
Hastings Av
Rosemary Crs
Crescent Road
Tressall Road
Hall Lane
Perran Av
Sharpley Av
Kingfisher Cl
Nelson Flds
Neville Dr
Blackwood
Castle Rock Drive
Willow Gn
Oakham Drive
St David's Crs
Abbott's Oak Drive
Crasmere
Thirlmere
Stamford Drive
Agar Nook La
York Pl
Jacquemart Cl
Romans Crs
Dauphine Cl
Kenmore Crs
Kirkhill Cl
Stonehaven Cl
Drome Cl
Kirton Rd
Charnborough Rd
Maplewell Dr
Northfield
Quorn Crs
Peldar Pl
Hamilton Rd
Smith Crs
Hall Gate
Clarke Rd
Swithland Rd
Garendon Rd
Beacon Crs
Longcliff Rd
Blackbrook Dr
St Ives
Cropston
Haslyn Wk
Rowan Av
Woodhouse Rd
Chestnut Gv
Linford Crs
Verdon Crs
Greenfields Dr
Dunbar Rd
Strathmore Cl
Staples Drive
Brooker Cl
Harker Dr
Kay Cl
Trent Br
The Oval
Surgery
PO
E F G H
1 2 3 4 5
27
47
45
46
15
16
14
Ivanhoe Way

28
A
B
C
D
450
51
Blackbird's Nest
use Lane
Dean's Lane
15
1
2
3
4
5
Beacon Hill Country Park
Beacon Road
Charley Road
Bawdon Castle Farm
14
Ulverscroft Lodge Farm
313
Priory Lane
Benscliffe Road
Joe
Benscliffe
1 grid square represents 500 metres

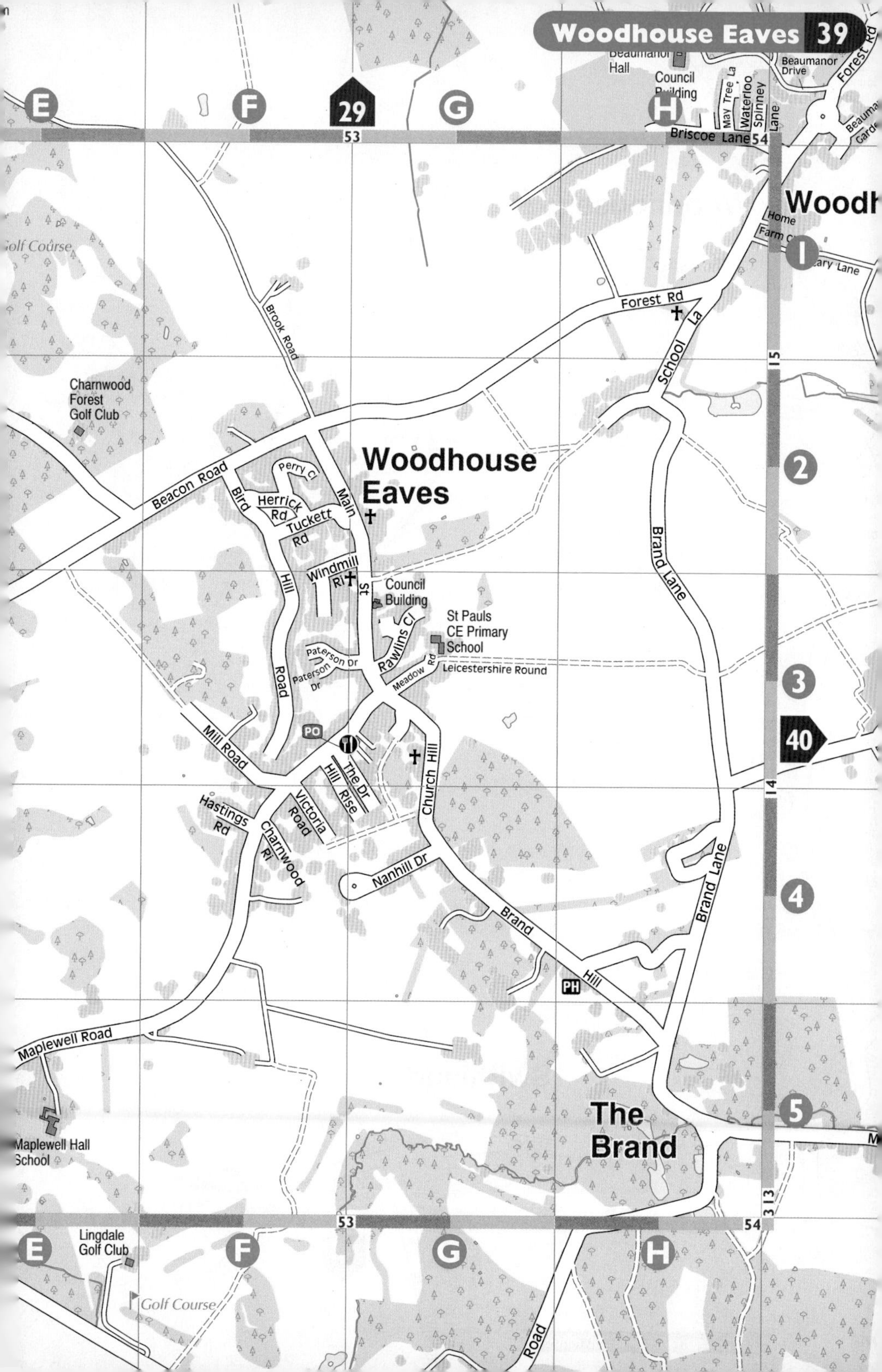
Beaumanor Hall
Council Building
May Tree La
Waterloo
Spinney
Lane
Beaumanor Drive
Forest Rd
Briscoe Lane
Woodh
Home Farm Cl
Forest Rd
School La
Golf Course
Charnwood Forest Golf Club
Brook Road
Woodhouse Eaves
Beacon Road
Perry Cl
Bird
Herrick Rd
Tuckett Rd
Main St
Hill Road
Windmill Ri
Council Building
St Pauls CE Primary School
Rawlins Cl
Paterson Dr
Meadow Rd
Leicestershire Round
Brand Lane
Mill Road
PO
The Dr
Hill Rise
Church Hill
Hastings Rd
Victoria Road
Charnwood Ri
Nanhill Dr
Brand Hill
PH
Maplewell Road
Maplewell Hall School
The Brand
Lingdale Golf Club
Golf Course
Road
E
F
G
H
29
40
53
54
1
2
3
4
5
15
14
13

40
Council Building
May Tree La
Waterloo
Spinney
Lane
Beaumanor Drive
Forest Rd
Briscoe Lane
454
A
B
30
C
D
55
Woodhouse
Home Farm Cl
Vicary Lane
Buddon Wood
Great Central Railway
School La
15
1
2
3
4
5
Brand Lane
Leicestershire Round
Rushey Fields Farm
39
14
Swithland
Main Street
Main Street
Swithland St Leonard CE Primary Sch
313
48
Charnia Gv
Leicester Lane
1 grid square represents 500 metres

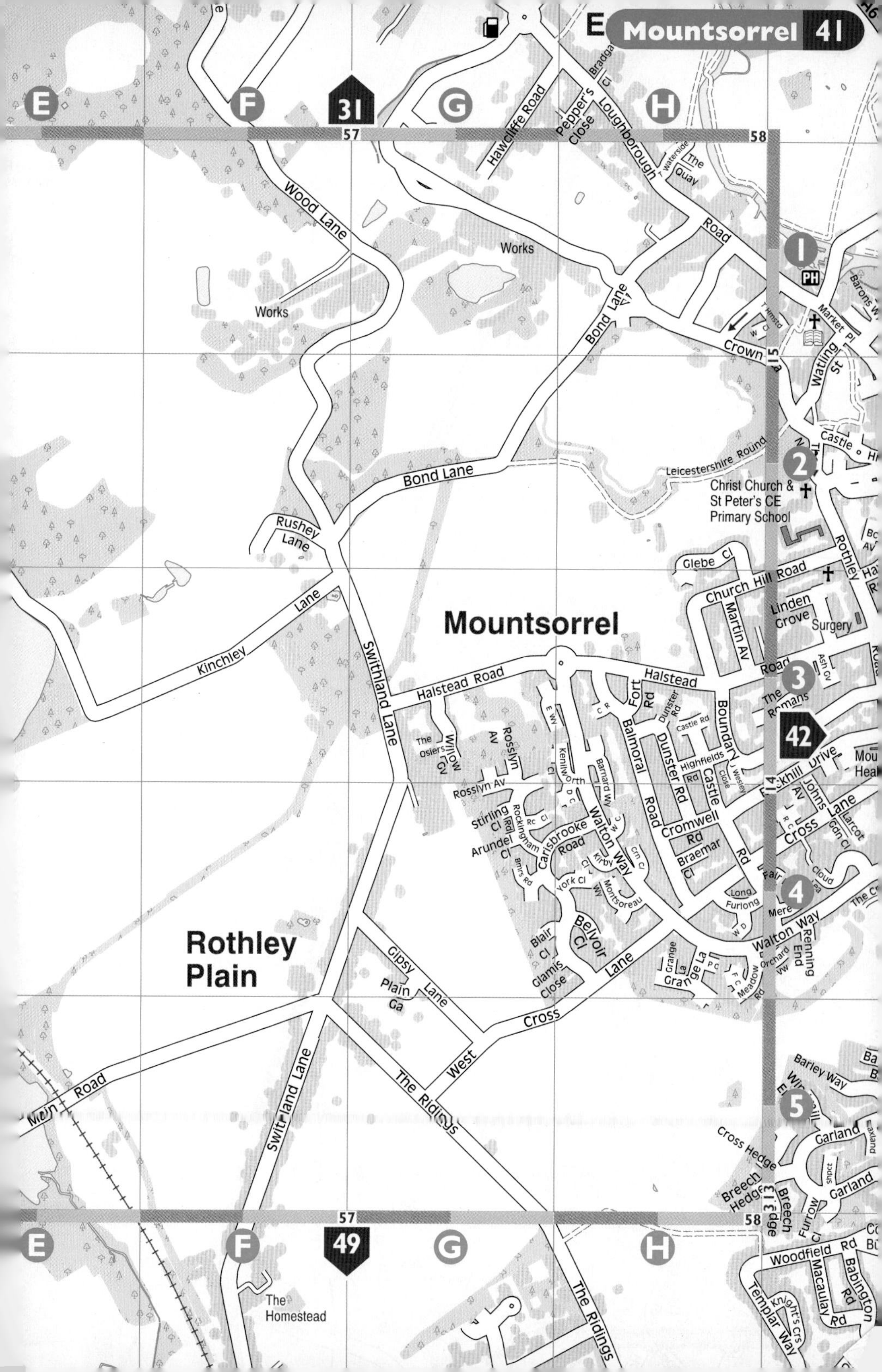
E
F
G
H
I
31
42
49
57
58
1
2
3
4
5
Wood Lane
Works
Hawcliffe Road
Pepper's Close
Loughborough Road
Bradgate Cl
The Quay
Bond Lane
Crown
Market Pl
Watling St
Castle
Leicestershire Round
Christ Church & St Peter's CE Primary School
Rushey Lane
Kinchley Lane
Swithland Lane
Glebe Cl
Church Hill Road
Martin Av
Linden Grove
Surgery
Rothley
Mountsorrel
Halstead Road
Fort Rd
Balmoral Road
Dunster Rd
Castle Rd
Boundary
The Romans
Highfields
Castle
The Osiers
Willow Gv
Rosslyn Av
Kenilworth
Barnard Way
Walton Way
Cromwell Rd
Braemar Cl
Stirling Cl
Rockingham Rd
Arundel Cl
Carisbrooke Road
York Cl
Kirby
Montsoreau
Belvoir Cl
Blair Cl
Glamis Close
Cross Lane
Grange La
Long Furlong
Mere
Meadow Rd
Orchard Vw
Renning End
Johns Av
Cloud
Rothley Plain
Gipsy Lane
Plain Ga
West Cross
Main Road
The Ridings
Barley Way
Garland
Cross Hedge
Breech Hedge
Furrow Cl
Woodfield Rd
Macaulay Rd
Babington Rd
Templar Way
Knight's Crs
The Homestead
A6
B5328

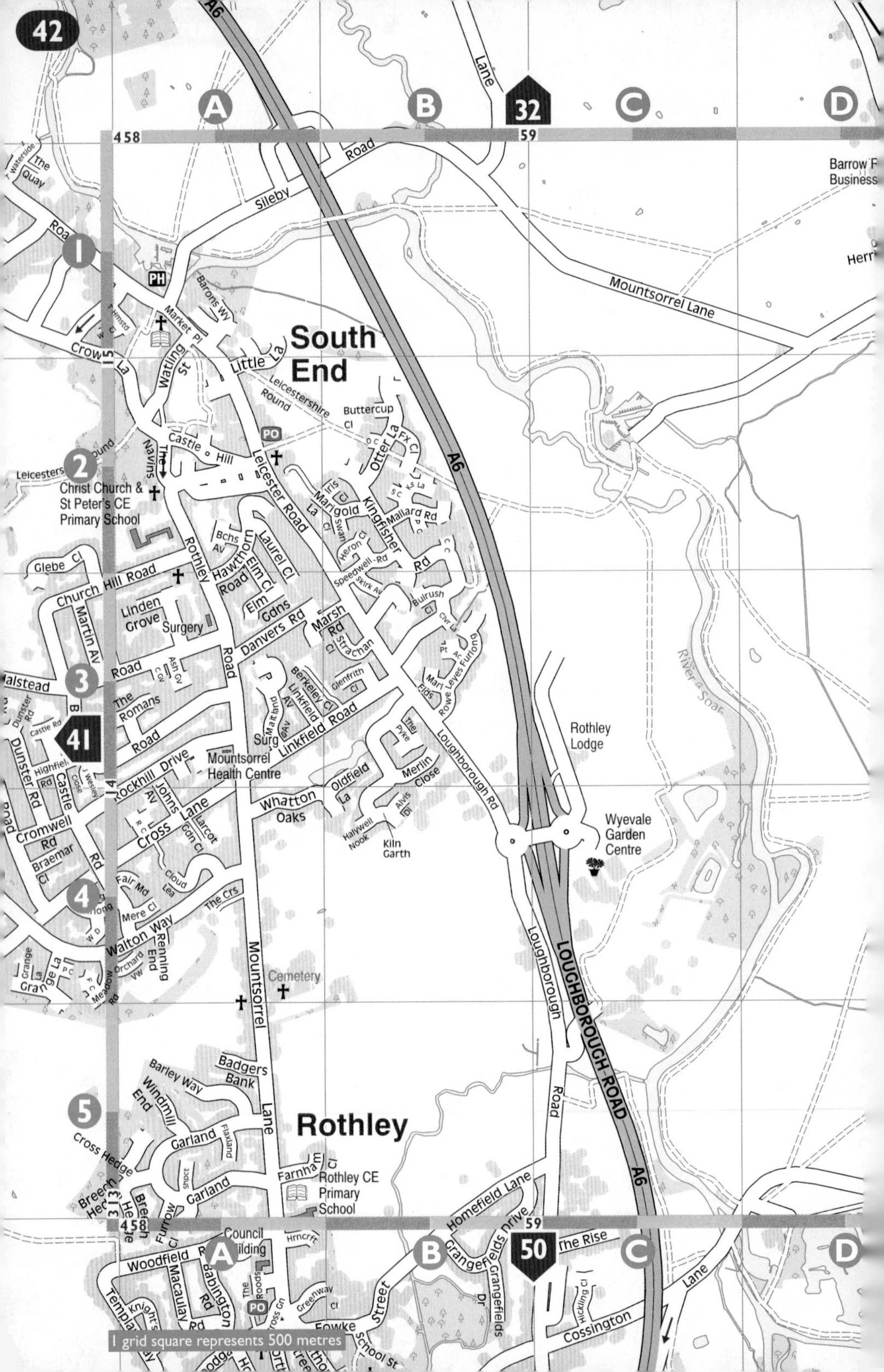
South End
Rothley
A6
LOUGHBOROUGH ROAD
Sileby Road
Mountsorrel Lane
Leicestershire Round
Leicester Road
Loughborough Rd
Loughborough Road
Mountsorrel Lane
Rothley Road
Church Hill Road
Linkfield Road
Cross Lane
Walton Way
Rockhill Drive
Danvers Rd
Kingfisher Rd
Rothley Lodge
Wyevale Garden Centre
River Soar
Cemetery
Christ Church & St Peter's CE Primary School
Mountsorrel Health Centre
Rothley CE Primary School
Council Building
Surgery
Homefield Lane
Grangefields Drive
The Rise
Cossington Lane
Woodfield Rd
School St
Barrow Business
1 grid square represents 500 metres

32
41
50

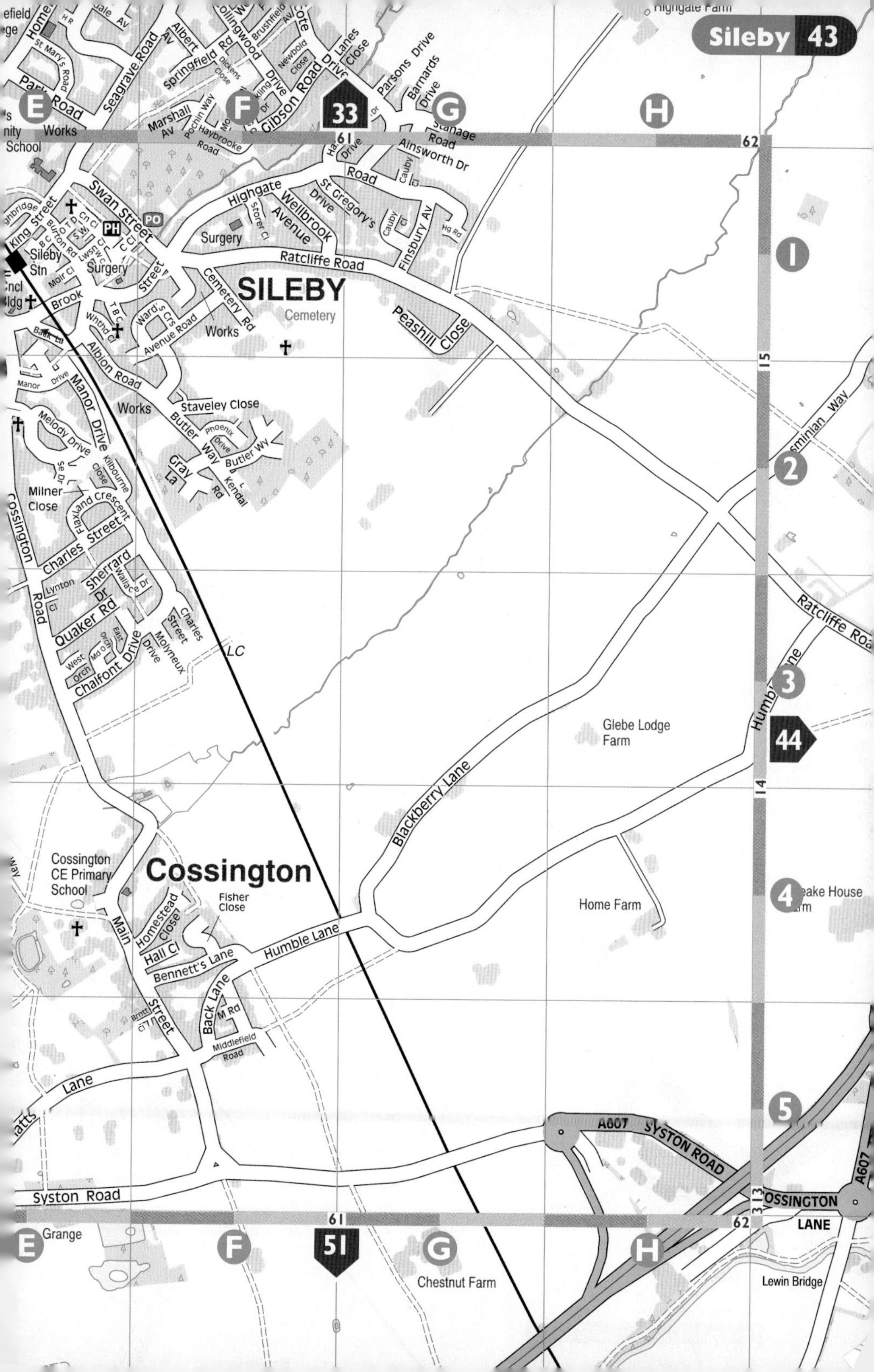
SILEBY
Cossington
Highgate Farm
Cemetery
Surgery
Works
Sileby Stn
Cncl Bldg
PH
PO
Cossington CE Primary School
Glebe Lodge Farm
Home Farm
Chestnut Farm
Lewin Bridge
Grange
Seagrave Road
Swan Street
King Street
Ratcliffe Road
Highgate Road
Wellbrook Avenue
St Gregory's Drive
Finsbury Av
Ainsworth Dr
Stanage Road
Parsons Drive
Barnards Drive
Gibson Road
Springfield Rd
Collingwood Drive
Haybrooke Road
Pochin Way
Marshall Av
Park Road
St Mary's Road
Albert Av
Dickens Close
Newbold Close
Brushfield Av
Storer Cl
Cauby Cl
Hg Rd
Peashill Close
Cemetery Rd
Avenue Road
Ward's Crs
Albion Road
Brook
Back La
Manor Drive
Melody Drive
Kilbourne Close
Staveley Close
Butler Way
Phoenix Drive
Butler Wy
Gray La
Kendal Rd
Milner Close
Flaxland Crescent
Charles Street
Sherrard Dr
Wallace Dr
Lynton Cl
Quaker Rd
Chalfont Drive
Molyneux Drive
Cossington Road
LC
Blackberry Lane
Humble Lane
Bennett's Lane
Hall Cl
Homestead Close
Fisher Close
Main Street
Back Lane
M Rd
Middlefield Road
Lane
Syston Road
A607 SYSTON ROAD
COSSINGTON LANE
A607
Rosminian Way
Peake House Farm
33
44
51
61
62
15
14
13
E
F
G
H
I
2
3
4
5

44
A
B
34
C
D
462
63
Spinney Farm
Leicestershire Way
Leicestershire Way
A46
1
15
Thrussington Road
Ratcliffe College
Rosminian Way
2
Main Street
Church La
Ratcliffe on the Wreake
Ratcliffe Road
Priory Farm
Humble Lane
3
Lodge
43
Broome Lane
14
River Wreake
Golf Course
4
Wreake House Farm
Beedles Lake Golf Centre
Industrial Estate
The Warren
The Warren
The Burrows
The Warren
The Warren
Craftsmans Way
Woodman Chase
Saddler Close
5
SYSTON ROAD
A607
COSSINGTON
LANE
313
462
63
A607
A
B
52
C
D
Lewin Bridge
New Zealand Lane
1 grid square represents 500 metres
Bourden Farm

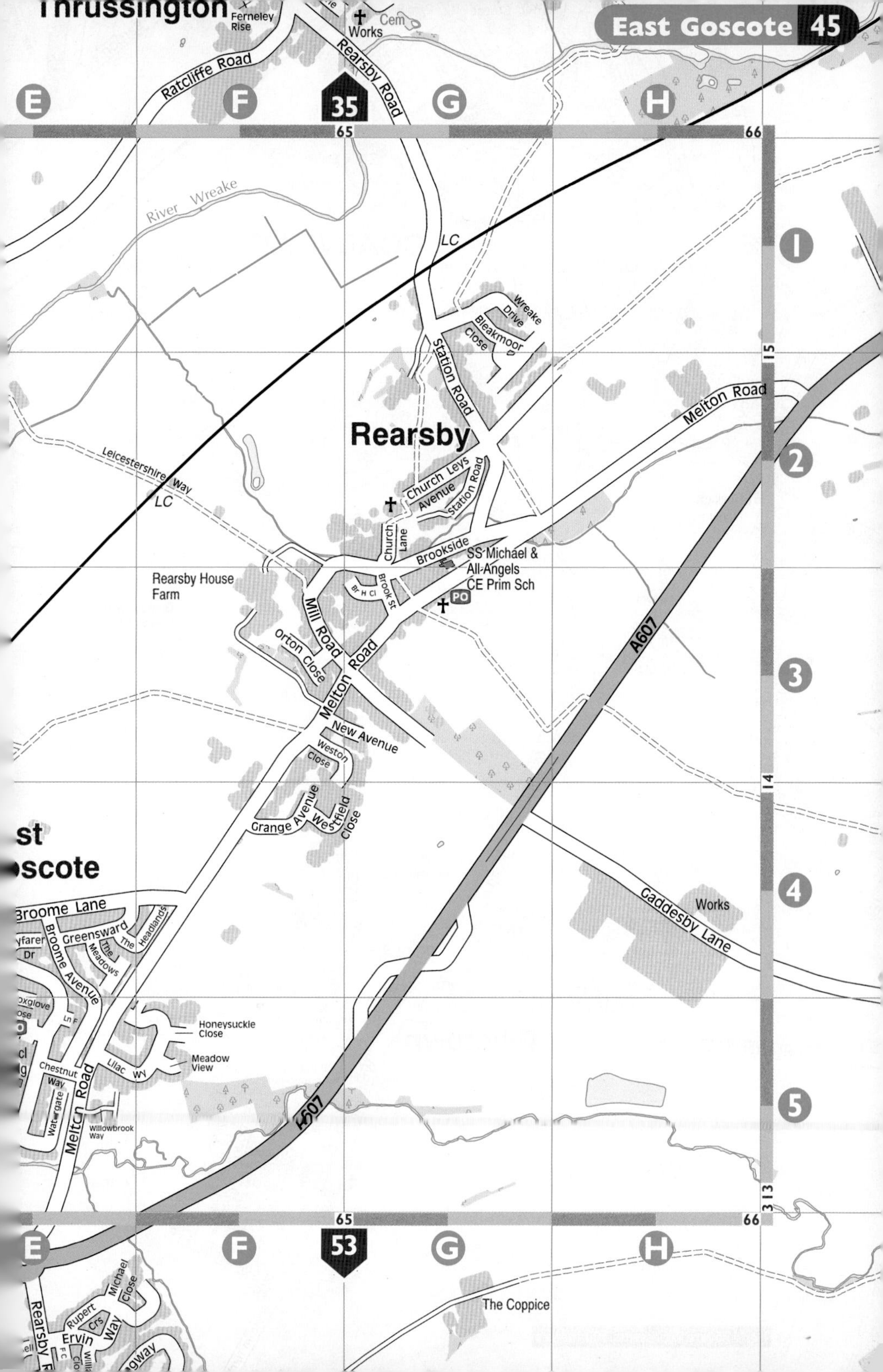
Thrussington
Ferneley Rise
Works
Cem
Ratcliffe Road
Rearsby Road
35
E
F
G
H
65
66
River Wreake
LC
Wreake Drive
Bleakmoor Close
Station Road
Melton Road
Rearsby
Leicestershire Way
LC
Church Leys Avenue
Station Road
Church Lane
Brookside
SS Michael & All Angels CE Prim Sch
PO
Rearsby House Farm
Br H Cl
Brook St
Mill Road
Orton Close
Melton Road
A607
New Avenue
Weston Close
Grange Avenue
Westfield Close
Caddesby Lane
Works
Broome Lane
Broome Avenue
Greensward
The Meadows
The Headlands
Honeysuckle Close
Meadow View
Lilac Wy
Chestnut Way
Watergate
Melton Road
Willowbrook Way
A607
53
The Coppice
Rearsby Rd
Rupert Crs
Ervin Way
Michael Close
I
2
3
4
5
15
14
313

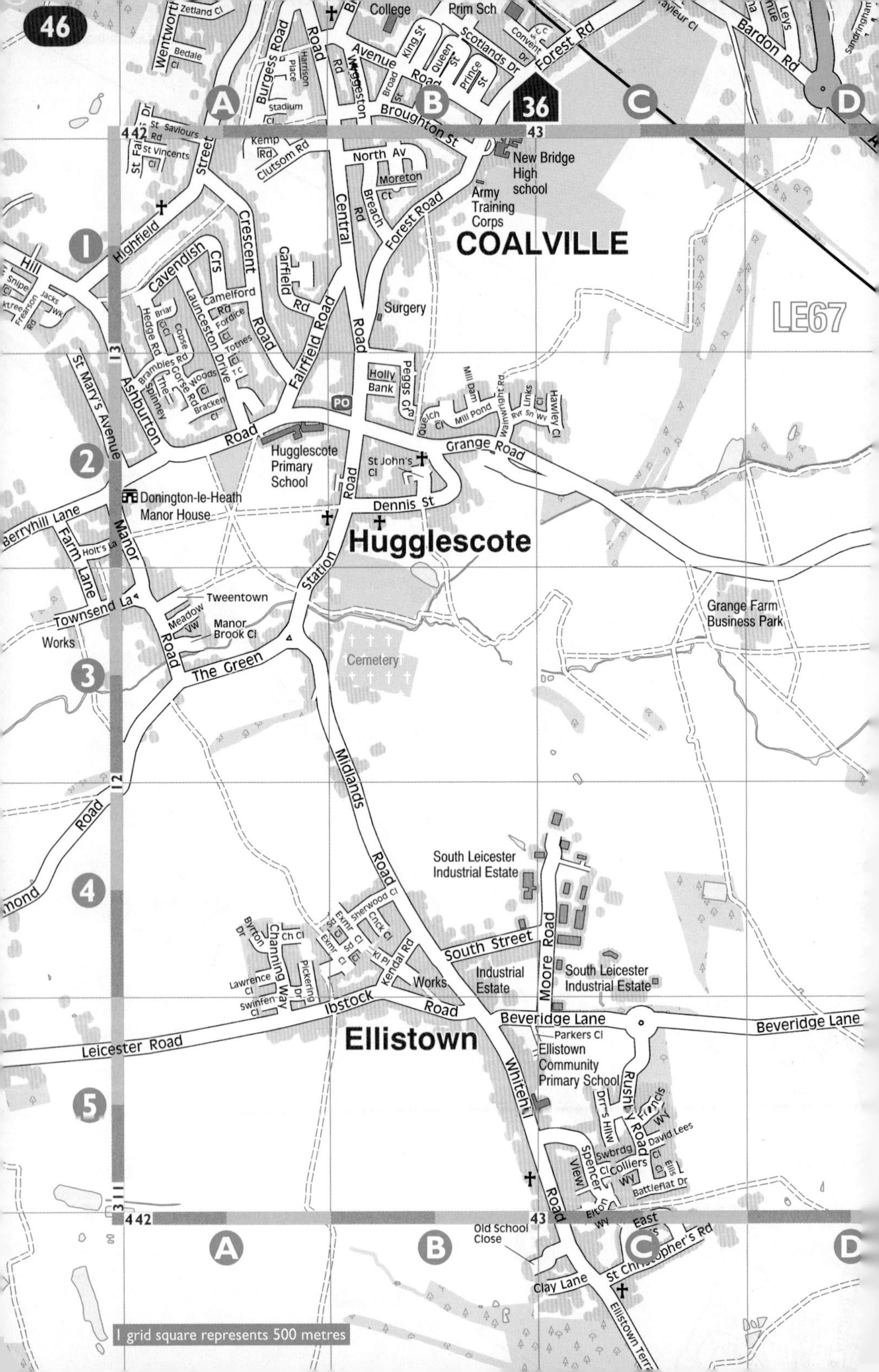

46
36
COALVILLE
Hugglescote
Ellistown
LE67
New Bridge High school
Army Training Corps
Surgery
PO
Hugglescote Primary School
Donington-le-Heath Manor House
Tweentown
Works
Cemetery
Grange Farm Business Park
South Leicester Industrial Estate
Industrial Estate
Ellistown Community Primary School
Old School Close
College
Prim Sch
Convent
Stadium
Forest Rd
Bardon Rd
Broughton St
North Av
Central Road
Forest Road
Highfield Street
Crescent Road
Cavendish Crs
Launceston Drive
Fairfield Road
Ashburton Road
St Mary's Avenue
Grange Road
Dennis St
Station Road
Berryhill Lane
Manor Road
Farm Lane
Townsend La
The Green
Midlands Road
South Street
Moore Road
Ibstock Road
Leicester Road
Beveridge Lane
Whitehill Road
Rushby Road
Spencer View
Clay Lane
St Christopher's Rd
Ellistown Terrace
Channing Way
Kendal Rd
Parkers Cl
Battleflat Dr
1 grid square represents 500 metres

Greenhill
Sycamore Rd
RAF Building
Forest Way School
Cropston
Swithland Rd
Beacon Crs
Longcliff Rd
Blackbrook Dr
Clarke Rd
Hall
Kay Cl
Harker Dr
Waterworks Road
Trent Br
The Oval
Bardon Cl
Brooker Cl
Staples Drive
Bradgate
Willn Cl
37
E
F
G
H
I
45
46
13
12
11
2
3
4
5
ROAD
Bardon
Works
LC
BARDON ROAD
A511
Bardon Hall
Brook Farm
Regs Way
Franks Road
Walker Rd
Walker Road
Tara St
Dromintee Rd
Forest Business Park
BEVERIDGE LANE
Beveridge Lane
East Lane
A511
SHAW LA
Hilltop Industrial Estate
Bardon Industrial Estate
Works
Interlink Way East
South Lane
WEST LANE
B585
Battle Flat
Quarry
Battleflat Lodge Farm
WEST LANE

48
Main Street
40
Main Street
Swithland St Leonard CE Primary Sch
Charnia Gv
Leicester Lane
Swithland Wood
Cropston Leys
Bybrook Lodge Farm
Swithland Road
Road
Bradgate
Roecliffe Road
Bradgate Rd
Lodge La
Reservoir Road
Cropston Reservoir
Guild Cl
Stamford Dr
Thistle
PO
Fox Hllw
Waterfield Rd
Outfields Dr
Waterfield Road
Ridley Cl
Causeway Lane
Lychgate Cl
Cropston Road
Cro
A
B
C
D
1
2
3
4
5
454
55
13
12
311
1 grid square represents 500 metres

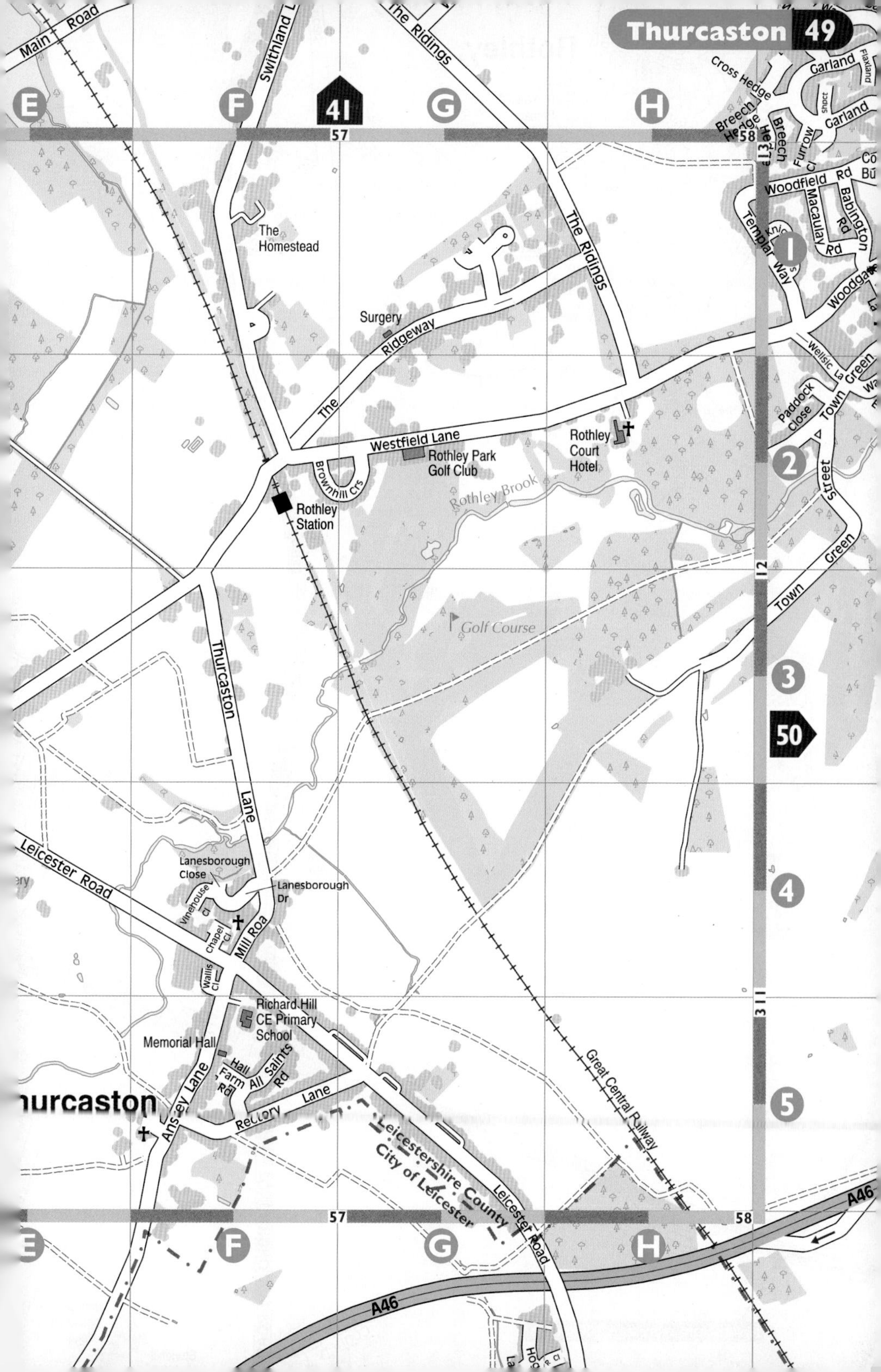
Main Road
Swithland L
The Ridings
41
E
F
G
H
57
58
Cross Hedge
Garland
Breech Hedge
Breech
Furrow Cl
Garland
Woodfield Rd
Macaulay Rd
Babington Rd
Templar Way
1
Woodgate
The Homestead
The Ridings
Surgery
Ridgeway
The
Wellsic La
Town Green
Paddock Close
Westfield Lane
Rothley Park Golf Club
Rothley Court Hotel
Brownhill Crs
Rothley Station
Rothley Brook
2
Street
Town Green
Golf Course
Thurcaston Lane
3
50
Leicester Road
Lanesborough Close
Lanesborough Dr
Vinehouse Cl
Chapel Cl
Mill Road
4
Wallis Cl
Richard Hill CE Primary School
Memorial Hall
Hall Farm Rd
All Saints Rd
Anstey Lane
Rectory Lane
Thurcaston
Great Central Railway
5
Leicestershire County
City of Leicester
Leicester Road
A46
57
58
E
F
G
H
A46

Rothley
Windmill End
Garland
Flaxland
Cross Hedge
Breech Hedge
Breach Hedge
Furrow Cl
Lane
Farnham Cl
Rothley CE Primary School
Homefield
42
Grangefields Drive
Grangefields Dr
Road
ROAD
The Rise
Hickling Cl
Lane
Council Building
Woodfield Rd
Macaulay Rd
Babington Rd
The Roods
PO
Cross Gn
Greenway Cl
Fowke Street
Templar Way
Knight's Crs
Woodgate
Howe La
North St
Anthony Street
School St
Cossington
Wellsic La
Green Street
Hallfields Lane
Walkers La
Forge End
Paddock Close
Town Green Street
Loughborough Rd
LOUGHBOROUGH ROAD
A6
Town Green
49
Wanlip Hill
Council Building
A46
Rectory
A46
A6 LOUGHBOROUGH ROAD
Connery Leys
Longslade Community College
Stonehill
A
B
C
D
1
2
3
4
5
458
59
13
12
311
1 grid square represents 500 metres

Platts Lane
Syston Road
Grange
43
A607 SYSTON ROAD
COSSINGTON LANE
A607
Chestnut Farm
Lewin Bridge
A46
Fosse Way
Works
Meadow Lane
Grand Union Canal
Ind Est
The Half Cft
High
Industrial Estate
Harcourt Close
52
Glebe Way
Wren Close
Teal Way
Swallow Drive
Mallard Drive
Martin Drive
Swift Close
St Columba Way
Glebe Way
Moorland Rd
Cygnet Cl
Blackthorn Dr
Iona Road
Priory Close
Lindisfarne Road
Abbotts Cl
Wolsey Way
Syston Station
Necton
Taylor Cl
A46
Wanlip Road
A607
Sedgefield Dr
Heath Avenue
Willow Walk
Corse Lane
Wanlip Road
Cranmer Dr
Hardwick Crs
Chatsworth Dr
Haddon Cl
The Pastures
Works
Industrial Estate
Archdale Street
Maiden Street
Fosse Way
Wanlip Road
Bruxby St
St Ad Av
Station Rd
Millers Close
The Firs
Lindum Close
Hadrian Close
Marcus Close
Augustus Close
Roundhill Close
Senator Cl
The Meadway
Roman Way
Trojan Wy
Fosse Way
Oliver Close
Dwyer Cl
Wilkes Wy
Simpson Close
Barkby Lane
Clover Wy
Watermead Country Park
nlip
61
62
Melton Road
Roundhill Community College
Britannia Way
Post Road
A607

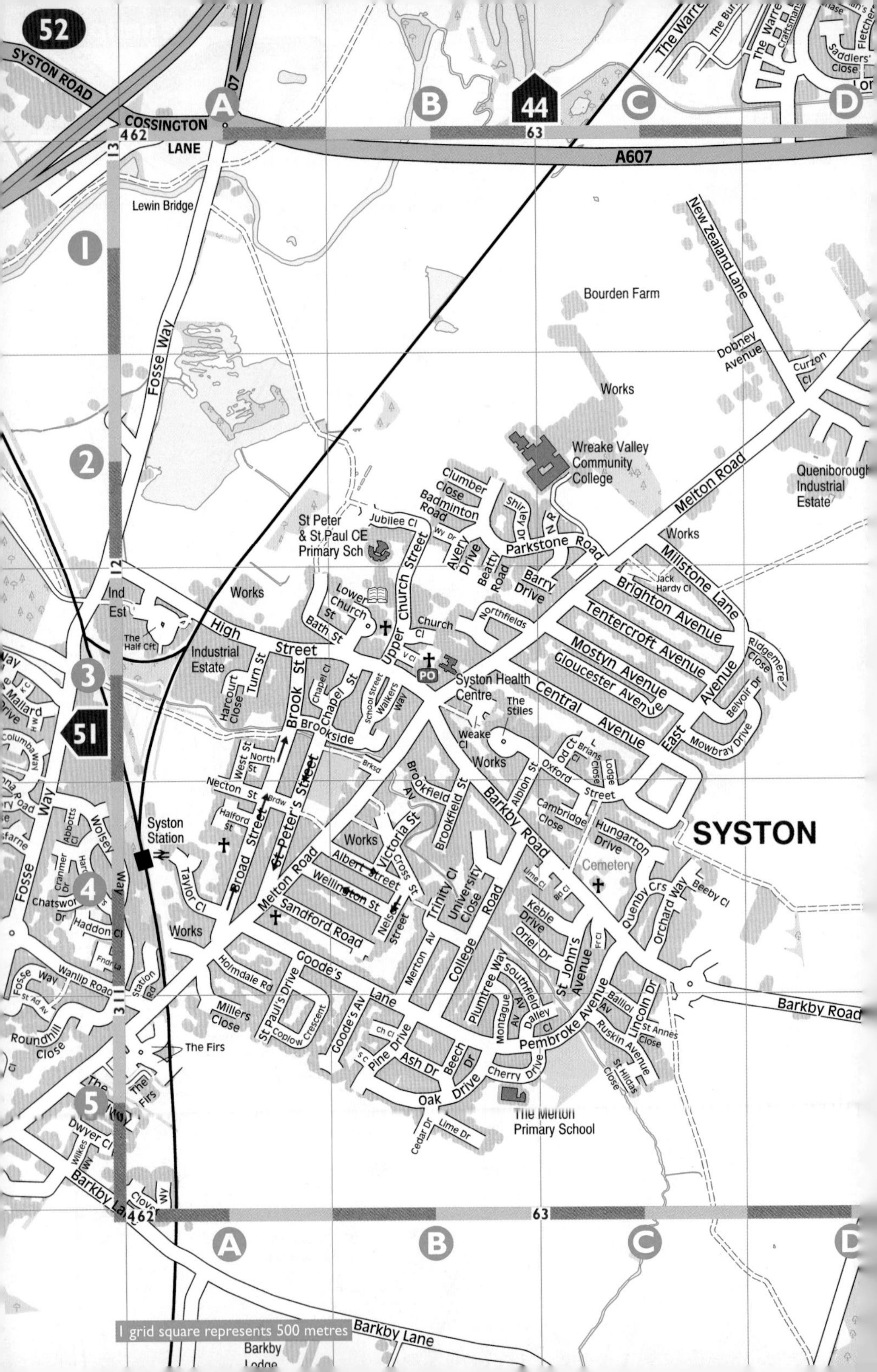
52
44
51
SYSTON ROAD
COSSINGTON LANE
A607
Lewin Bridge
Fosse Way
Bourden Farm
New Zealand Lane
Works
Dobney Avenue
Curzon Cl
Wreake Valley Community College
Queniborough Industrial Estate
Melton Road
St Peter & St Paul CE Primary Sch
Jubilee Cl
Upper Church Street
Clumber Close
Badminton Road
Parkstone Road
Millstone Lane
Brighton Avenue
Tentercroft Avenue
Mostyn Avenue
Gloucester Avenue
Central Avenue
East Avenue
Mowbray Drive
Belvoir Dr
Ridgemere Close
Avery Drive
Beatty Road
Barry Drive
Northfields
Lower Church St
Bath St
Church Cl
Ind Est
The Half Cft
High Street
Industrial Estate
Turn St
Harcourt Close
Brook St
Chapel St
Chapel Cl
School Street
Walkers Way
Brookside
Syston Health Centre
The Stiles
Weake Cl
Works
Albion St
Oxford Street
Brians Close
Lodge Close
SYSTON
Hungarton Drive
Cambridge Close
Cemetery
Beeby Cl
Orchard Way
Quenby Crs
Barkby Road
Brookfield St
Brookfield Av
Victoria St
Cross St
Albert Street
Wellington St
Nelson Street
Trinity Cl
University Close
College Road
Keble Drive
Oriel Dr
St John's Avenue
Lincoln Dr
Balliol Av
Ruskin Avenue
St Annes Close
St Hildas Close
Pembroke Avenue
Dalley Cl
Southfield Av
Montague Av
Plumtree Way
Cherry Drive
The Merton Primary School
Oak Drive
Beech Dr
Ash Dr
Pine Drive
Ch Cl
Cedar Dr
Lime Dr
Goode's Lane
Goode's Av
St Paul's Drive
Coplow Crescent
Holmdale Rd
Millers Close
Sandford Road
Melton Road
St Peter's Street
Broad Street
West St
North St
Necton St
Halford St
Syston Station
Taylor Cl
Works
Fosse Way
Wolsey Way
Abbotts Cl
Cranmer Dr
Chatsworth Dr
Haddon Cl
Wanlip Road
Station Rd
Roundhill Close
The Firs
Dwyer Cl
Wilkes Wy
Barkby La
Clover Wy
Barkby Lane
Barkby Lodge
Columba Way
Mallard Drive
1 grid square represents 500 metres

45
E
F
G
H
65
66
A607
Melton Road
Chestnut Way
Watergate
Willowbrook Way
The Coppice
Rearsby Road
Rupert Crs
Michael Close
Ervin Way
William Close
Bluebell
The Ringway
Coppice Lane
Queniborough Road
PO
Gascoigne Avenue
Glebe Road
The Banks
Queniborough CE Primary School
Peggs Lane
Main Street
Queniborough Hall
Hall Farm Close
School Lane
Mere Lane
Queniborough
Croxton Road
Cemetery
Ridge Farm
gemere Lane
Ridgemere Lane
New
1
2
3
4
5
13
12
11

A
B
C
D
474
75
1
2
3
4
5
21
20
319
A606
NOTTINGHAM ROAD
Scalford Road
John Ferneley
High School
Sysonby
Lodge
St Bartholomews Way
Sthwll Cl
Wn Dr
Canterbury Dr
W Cl
Brampton Rd
St Marys
CE Primary
School
Coniston Rd
Lynton Rd
Krtn Dr
Cavalry Cl
Palmerston Rd
Abingdon Road
Lancers Dr
Dulverton Rd
Alvs Rd
Gldstn Av
Grnvll
Road
Beaconsfield
Road
Hillside Av
Nttnghm Rd
Highfield Avenue
Everest
Drive
James Lm Dr
Newbury Av
Elmhurst Av
Welby Lane
Garden La
Grdn La
Mayfield St
Bd St
Sd St
Horse Fld Vw
Wellington Wy
PO
Morley
Close
Horse Field
View
Sysonby St
Avenue
East Av
Jrvs Dr
Douglas
Jane Cl
Greaves Av
Staveley
Road
West
Rockingham
Dr
Arden
Dr
Charnwood Dr
Sherwood Dr
Brightside
Avenue
Dorothy Avenue
Rudbeck Avenue
Petersfield Rd
Weaver Gn
Stirling Road
West Avenue
Council
Building
Quorn
Lodge
Hotel
Fernie Av
Ct Av
A6006
Darcy Gdns
Scalford
Road
Bnntt Dr
M H Cl
Fld L
Dickens Drive
Glswrt Crs
Melbray Drive
Brwnng
Close
Burns Cl
Tennyson Way
K Cl
Tn Wy
Tn Wy
Kipling Dr
Sh Av
Milton
Close
Byron Way
Shphds Cft
Dieppe Way
Dieppe Wy
Dpp Way
Balmoral Rd
Ludlow
Drive
Hn Dr
Conway
Drive
St John's
Maple
Cl
Birch Cl
Ash Gv
Lilac Wy
Cedar Dr
D Mntfrt
Sycmr
Close
The Crescent
Newport A
Clumber St
Road
Nrthfld Cl
Layc
Elgin
Elgin Dr
County
Court
Scalford
North
Tdg &
Ind Est
Soho St
Cht St
A607
WILTON RD
Pk Rd
Wilton Ter
Nottingham St
Cts
Grove
Primary
School
P
Brooksby Melton
College (Melton
Campus)
High St
Market Pl
LEICESTER ST
LE13
Park Av
ASFORDBY
ROAD
Clingw Cl
Collingwood Crs
Melbourne
Drive
Sysonby Knoll
Hotel
Chetwynd Dr
Sysonby Grange Lane
Riverside Rd
Egerton Vw
LEICESTER ROAD
Leisure
Pools
56
Lake Ter
Rd
Oxbow
Close
Lake Ter
A607
Council
Bldg
Birch Wood
School
Navigation
Close
The
Uplands
Pochin Cl
Melton
Mowbra
Station
DALBY
Park La
1 grid square represents 500 metres

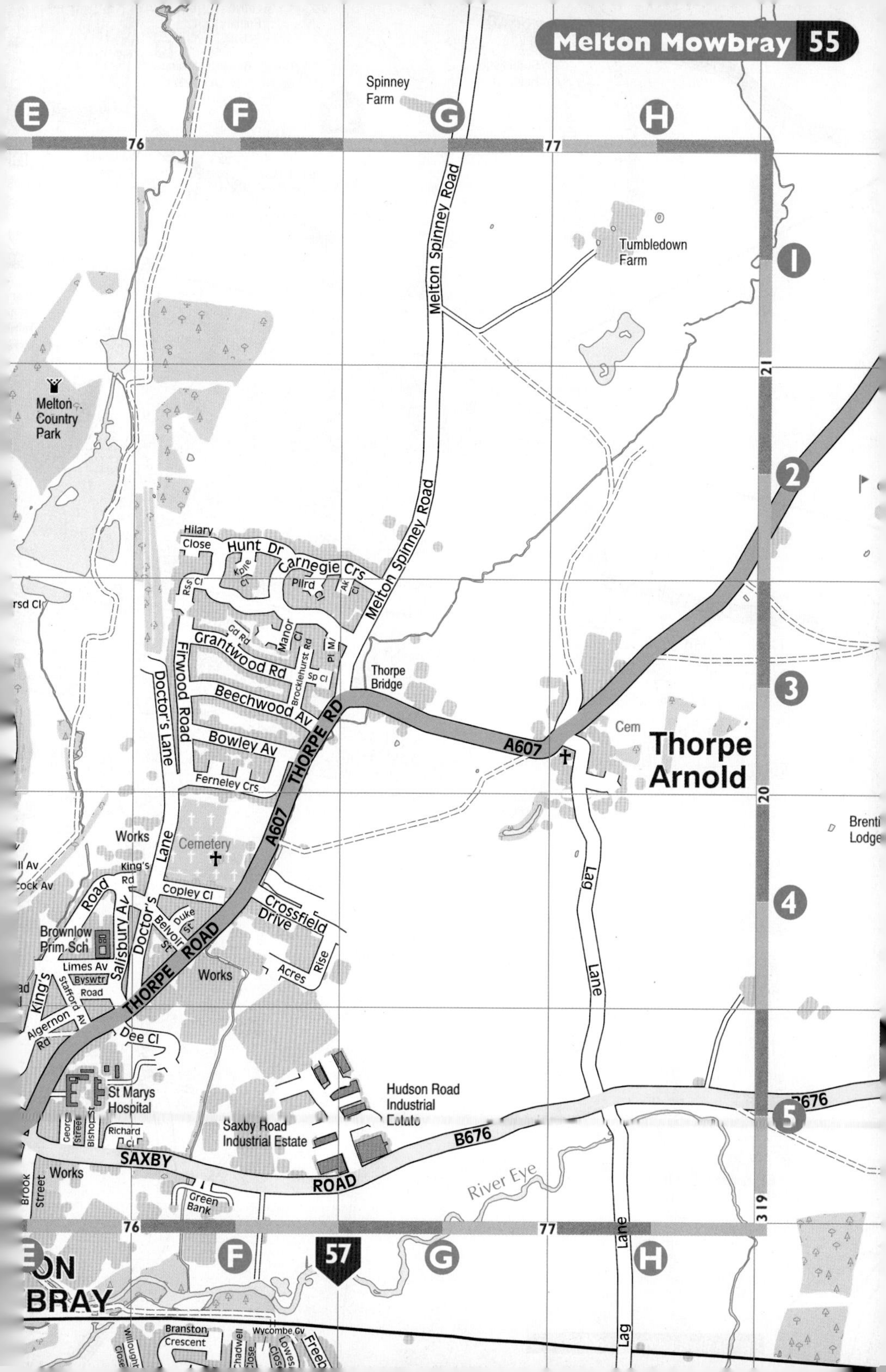
Spinney Farm
E
F
G
H
76
77
Melton Spinney Road
Tumbledown Farm
1
Melton Country Park
21
2
Hilary Close
Hunt Dr
Carnegie Crs
Rss Cl
Pllrd Cl
Ak Cl
Grantwood Rd
Manor Cl
Brocklehurst Rd
Sp Cl
Firwood Road
Doctor's Lane
Beechwood Av
Thorpe Bridge
3
Bowley Av
THORPE RD
A607
Cem
Thorpe Arnold
Ferneley Crs
20
Brenti Lodge
Works
Cemetery
King's Rd
Copley Cl
Crossfield Drive
Lag Lane
Road
4
Brownlow Prim Sch
Salisbury Av
Doctor's
Belvoir St
Duke St
THORPE ROAD
Limes Av
Byswtr
Stafford Av
Road
Works
Acres Rise
King's
Algernon Rd
Dee Cl
Hudson Road Industrial Estate
St Marys Hospital
B676
5
Saxby Road Industrial Estate
Richard Cl
Bishop St
George Street
SAXBY ROAD
Works
Brook Street
River Eye
Green Bank
319
57
ON BRAY
Branston Crescent
Wycombe Gv
Chadwell Close
Lowes Close
Freeb
Willoughby Close
Lag Lane

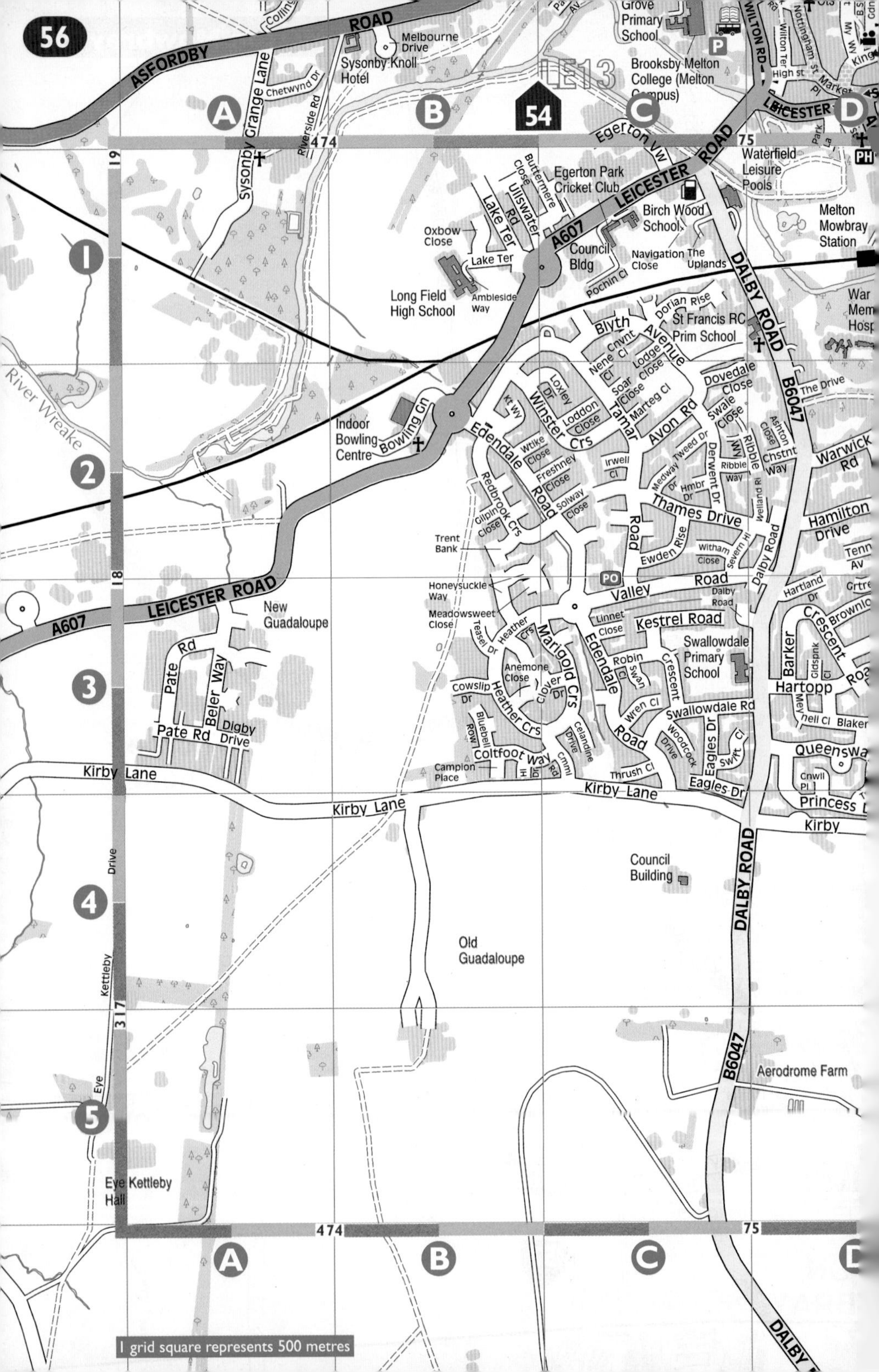
ASFORDBY ROAD
Melbourne Drive
Sysonby Knoll Hotel
Chetwynd Dr
Sysonby Grange Lane
Riverside Rd
LE13
54
Grove Primary School
Brooksby Melton College (Melton Campus)
WILTON RD
Wilton Ter
Nottingham St
High St
Market Pl
LEICESTER
Egerton Vw
LEICESTER ROAD
A607
Waterfield Leisure Pools
Melton Mowbray Station
Buttermere Close
Ullswater Rd
Lake Ter
Oxbow Close
Egerton Park Cricket Club
Birch Wood School
Council Bldg
Navigation Close
The Uplands
Pochin Cl
Long Field High School
Ambleside Way
Dorian Rise
Blyth Avenue
St Francis RC Prim School
DALBY ROAD
War Mem Hosp
River Wreake
Nene Cl
Cnvnt Cl
Lodge Close
Soar Close
Loxley Dr
Winster Crs
Loddon Close
Tamar Road
Marteg Cl
Avon Rd
Dovedale Close
Swale Close
B6047
The Drive
Kt Wy
Indoor Bowling Centre
Bowling Gn
Edendale Road
Wtlke Close
Freshney Close
Irwell Cl
Medway
Tweed Dr
Hmbr Dr
Derwent Dr
Wy
Ribble Way
Ribble
Ashton Close
Chstnt Way
Warwick Rd
Redbrook Crs
Gilpin Close
Solway Close
Thames Drive
Welland Rl
Hamilton Drive
Trent Bank
Ewden Rise
Witham Close
Severn Hl
Dalby Road
Tenn Av
PO
Valley Road
Dalby Road
Hartland Dr
Grtre
Honeysuckle Way
Meadowsweet Close
LEICESTER ROAD
A607
New Guadaloupe
Linnet Close
Kestrel Road
Barker Crescent
Brownlo
Teasel Dr
Heather Crs
Marigold Crs
Edendale Road
Robin Cl
Swan
Crescent
Swallowdale Primary School
Gldspnk Cl
Pate Rd
Beler Way
Anemone Close
Clover Dr
Hartopp Ro
Cowslip Dr
Heather Crs
Wren Cl
Swallowdale Rd
Meynell Cl
Blaker
Digby Drive
Pate Rd
Bluebell Row
Celandine Drive
Woodcock Drive
Eagles Dr
Swift Cl
Queensway
Coltfoot Way
Campion Place
Hl
Rd
Cnml
Thrush Cl
Cnwll Pl
Kirby Lane
Kirby Lane
Kirby Lane
Eagles Dr
Princess D
Kirby
Council Building
Kettleby Drive
Old Guadaloupe
Aerodrome Farm
Eye Kettleby Hall
DALBY ROAD
DALBY
474
75
19
18
317
A
B
C
D
1
2
3
4
5
1 grid square represents 500 metres

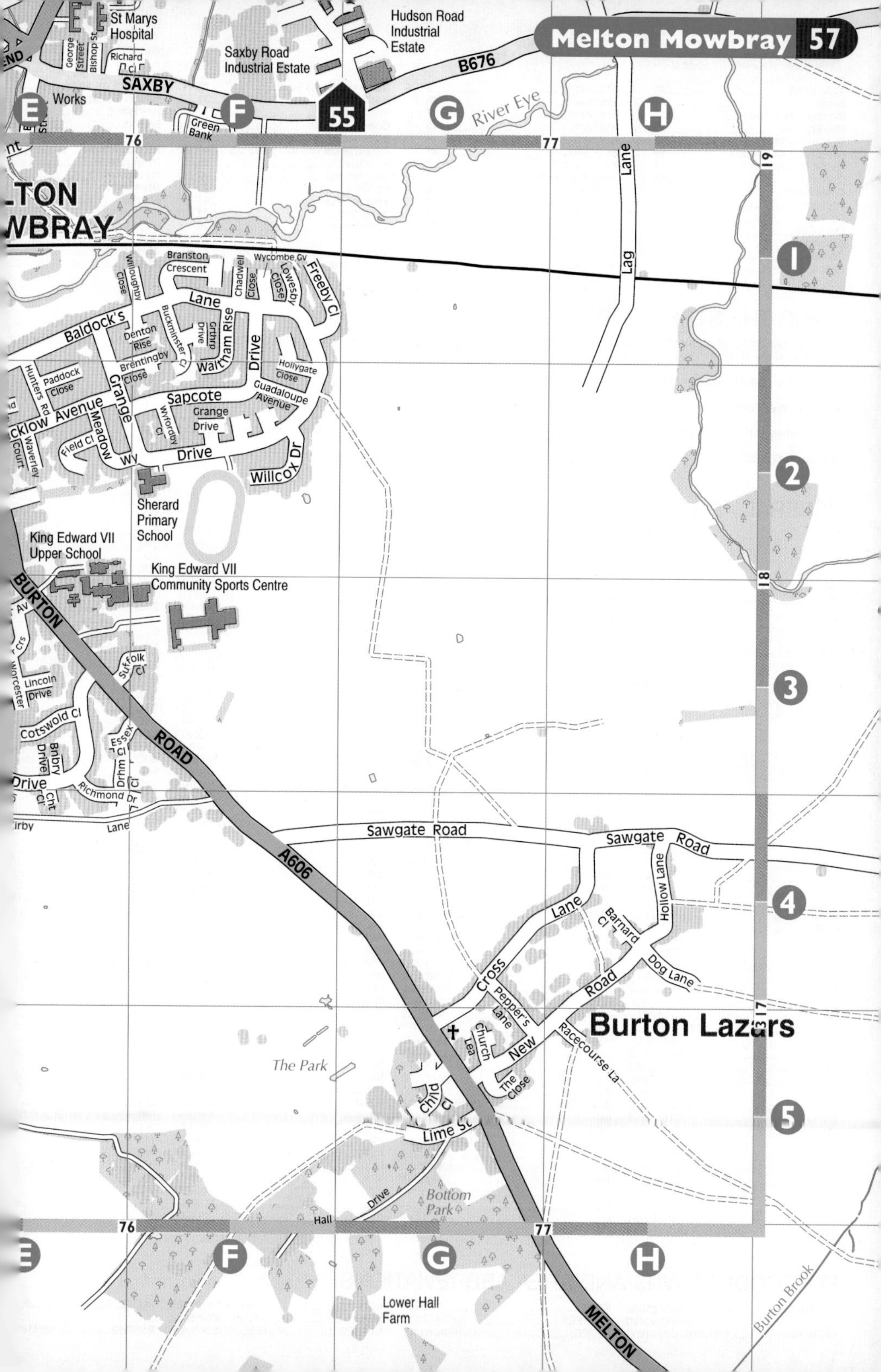
St Marys Hospital
Hudson Road Industrial Estate
Saxby Road Industrial Estate
George Street
Bishop St
Richard Cl
SAXBY
B676
Works
55
River Eye
Green Bank
Lag Lane
MELTON MOWBRAY
Branston Crescent
Wycombe Gv
Willoughby Close
Chadwell Close
Lowesby Close
Freeby Cl
Baldock's Lane
Denton Rise
Buckminster Cl
Grthrp Drive
Waltham Rise
Drive
Hollygate Close
Brentingby Close
Hunters Rd
Paddock Close
Grange
Sapcote
Guadaloupe Avenue
Avenue
Meadow
Wyfordby Cl
Grange Drive
Field Cl
Waverley Court
Drive
Willcox Dr
Sherard Primary School
King Edward VII Upper School
King Edward VII Community Sports Centre
BURTON ROAD
Suffolk Cl
Lincoln Drive
Worcester
Cotswold Cl
Essex Cl
Bnbry Drive
Drhm Cl
Drive
Cht Cl
Richmond Dr
Lane
Sawgate Road
A606
Hollow Lane
Barnard Cl
Cross Lane
Dog Lane
Pepper's Lane
New Road
Burton Lazars
Church Lea
Racecourse La
The Close
The Park
Child Cl
Lime St
Bottom Park
Hall Drive
Lower Hall Farm
MELTON
Burton Brook
76
77
E
F
G
H
1
2
3
4
5
19
18
17

USING THE STREET INDEX

Street names are listed alphabetically. Each street name is followed by its postal town or area locality, the Postcode District, the page number, and th reference to the square in which the name is found.

Standard index entries are shown as follows:

Abberton Wy *LBORO* LE11 ....**22** A4

Street names and selected addresses not shown on the map due to scale restrictions are shown in the index with an asterisk:

Beaumont Ct *LBORO* LE11 * **16** C5

GENERAL ABBREVIATIONS

ACC ACCESS
ALY ALLEY
AP APPROACH
AR ARCADE
ASS ASSOCIATION
AV AVENUE
BCH BEACH
BLDS BUILDINGS
BND BEND
BNK BANK
BR BRIDGE
BRK BROOK
BTM BOTTOM
BUS BUSINESS
BVD BOULEVARD
BY BYPASS
CATH CATHEDRAL
CEM CEMETERY
CEN CENTRE
CFT CROFT
CH CHURCH
CHA CHASE
CHYD CHURCHYARD
CIR CIRCLE
CIRC CIRCUS
CL CLOSE
CLFS CLIFFS
CMP CAMP
CNR CORNER
CO COUNTY
COLL COLLEGE
COM COMMON
COMM COMMISSION
CON CONVENT
COT COTTAGE
COTS COTTAGES
CP CAPE
CPS COPSE
CR CREEK
CREM CREMATORIUM
CRS CRESCENT
CSWY CAUSEWAY
CT COURT
CTRL CENTRAL
CTS COURTS
CTYD COURTYARD
CUTT CUTTINGS
CV COVE
CYN CANYON
DEPT DEPARTMENT
DL DALE
DM DAM
DR DRIVE
DRO DROVE
DRY DRIVEWAY
DWGS DWELLINGS
E EAST
EMB EMBANKMENT
EMBY EMBASSY
ESP ESPLANADE
EST ESTATE
EX EXCHANGE
EXPY EXPRESSWAY
EXT EXTENSION
F/O FLYOVER
FC FOOTBALL CLUB
FK FORK
FLD FIELD
FLDS FIELDS
FLS FALLS
FM FARM
FT FORT
FTS FLATS
FWY FREEWAY
FY FERRY
GA GATE
GAL GALLERY
GDN GARDEN
GDNS GARDENS
GLD GLADE
GLN GLEN
GN GREEN
GND GROUND
GRA GRANGE
GRG GARAGE
GT GREAT
GTWY GATEWAY
GV GROVE
HGR HIGHER
HL HILL
HLS HILLS
HO HOUSE
HOL HOLLOW
HOSP HOSPITAL
HRB HARBOUR
HTH HEATH
HTS HEIGHTS
HVN HAVEN
HWY HIGHWAY
IMP IMPERIAL
IN INLET
IND EST INDUSTRIAL ESTATE
INF INFIRMARY
INFO INFORMATION
INT INTERCHANGE
IS ISLAND
JCT JUNCTION
JTY JETTY
KG KING
KNL KNOLL
L LAKE
LA LANE
LDG LODGE
LGT LIGHT
LK LOCK
LKS LAKES
LNDG LANDING
LTL LITTLE
LWR LOWER
MAG MAGISTRATES'
MAN MANSIONS
MD MEAD
MDW MEADOWS
MEM MEMORIAL
MI MILL
MKT MARKET
MKTS MARKETS
ML MALL
MNR MANOR
MS MEWS
MSN MISSION
MT MOUNT
MTN MOUNTAIN
MTS MOUNTAINS
MUS MUSEUM
MWY MOTORWAY
N NORTH
NE NORTH EAST
NW NORTH WEST
O/P OVERPASS
OFF OFFICE
ORCH ORCHARD
OV OVAL
PAL PALACE
PAS PASSAGE
PAV PAVILION
PDE PARADE
PH PUBLIC HOUSE
PK PARK
PKWY PARKWAY
PL PLACE
PLN PLAIN
PLNS PLAINS
PLZ PLAZA
POL POLICE STATION
PR PRINCE
PREC PRECINCT
PREP PREPARATORY
PRIM PRIMARY
PROM PROMENADE
PRS PRINCESS
PRT PORT
PT POINT
PTH PATH
PZ PIAZZA
QD QUADRANT
QU QUEEN
QY QUAY
R
RBT RO
RD
RDG
REP
RES
RFC RUGBY FOO
RI
RP
RW
S
SCH
SE
SER SE
SH
SHOP
SKWY
SMT
SOC
SP
SPR
SQ
ST
STN
STR
STRD
SW
TDG
TER
THWY T
TNL
TOLL
TPK
TR
TRL
TWR
U/P
UNI
UPR
V
VA
VIAD
VIL
VIS
VLG
VLS
VW
W
WD
WHF
WK
WKS
WLS
WY
YD
YHA Y

POSTCODE TOWNS AND AREA ABBREVIATIONS

CDON/KEG Castle Donington/Kegworth
CFTN/RUD Clifton/Ruddington
COAL Coalville
GBY/RBY Groby/Ratby
LBORO Loughborough
LEIN Leicester north
MMWB Melton Mowbray
RLBORO Rural Loughborough
RLEINE/SYS Rural Leic
RMMWB Rural Me

A

B

C

D

E

F

G

H

I

J

K

L

M

N

O

Orton Cl *RLEINE/SYS* LE7 45 F3
Orwell Cl *LBORO* LE11 15 H5
Osborne Rd *LBORO* LE11 15 G5
Osier Flds *RLBORO* LE12 8 C3
The Osiers *CDON/KEG* DE74 7 E3
LBORO LE11 29 G2
RLEINE/SYS LE7 41 G3
Osterley Cl *LBORO* LE11 22 C2
Otter La *RLBORO* LE12 42 B2
Outfields Dr *RLEINE/SYS* LE7 48 D5
Outwoods Dr *LBORO* LE11 23 F4
Outwoods Rd *LBORO* LE11 29 F1
The Oval *COAL* LE67 47 E1
Owen Crs *MMWB* LE13 55 E4
Owen Dr *MMWB* LE13 55 E3
Owen St *COAL* LE67 36 A4
Oxbow Cl *MMWB* LE13 56 B1
Oxburgh Cl *LBORO* LE11 22 C1
Oxford Ct *RLEINE/SYS* LE7 52 C3
Oxford Dr *MMWB* LE13 56 D3
Oxford St *COAL* LE67 36 C4
LBORO LE11 2 D3
RLBORO LE12 20 D4
RLEINE/SYS LE7 52 C3
Oxley Cl *RLBORO* LE12 20 C3

P

Packe St *LBORO* LE11 3 F4
Pack Horse La *LBORO* LE11 3 H5
Packington Hl *CDON/KEG* DE74 6 C3
Paddock Cl *CDON/KEG* DE74 4 B2
MMWB LE13 57 E2
RLBORO LE12 31 E4
RLEINE/SYS LE7 50 A2
The Paddocks *RLBORO* LE12 13 F2
The Paddock *RLBORO* LE12 20 D3
Paddock Vw *RLEINE/SYS* LE7 51 H4
Page La *CDON/KEG* DE74 10 C3
Paget St *LBORO* LE11 2 D3
Pall Ml *MMWB* LE13 55 F3
Palmer Av *LBORO* LE11 2 C1
Palmerston Rd *MMWB* LE13 54 B2
Pantain Rd *LBORO* LE11 29 E1
Pares Cl *COAL* LE67 26 C5
Park Av *CDON/KEG* DE74 4 B2
LBORO LE11 23 H5
MMWB LE13 54 C5
RLBORO LE12 21 E4
Park Cl *RLBORO* LE12 20 D2
Parkers Cl *COAL* LE67 46 C5
Parkers Flds *RLBORO* LE12 31 E2
Park Hill La *RLBORO* LE12 34 A2
Parklands Dr *LBORO* LE11 29 G1
Park La *CDON/KEG* DE74 4 C2
MMWB LE13 54 D5
RLBORO LE12 13 F2
Park Ri *RLBORO* LE12 20 D3
Park Rd *COAL* LE67 36 B4
LBORO LE11 3 F6
LBORO LE11 29 G1
MMWB LE13 54 D5
RLBORO LE12 33 E5
Parkstone Rd *RLEINE/SYS* LE7 52 B2
Park St *LBORO* LE11 3 G6
Parkyns Piece *RLBORO* LE12 8 C3
Parsons Dr *RLBORO* LE12 33 G5
Parsonwood Hl *COAL* LE67 26 C5
Partridge Cl *RLBORO* LE12 42 B2
RLEINE/SYS LE7 51 H3
Pasture La *RLBORO* LE12 15 E2
The Pastures *RLBORO* LE12 32 A3
RLEINE/SYS LE7 51 G4
Pate Rd *MMWB* LE13 56 A3
Paterson Dr *RLBORO* LE12 39 F3
Paterson Pl *RLBORO* LE12 20 D1
Patterdale Dr *LBORO* LE11 22 C5
Pavilion Wy *LBORO* LE11 16 C4
Peartree Av *RLBORO* LE12 21 F3
Peartree Cl *CDON/KEG* DE74 4 C2
Pear Tree La *LBORO* LE11 15 F5
Peashill Cl *RLBORO* LE12 43 G1
Peel Dr *LBORO* LE11 3 J3
Peggs Gra *COAL* LE67 46 B2
Peggs La *RLEINE/SYS* LE7 53 F2
Peldar Pl *COAL* LE67 37 F5
Pell Cl *RLBORO* LE12 32 A1
Pembroke Av *RLEINE/SYS* LE7 52 B5
Pennine Cl *RLBORO* LE12 21 E4
Penrith Av *RLBORO* LE12 20 B4
Pentland Av *RLBORO* LE12 21 F4
Pepper Dr *RLBORO* LE12 30 D2
Pepper's Cl *RLBORO* LE12 31 H5
Peppers Dr *CDON/KEG* DE74 6 B3
Pepper's La *RMMWB* LE14 57 G4
Perkins Cl *RLBORO* LE12 25 G5
Perran Av *COAL* LE67 37 E3
Perry Cl *RLBORO* LE12 39 F2
Perry Gv *LBORO* LE11 24 A5
Peterfield Rd *COAL* LE67 37 E2
Peter McCaig Wy *RLBORO* LE12 31 E2
Petersfield Rd *MMWB* LE13 54 B4
Petworth Dr *LBORO* LE11 22 C1
Pevensey Rd *LBORO* LE11 2 A1
Phoenix Dr *RLBORO* LE12 43 F2
Pickering Dr *COAL* LE67 46 A4
Pick St *RLBORO* LE12 20 D2
Pine Cl *LBORO* LE11 29 G2
RLBORO LE12 8 B5
Pine Dr *RLEINE/SYS* LE7 52 B5
Pinfold Gdns *LBORO* LE11 3 H3
Pinfold Ga *LBORO* LE11 3 H4
The Pingle *RLBORO* LE12 30 C4
Piper Cl *LBORO* LE11 23 F5
RLBORO LE12 14 A1
Piper Dr *RLBORO* LE12 12 A5
Pitsford Dr *LBORO* LE11 22 A4
Plain Ga *RLEINE/SYS* LE7 41 G4
Platts La *RLEINE/SYS* LE7 43 E5
Pleasant Cl *LBORO* LE11 2 E3
Pleasant Pl *CDON/KEG* DE74 6 D3
Plough Cl *RLBORO* LE12 41 H4
Ploughmans Dr *RLBORO* LE12 21 E1
Ploughman's Lea
RLEINE/SYS LE7 44 D5
Plumtree Cl *LBORO* LE11 16 B5
Plumtree Wy *RLEINE/SYS* LE7 52 B5
Pochin Cl *MMWB* LE13 56 C1
Pochin Wy *RLBORO* LE12 33 F5
Pocket End *LBORO* LE11 28 D1
Polden Cl *RLBORO* LE12 21 E4
Pollard Cl *MMWB* LE13 55 F3
Pond St *RLBORO* LE12 33 H2
Poplar Av *RLBORO* LE12 8 B5
Poplar Rd *LBORO* LE11 29 H1
Poppy Cl *COAL* LE67 37 E5
LBORO LE11 29 G3
Porlock Cl *RLBORO* LE12 21 E4
Pott Acre *RLEINE/SYS* LE7 42 B3
Potters La *RLBORO* LE12 8 C5
Poulteney Dr *RLBORO* LE12 30 C3
Prestbury Rd *LBORO* LE11 22 B2
Preston Cl *RLBORO* LE12 43 E2
Prestwold La *RLBORO* LE12 18 C2
Primerose Wy *RLEINE/SYS* LE7 53 E1
Princess Dr *MMWB* LE13 56 D4
Prince St *COAL* LE67 36 B5
Prince William Rd *LBORO* LE11 16 C5
Priory Cl *COAL* LE67 26 A2
RLEINE/SYS LE7 51 H4
Priory Rd *LBORO* LE11 29 E1
Proctor's Park Rd *RLBORO* LE12 31 G2
Pryor Rd *RLBORO* LE12 33 F5
Pulteney Av *LBORO* LE11 29 H1
Pulteney Rd *LBORO* LE11 29 H1
Purbeck Av *RLBORO* LE12 21 F3
Purley Ri *RLBORO* LE12 21 E4
The Pyke *RLEINE/SYS* LE7 42 B3
Pytchley Dr *LBORO* LE11 29 F1

Q

Quaker Rd *RLBORO* LE12 43 E3
Quantock Ri *RLBORO* LE12 21 E4
The Quay *RLBORO* LE12 41 H1
Queens Rd *CDON/KEG* DE74 6 D2
Queen's Rd *LBORO* LE11 3 J2
Queen St *COAL* LE67 36 B5
LBORO LE11 3 J5
RLBORO LE12 21 E2
Queensway *CDON/KEG* DE74 4 B1
MMWB LE13 56 D3
Quelch Cl *COAL* LE67 46 B2
Quenby Crs *RLEINE/SYS* LE7 52 C4
Queniborough Rd
RLEINE/SYS LE7 53 E2
Quorn Av *MMWB* LE13 54 C5
Quorn Cl *LBORO* LE11 24 A4
Quorn Crs *COAL* LE67 37 F5
Quorndon Ter *RLBORO* LE12 30 D3
Quorndon Waters
RLBORO LE12 30 D3

R

Racecourse La *RMMWB* LE14 57 H5
Radmoor Rd *LBORO* LE11 2 C5
Radnor Dr *RLBORO* LE12 20 D1
Railway Ter *LBORO* LE11 3 K1
Ralph Cl *LBORO* LE11 28 D1
Ratcliffe Rd *LBORO* LE11 3 J1
RLBORO LE12 43 F1
Ravensthorpe Dr *LBORO* LE11 22 B3
Rawdon Cl *CDON/KEG* DE74 4 C1
Rawlins Cl *RLBORO* LE12 39 G3
Raymond Av *LBORO* LE11 15 H5
Raynham Dr *LBORO* LE11 22 C1
Rearsby Rd *RLEINE/SYS* LE7 53 E1
Rectory La *RLEINE/SYS* LE7 49 F5
Rectory Pl *LBORO* LE11 3 G3
Rectory Rd *LBORO* LE11 3 H2
RLEINE/SYS LE7 50 D5
Redbrook Crs *MMWB* LE13 56 B2
Redhill La *COAL* LE67 26 A5
Redmires Cl *LBORO* LE11 22 B3
Redwood Av *MMWB* LE13 54 D4
Redwood Rd *LBORO* LE11 29 G2
Regent Pl *MMWB* LE13 55 E5
Regent St *LBORO* LE11 2 E3
MMWB LE13 57 E1
RLEINE/SYS LE7 35 F5
Regs Wy *COAL* LE67 47 F4
Rempstone Rd *RLBORO* LE12 8 B5
Rendell St *LBORO* LE11 3 G1
Renning End *RLBORO* LE12 42 A4
Reservoir Rd *RLEINE/SYS* LE7 48 B4
The Retreat *RLBORO* LE12 31 H1
Revell Cl *RLBORO* LE12 31 F3
Ribble Dr *RLBORO* LE12 31 H3
Ribble Wy *MMWB* LE13 56 C2
Richard Cl *MMWB* LE13 55 E5
Richmond Dr *MMWB* LE13 57 E3
Ridgemere Cl *RLEINE/SYS* LE7 52 D3
Ridgemere La *RLEINE/SYS* LE7 53 E4
The Ridgeway *RLEINE/SYS* LE7 49 F2
The Ridings *RLEINE/SYS* LE7 49 H1
RLEINE/SYS LE7 53 E2
Ridley Cl *RLEINE/SYS* LE7 48 C5
The Rigsty *RLBORO* LE12 30 C3
Ring Fence *RLBORO* LE12 20 D4
The Ringway *RLEINE/SYS* LE7 53 E1
Ringwood Rd *RLBORO* LE12 20 D1
The Rise *RLEINE/SYS* LE7 50 C1
River Sence Wy *COAL* LE67 46 B2
Riverside Ms *RLEINE/SYS* LE7 51 E5
Riverside Rd *MMWB* LE13 56 A1
River Vw *RLBORO* LE12 32 A3
Rivington Dr *LBORO* LE11 22 B4
Robert Hardy Whf *LBORO* LE11 24 B2
Roberts Cl *CDON/KEG* DE74 6 C4
Robin Crs *MMWB* LE13 56 C3
Robin Ms *LBORO* LE11 2 E6
Robin Rd *COAL* LE67 36 D5
Robinson Rd *COAL* LE67 26 B5
Roby Lea *CDON/KEG* DE74 4 B1
Rochdale Crs *COAL* LE67 37 H4
Rochester Cl *RLBORO* LE12 41 G4
Rockhill Dr *RLBORO* LE12 41 H4
Rockingham Cl *RLBORO* LE12 20 C4
Rockingham Dr *MMWB* LE13 54 B4
Rockingham Rd *LBORO* LE11 16 A5
RLBORO LE12 41 G4
Rockland Ri *COAL* LE67 26 D4
Romans Crs *COAL* LE67 37 H4
The Romans *RLBORO* LE12 42 A3
Roman Wy *RLEINE/SYS* LE7 51 G5
Romway Cl *RLBORO* LE12 21 E3
Ronald West Ct *LBORO* LE11 22 D5
The Roods *RLEINE/SYS* LE7 50 A1
The Rookery *RLBORO* LE12 31 G1
Ropewalk *CDON/KEG* DE74 6 C3
Rope Wk *RLBORO* LE12 8 B4
Rosebery Av *MMWB* LE13 55 E5
Rosebery St *LBORO* LE11 2 C3
Rosedale *COAL* LE67 26 C4
Rosehill *LBORO* LE11 22 C2
Rosemary Crs *COAL* LE67 37 E1
Rosewood Wy *LBORO* LE11 29 F3
Rosminian Wy *RLEINE/SYS* LE7 44 A2
Ross Cl *MMWB* LE13 55 F3
Rosslyn Av *RLEINE/SYS* LE7 41 G4
Rosslyn Rd *COAL* LE67 36 D1
Rothley Rd *RLBORO* LE12 42 A2
Roulstone Crs *RLBORO* LE12 9 C2
Roundhill Cl *RLEINE/SYS* LE7 51 H5
Roundhill Wy *LBORO* LE11 22 B3
Routh Av *CDON/KEG* DE74 4 D3
Rowan Av *COAL* LE67 37 F5
RLBORO LE12 15 E1
Rowbank Wy *LBORO* LE11 22 B3
Rowe Leyes Furlong
RLEINE/SYS LE7 42 B3
Rowena Ct *RLBORO* LE12 42 A4
Royal Wy *LBORO* LE11 16 C5
Roydale Cl *LBORO* LE11 16 A5
Royland Rd *LBORO* LE11 3 F6
Rudbeck Av *MMWB* LE13 54 B5
Rudyard Cl *LBORO* LE11 22 B4
Rufford Cl *LBORO* LE11 22 B1
Rumsey Cl *COAL* LE67 26 A2
RLBORO LE12 30 C3
Rupert Brooke Rd *LBORO* LE
Rupert Crs *RLEINE/SYS* LE7
Rupert Law Cl *RLBORO* LE12
Rushby Rd *COAL* LE67
Rushcliffe Gv *RLBORO* LE12
The Rushes *LBORO* LE11
Rushey La *RLEINE/SYS* LE7
Ruskin Av *RLEINE/SYS* LE7
Russ Cl *RLBORO* LE12
Russell St *LBORO* LE11
Rutland St *LBORO* LE11
MMWB LE13
Rydal Av *LBORO* LE11
Ryeholm Cl *RLBORO* LE12

S

Saddlers Cl *LBORO* LE11
Saddlers' Cl *RLEINE/SYS* LE7
Sage Cross St *MMWB* LE13
St Aidan's Av *RLEINE/SYS* LE
St Andrew's Cl *COAL* LE67
St Andrews Cl *RLBORO* LE12
St Andrew's Ri *CDON/KEG* D
St Annes Cl *RLEINE/SYS* LE7
St Anne's La *CDON/KEG* DE7
RLBORO LE12
St Barnard's Rd *COAL* LE67
St Bartholomews Wy
MMWB LE13
RMMWB LE14
St Bernard's Cl *RLBORO* LE1
St Botolph Rd *RLBORO* LE12
St Christophers Pk *COAL* LE
St Clares Ct *COAL* LE67
St Columba Wy *RLEINE/SYS*
St Davids Ct *COAL* LE67
St David's Crs *COAL* LE67
St Edward's Rd
CDON/KEG DE74
St Faiths Rd *COAL* LE67
St Gregory's Dr *RLBORO* LE
St Hildas Cl *RLEINE/SYS* LE7
St Ives *COAL* LE67
St James Cl *RLBORO* LE12
St James Rd *RLBORO* LE12
St John's Av *RLEINE/SYS* LE
St John's Cl *COAL* LE67
St Johns Ct *MMWB* LE13
St John's Dr *MMWB* LE13
St Leonards Cl *RLBORO* LE
St Mary's Cl *LBORO* LE11
St Marys Cl *RLBORO* LE12
St Mary's Crs *RLBORO* LE12
St Mary's Rd *RLBORO* LE12
St Mary's Wy *MMWB* LE13
St Olaves Cl *LBORO* LE11
St Paul's Dr *RLEINE/SYS* LE
St Peters Av *RLBORO* LE12
St Peter's St *RLEINE/SYS* L
St Philips Rd *RLBORO* LE12
St Saviours Rd *COAL* LE67
St Vincents Cl *COAL* LE67
St Winefride Rd *RLBORO* L
St Winifreds Ct
CFTN/RUD NG11
Salisbury Av *MMWB* LE13
RLBORO LE12
Salisbury St *LBORO* LE11
Salter Cl *CDON/KEG* DE74
Samson Rd *COAL* LE67
Sandalwood Rd *LBORO* LE
Sanders Rd *RLBORO* LE12
Sandford Rd *RLEINE/SYS*
Sandham Bridge Rd
RLEINE/SYS LE7
The Sandhills *RLBORO* LE1
Sandhole La *RLBORO* LE12
Sandringham Dr *LBORO* L
Sandringham Ri *RLBORO*
Sandringham Rd *COAL* LE
Sandy La *MMWB* LE13
Sapcote Dr *MMWB* LE13
Sarson St *RLBORO* LE12
Saville Dr *RLBORO* LE12
Sawbridge Cl *COAL* LE67
Sawgate Rd *RMMWB* LE1
Saxby Rd *MMWB* LE13
Scalford Rd *MMWB* LE13
Schofield Rd *LBORO* LE11
School Gn *RLBORO* LE12
School La *CDON/KEG* DE7
COAL LE67
RLBORO LE12
RLBORO LE12
RLEINE/SYS LE7
School St *LBORO* LE11

T

U

V

W

Y

Z

Index - featured places

knowledgements

data provided by Education Direct.

rmation supplied by Johnsons.

formation provided by:

ssociation Britains best garden centres

Centres 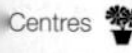

the front cover of this atlas is sourced, selected and quoted
mment and feedback form received in 2004